PROFESSIONAL RESOURCES

D1450127

The Four-Blocks™ Literacy Model

True Stories
from Four-Blocks™ Classrooms

Edited by
Patricia Cunningham
and Dorothy Hall

Editors
Tracy Soles
Joey Bland

Cover
Julie Webb

· · · · · · · · · · · · · · · · Table of Contents · · · · · · · · · · · · · · · ·

Table of Contents

ISBN 0-88724-628-1

Introduction: The True Story of
True Stories from Four-Blocks™ Classrooms • • • • • • • • • • • • •

All teachers have stories to tell. Many teachers are natural storytellers. As we traveled around the country talking about Four-Blocks™, we heard marvelous stories. When one of us heard a particularly poignant story, we would call the other one and tell her:

Hello, Dottie. It's Pat. You just won't believe what I learned in Indianapolis this week! This teacher came up to me at the break and said that she could see how using the *Weekly Reader* or *Scholastic News* one day for Guided Reading would provide some variety and some informational text, but she is from a poor school that doesn't have money for extras like some suburban schools do. Before I could open my mouth, another teacher piped up, 'Well, we don't have any money either, but we pooled our own money and for $48.00 ordered 12 copies of one of those magazines. There were four of us at second grade, but we ordered the first-grade version to have some easier reading material. Then, we each decided on a day to use them. One teacher got them on Monday, one on Tuesday, and so on. At the end of the week, we each got three copies. I put two copies in the baskets for Self-Selected Reading and laminated one copy to keep year after year. That was three years ago, and I have several baskets of them now. My children pore over those laminated magazines at SSR time; and Tuesday, the day we get them for Guided Reading, is their favorite Guided Reading day!' Isn't that brilliant?! Look what those four teachers got for their $48.00! I am going to tell that story everywhere I go. It was worth the trip—even though my flight was cancelled again, and it was almost 3:00 a.m. before I got home!

For years, we would share the stories we heard and the stories we saw while visiting in schools. "We should write these down," one of us would periodically chide the other.

Then, last March as our U.S. Census forms arrived, we got the brainstorm to do a Four-Blocks census. We got together that weekend and made up the form—a short form with quick answers on one side and a long form with room for lots of details on the other side. We printed out copies to take on our "road trips," and posted the form on the Four-Blocks mailrings. Soon, our census forms started pouring in, by E-mail, fax, "snail mail," and hand-delivered at workshops. We began reading and coding them—and wondering whose idea this was anyway!

The census responses were full of stories—like the story of a stuffed worm named Wally who introduces the new Word Wall words to the kids each week. "I love that idea—how clever!" Another story told about some fourth-graders whose reading levels were way below where they should be, and a clever reading specialist who rounded up the kids, the teachers, and two interns each day for two hours in the library and supported them as they all learned together how to do Four-Blocks with older, struggling readers.

Teachers told stories of doing Four-Blocks in multiage classrooms; with English Language Learners; in Spanish; in both English and Spanish in the same classrooms. Some of our favorite stories came from first-year teachers—teachers who were working hard to teach reading, but not feeling particularly successful at it. Somehow, they heard about Four-Blocks, and on their own (they were the only teachers doing it in their schools), began using Four-Blocks as their organizing framework. "Gutsy ladies," we concluded, as we marveled at these beginning teachers taking on their first year of teaching and Four-Blocks simultaneously.

Of course, we wanted to know more. How exactly does Wally introduce the Word Wall words? How do you do Four-Blocks in the library with all the fourth-graders, many of whom struggle with reading? How do you do it in a multiage classroom? With English Language Learners? In Spanish? How do you implement Four-Blocks as a beginning teacher? What is most difficult? What mistakes do you make, and how will you change it next year?

As we shared the stories we heard at meetings, saw played out in classrooms, and read about on our census forms, we conceived the idea for this book. "Let's collect them and put them together so that others can learn and marvel as we did," one of us (We're not sure which one!) suggested.

Of course, conceiving the book is a lot easier than developing and delivering it. But, at the moment of conception and in the first few months of endless possibilities, you never think about the months of work and labor that lie ahead. And when—almost exactly nine months later—the book is born, you forget you ever had any second thoughts! *True Stories from Four-Blocks™ Classrooms* was truly a "labor of love." And many people shared in that labor. We are most grateful to all the storytellers—teachers and administrators—who answered the call (actually the E-mail, in most cases) to share their stories with you. Even when the final editing, which we had planned to be doing in the lazy days of August, crept up into the frantic days of September when a new school year was starting, our storytellers worked late and on weekends to answer our questions and dig up test data.

We are delighted that all of these professional educators so willingly shared their stories with us and allowed us to share them with you. We dedicate this book to teachers everywhere who inspire each other as they share their stories, but especially to the storytellers/educators you are about to meet as you enter their worlds through their stories. Enjoy!

— Pat Cunningham and Dottie Hall

Making the Four-Blocks™ My Own and Having Fun Working with Words

by Lucie Rossi (with Dottie Hall)

Lucie, like many caring, competent teachers, is always searching for new and better ways to work with her young students. Lucie learned about the Four-Blocks™ as she searched for new and better methods of teaching reading. Like many other teachers, she "fine-tunes" these activities so that her students can profit more from the instruction; or in her words, "I make it my own by adding little touches that enhance learning and make it even more enjoyable." We continue to learn and grow, thanks to teachers like Lucie Rossi. Here is her story:

I have been a teacher in the San Lorenzo Valley Unified School District in California for the past thirteen years. Twelve of those years were at Boulder Creek School. I have also served as an Early Literacy Mentor for the past four years and led a Four-Blocks™ support group for teachers in this district. Boulder Creek Elementary School is a school of approximately 500 students, K–6, nestled among beautiful Redwood trees in the Santa Cruz Mountains. It is one of four elementary schools, along with a junior high and high school, that make up the San Lorenzo Valley Unified School District.

There is a broad spectrum of socioeconomic levels among our families, with approximately 20% of the students receiving free and reduced lunch services. We are less than 2% non-English speaking. Many parents work "just over the hill," a 40-minute drive to the Silicon Valley. We are 20 minutes from the Santa Cruz beaches of the Pacific Ocean. Although it is in a rural setting, the district has been at the forefront of literacy education for its teachers and actively seeks out and supports innovative teaching methods and interventions for students at risk. All primary teachers in the district were trained in Effective First Teaching (which was my first introduction to many of the strategies and activities of Four-Blocks) five years ago. Many teachers formed a Four-Blocks support group in which to further explore teaching practices. At Boulder Creek Elementary, the first-graders have been served by three Reading Recovery teachers for the past four years, and our Resource Specialist works collaboratively in second- and third-grade classrooms helping at-risk students with reading. In spring 2000, Boulder Creek Elementary was awarded the California Distinguished School Award. Some of the main considerations in this award were the many interventions we have in place to ensure that no child "falls through the cracks."

Five years ago I was assigned to teach a multiage (kindergarten/first grade) class. At that time I had eight years of teaching experience, four of those in kindergarten. But nonetheless, I was terrified of the task before me. I had always believed that first grade was by far the hardest grade to teach. I had no interest in taking on that bigger-than-life task of teaching six-year-olds to read. I cried for a day (partly from fear, partly from frustration), and then set out to prepare myself for the task ahead. Luckily, it was a good time to be learning new literacy methods. Our local county office of education was offering some courses in what would soon become a "reading academy" for teachers. During the first course, I was introduced to methods, strategies, and activities that were totally new to me. I learned about morning messages, interactive writing, Word Walls, Making Words, running records, and shared and guided reading. I took these new strategies back to my classroom and was excited. This was good stuff. The students loved the activities, and so did I. We were learning together.

Finding Four-Blocks™

The next year, I taught first grade. I had learned a lot about teaching children to read during my K-1 year, but something still troubled me. I was fitting activities in wherever I could, but it seemed haphazard. I knew it was good teaching, but I didn't feel organized. I was looking for something, but I didn't know quite what. Then one day I found it, or at least my first clue, at the local teachers' supply store. It was a single copy of a very slim, spiral-bound book titled *Implementing the 4-Blocks™ Literacy Model*. It seemed to be an organizational overview of many of the wonderful strategies and activities I had been introduced to, but it didn't seem quite complete. It was almost like a resource that should have accompanied a workshop or seminar. I combed through every book in the store and questioned the store owner: "What is Four-Blocks, and where can I learn more?" No one could answer my question, and so began a half-year quest in search of the answer. At the time I had sitting on my bookshelf two wonderful books, *Phonics They Use* and *Classrooms That Work*. I could have saved myself a lot of time and frustration if I had only opened them, but I didn't.

I asked all my friends and colleagues to be on the lookout for any information and started searching the Internet. I tried in vain to find anything about one of the model's authors, Pat Cunningham. I finally "visited" the Wake Forest University Web site, not sure if she was still an instructor there. She was listed in the faculty directory, and from there I found a Web site. As the pictures from the site slowly appeared on my computer screen, I saw a very warm and friendly smiling face, and then a picture of a beach cove that closely resembled my grandmother's home where I spent my childhood summers. It was feeling like home. And then, like magic, four brightly-colored blocks appeared at the bottom of the screen, along with the words "click here for more information on the Four-Blocks." (I should say here that you really have to be teaching first grade for the first time to appreciate my excitement.) One click, and there it was—a full, detailed description of the Four-Blocks™ Literacy Model. It had a name; it had a shape; it had a format. This was very exciting. And, it was just the beginning.

As anyone familiar with the model knows, the blocks are: Guided Reading, Self-Selected Reading, Writing, and Working with Words. Each of these approaches to teaching reading is given a block of time each day, and a variety of multilevel activities are used in each block. I was already doing some form of Self-Selected Reading, Guided Reading, and Writers' Workshop in my class, but the Working with Words Block was new to me, and has since become my favorite block.

There seems to be a small amount of controversy regarding how closely the details of the blocks must be followed. Four-Blocks has become very popular across the country (and even around the world), and has a very active and vocal mailring on the Web. There are even good-natured references to "the Four-Blocks police." I believe strongly in the basic premise of the Four-Blocks—not all children can best be taught to read with one literacy method. A balanced, multimethod, multi-level program is required, and each component of the program must be present in the schedule each day. Careful to follow these basic principles, I have added many details of my own. Some changes were made to fit in with my physical environment or resources, while others were made to add a touch of fun or whimsy to an activity. This model has enhanced my enthusiasm for teaching, as well as greatly enriched my students' literacy learning. I would like to share some of the ways in which I have "made it my own."

The Writing Block

At the beginning of the year in first grade, we do names activities during our writing time. Thinking and organizing skills are modeled as well as actual writing. With the children gathered on the carpet, we look to our "magic slate" to identify the day's special person and subject of our names activity. The "slate" is a white sheet of construction paper on which I have used a white crayon to print the letters of a student's name (the letters are placed randomly around the paper, out of order, but always right-side-up). They are invisible until the previous day's special person comes up and begins to watercolor over the paper so that the letters "magically" appear. (I modified this activity from an idea I heard at a Jim Heaton Kindergarten Activities seminar.) When all the letters are visible, we find the one capital letter that gives us a clue on where to start. We also count the letters. It can get very quiet while each student thinks about his/her own name and tries to figure out if this could possibly be it. Once we figure it out, we print each letter on a card and place them in the pocket chart. We then continue with the traditional activities of chanting, cheering, and "being" the name. We mix up the letters and find little words that can be made with them. When finished, the special person chooses a friend to come up and rebuild the name in the pocket chart from memory (a great motivator for learning how to spell the names). It is then time to interview the special person. I make a big starburst or some other type of graphic organizer on a half-size chart. I print the name in the center and the students offer suggestions of what they would like to learn about this person (favorite food, play activity, school subject, family, pets, sports, etc.). I label six subcategories and the interview begins. Students raise their hands with questions for the S.P. (Special Person). He/She hands them a microphone, and they ask the question into it. The S.P. answers the questions using the microphone as well. It really looks a bit like a newscaster's interview. I jot down one or two word answers under the appropriate headings on the graphic organizer until the chart is full. The S.P. then chooses four of the six subcategories to be included in the message about him/her. The students use the information to form complete sentences and tell me what to write (on a new half-size chart). We end up with a four-sentence paragraph describing the special person, but we also have heard a lot of other information about him/her. The S.P. uses a pointer to track the print, and the whole class reads the message together. It is now time for the students to go to their desks and draw a picture of and write about the S.P. independently. When all the students are finished, we make a book, read it out loud, and present it to the S.P. to take home.

During the rest of the year, our Writing Block closely resembles the one described in *The Teacher's Guide to Four-Blocks™*. We have a minilesson, a time for independent writing, and a sharing time. Last year I bought a cute little plastic chair and decorated it with letter stickers. We called it the "share chair." Unfortunately, it was very light and kept tipping over accidentally. I solved this by placing the chair directly in front of my chair while the child read to the class. Even though I will be using a sturdier chair this year, I will continue to sit directly behind the sharer for sharing of both reading and writing. It gives me a great opportunity to monitor the child and see what strategies are being used in both reading and writing.

The Guided Reading Block

My favorite thing about the Guided Reading Block is the flexibility. Guided Reading is meant as just that—a reading experience that is supported, or guided (in a variety of ways) by the teacher. It is not a lock-step, scripted procedure, as some reading group experiences can be. It never feels contrived, but rather, feels exciting and authentic. Many of my first graders ask as they enter the classroom in the morning, "How are we doing reading today? I hope it's book clubs (or partners, etc.)." They are so aware of the purpose and excitement of reading.

My one concern with this block is that I can totally empathize with a teacher who is confused by it. To have Guided Reading the Four-Blocks way work, a teacher must use many before, during, and after reading strategies; be confident; and naturally flexible. Many excellent, experienced teachers are not that flexible, especially when it comes to teaching reading. I understand that the students also need a predictable routine and need to know what is expected of them. Initially, some students may be confused by the variety of reading formats, but they learn the names and procedures quickly. In fact, they truly buy into it as they develop preferences and come to really care about how reading is done every day. Another wonderful benefit is watching the lower students truly "rise to the challenge" of reading. I love the fluid and flexible grouping, and also the whole group lessons and emphasis on comprehension strategies.

Self-Selected Reading

The Self-Selected Reading Block competes with the Working with Words Block as my favorite. This is where the students soar—in skills, confidence, maturity, and appreciation for reading. This is where each child develops his/her own special relationship with books and stories. This is probably also the most difficult block to implement, at least in a practical sense, as it requires quite a monetary investment in books. It is a block that I have very much "made my own."

Like many teachers, I have invested thousands of dollars in books for my classroom. Along with the beautiful story, picture, and theme books, I have purchased many easy readers and leveled books. After reading each book, I level it very simply. The easiest books get a red sticker on the cover and are placed in a red box, the medium books get a blue sticker and are placed in a blue box, and the more difficult books get a yellow sticker and go in a yellow box. I print an "n" on the stickers of nonfiction books. Chapter books such as *The Magic Tree House* series get two yellow stickers as I think they can be quite challenging for most first-graders (but boy, do those kids aim for reading double yellows, usually with great success!).

Very early in the year, I model how to choose books and decide if they are right for you. I then take small groups and show them the independent reading book boxes. We really look through the books in the boxes, and the students get very anxious to start choosing. I guide them individually toward the books which I think would be just right for them, and then let them choose no less than four and no more than six books to keep in their independent reading folders. (I purchase pleated manila folders which are closed on the sides; twenty full folders can be stored in two dishpan tubs.) As a general rule, the students may have one book that they consider too easy and one too difficult in their folders, but the rest should feel "just about right."

When I first started Four-Blocks, I managed the Self-Selected Reading Block as described in the model. In the model, a small crate or tub of books of many genres and reading levels is placed at each table of students. They select reading materials from that crate each day for a week, and after that, the crates are rotated. If there was a book the student wanted to read again, he or she was to put a personalized bookmark in it and return it to the crate. I found, however, that a lot of reading time was spent going through the tubs on the tables and selecting books, rejecting books, and arguing over books. I wanted this to be a time for the student to "bond" with the book itself; the social aspect could come later when it was time to share-read the book aloud to the class. I wanted the child to anticipate reading the book they would be getting back to, and to already feel a bond with the books just waiting to be read.

After getting many great suggestions from the Four-Blocks mailring on *Teachers.Net*, I made up my own procedures for the Self-Selected Reading Block. On the first day of implementing the block, I meet with the whole class and describe where to find different kinds of books in the classroom. I describe how to select books and how to put books away. I then meet with small groups and help individuals select from four to six books by themselves. They are to keep these books in their reading folders (described previously). When everyone has their books, and they are bursting to get to them, we begin our "reading workshop." The boys sit at their seats and the girls may sit anywhere in the room (we alternate girl/boy every day), but everyone must have their own space, not too close to another student. I give the students one minute to settle in (no getting up for any reason during reading time), and set the timer for 15 minutes. When the 15 minutes are up, I announce that they have five more minutes in which they can continue to read, select new books and trade in old ones, or read/share their books with a friend. I set the timer again for five minutes. When the time is up, the students put their books in their envelopes and return the filled envelopes to the tubs. The only time to select new books (which involves a degree of wandering around the room) is during these five minutes. When we start reading the next day, the students are all ready to go, with a minimum of time spent settling in.

The students can keep the same books for as long as they like. If I notice during conferencing that one student has mastered a book and keeps reading that same book every day, I help him/her find a few others with which he/she will feel comfortable, and give him/her a little support so he/she feels ready to move on. We end Reader's Workshop (my name for Self-Selected Reading) with four or five children reading a page or two from their books each day.

The Working with Words Block

My favorite block is Working with Words. These are the activities that I feel have really changed the way I teach. My training as a teacher came during a time when "phonics" was a bad word, and I was never comfortable with that. I viewed phonics as a potentially useful tool in which every child should be trained and encouraged to use in their task of learning to read. Unfortunately, most of the phonics tools available to both teachers and students amounted to little more than drill and practice worksheets; they had very little to do with the process of learning to read or reading itself. Because these worksheets were done during reading time, many children came to think that was what reading was all about, and of course, they came to view reading as boring and unrelated to just about anything of interest to them. Although phonics is a good and necessary tool, and many students found the worksheets and drill fun and easy, it confused many students in understanding what reading was really all about. What they may have gained in word-attack skills, they lost in motivation and desire to read.

During the first week of school, my students meet "Wally, the Word Wall Worm." Wally is a little stuffed-animal worm, about seven inches long. He lives in an apple-shaped pocket chart, and each week he brings us five new words to learn and put on our Word Wall. These words become known as "Wally Words." Each Monday, before being introduced to the week's new words, each student takes out his/her own Wally (a four-inch piece of pink yarn), and we sing and dance to the Wally song (a tape of Hap Palmer's "Walter the Waltzing Worm" with a few changes in the words). Then, we chant, clap, and spell the five words for that week. The words stay on the apple-shaped pocket chart all week and are moved to the Word Wall at the end of the week. As the number of words on the Word Wall grows, we do many of the Working with Words activities such as On-the-Back Endings, On-the-Back Rhymes, and Be a Mind Reader. As words are added to the wall, each student makes a card for each word and keeps it in his/her own special word can. (The little specialty coffee cans can be covered with colored paper and are a perfect size for storing cards.)

I follow the Four-Blocks™ Model closely with Rounding Up the Rhymes, Guess the Covered Word, Using Words You Know, and Reading/Writing Rhymes, but have made a few changes to how I introduce the lessons in Making Words. At the beginning of the year, I start my first-graders with lessons from a book published by Scholastic, *Easy Lessons for Teaching Word Families* by Judy Lynch. These are very simple lessons and introduce one, two, or three similar word patterns at a time. As we learn each, we put up a small chart with examples from that pattern. We do Making Words lessons two or three times a week, and after learning about thirty patterns, we start using lessons from the *Making Words* books. These are theme- related, and the students are not only motivated to find and spell words, but very capable because they have had so much practice with word families.

Storage and accessibility of letters seems to be a recurring concern for teachers doing Making Words. I use a blank grid of eight by five rectangles, forty rectangles total. I make dozens of copies of this grid. For each lesson, I print the letters each student will need in a row across the grid (one paper is enough for five students) and make four copies. I cut out the strips of letters and have the students snip them apart and lay them out. They build their words on a piece of manila tagboard with a green sticker dot on the left side ("go" or start here). At the end of the lesson, we recycle or take home the letters. Although it seems wasteful, each lesson only uses five sheets of paper (one master and four copies), and we save lots of time doing it this way.

I prepare my Making Words lessons well in advance on white and colored index cards and store them in clear, resealable plastic bags. I include all letter and word cards needed in the bag, along with a list of words and directions. I store the bags sequentially in a small basket and can use them year after year. What I love most about Making Words and all the other Working with Words activities is that children are so involved in actually working with the words. They make discoveries and connections and begin to get a real understanding for how our language works.

All of the Working with Words activities involve a degree of problem solving and analyzing. There is no rote memorization here, but rather, opportunities built one upon another for applying learned skills to learn and understand even more. It is truly exciting when beginning readers discover the words (or similar words) in their real reading during the Guided Reading or Self-Selected Reading Blocks that they have just learned during the Working with Words Block. Every day they have the opportunity to apply and extend what they have learned.

Looking Forward to the Coming Year

I often think back to that day five years ago when I was assigned to teach first grade. I was terrified. Teaching children to read seemed a task far beyond my capabilities. Little did I know that teaching children to read is the most exciting teaching of all. The Four-Blocks™ Model has provided me with a framework and a huge selection of activities which I implement confidently, knowing that these are truly the best practices.

After teaching in the San Lorenzo Valley District for thirteen years, I made the huge decision to make a change in my life and am now teaching "over that hill" in the Silicon Valley at Blossom Hill Elementary School in the Los Gatos Union School District. I find myself once again at a wonderful school in a beautiful setting, and once again teaching a K-1 multiage class. My new challenge will be combining the methods of Four-Blocks with Building Blocks™ to best meet the needs of all my students. I look forward to that challenge of teaching this class this year, because I understand both how children learn to read and the activities they need to find success.

Four-Blocks™ Finds Its Way to Georgia ● ● ● ● ● ● ● ● ● ● ● ● ● ● ● ●

by Cece Tillman (with Dottie Hall)

In the summer of 1997, I did some Phonics and Four-Blocks™ workshops in Georgia. The legislature was pushing "phonics" as the answer to all the reading problems, but teacher leaders at the Regional Educational Service Centers were looking for balance. Every time I talked, these educational leaders would be in the audience, and they understood that balance was needed and that phonics alone would not solve all children's reading problems. I did not meet Cece that summer, even though I was working close by. I am sure I met and talked with the reading consultant who worked with Cece. I met Cece in Atlanta in the fall of 1999, and again at the Leadership Conference in January, 2000. I was delighted to meet her because I had so enjoyed all her practical and thoughtful postings on the mailrings. Cece's story reminds me of all the wonderful teachers all over the country who are helping other teachers find ways to reach all the children they teach. This is Cece's story:

My name is Cece Tillman, and I teach first grade at Davis Elementary in Dade County, Georgia. Dade County is in northwestern Georgia, in the mountains very close to the Alabama line. I have taught for a total of 10 years—four years in kindergarten, three years in second grade, and I just completed my third year in first grade.

I first heard about Four-Blocks™ during post-planning in the summer of 1999, when a reading consultant visited our school. Many teachers in my school had expressed concern to our principal about our reading instruction. As a former English teacher, our principal knew the importance of reading and how critical the early grades are to developing good readers. He arranged for the regional reading consultant to come to our school to help revitalize our reading program.

Before Four-Blocks, I had been doing a fairly traditional first-grade reading program, meeting my reading groups and providing work for the children I wasn't working with. I felt that my instruction didn't do much for those "struggling readers," who weren't learning disabled, just slow learners. These children didn't make much progress, and I blamed myself for not meeting the needs of <u>all</u> my students. No matter which group I was working with, I felt guilty about the group I wasn't working with. I also had problems keeping kids on task that weren't in my group.

In addition, teaching the groups took all my time and energy. Even though I knew it was critical, I never had enough time to share all the wonderful books in my classroom or instill in my students my love of books and reading.

My Introduction to the Four-Blocks™

At our first meeting, the reading consultant divided a piece of paper into "Four-Blocks" and showed me how I could arrange my reading instruction into each of these blocks. She never really told me about the program *"Four-Blocks,"* but everything she talked about really made sense. That summer, she and another consultant conducted a three-day conference on phonics, and they referred to the *Month-by-Month Phonics* books. I went out and bought *Month-by-Month Phonics for First Grade* and was immediately won over by the information I read. From there, I purchased *The Teacher's Guide to the Four-Blocks™* and began to read about Four-Blocks. I had already used many of the activities in the Working with Words and Guided Reading Blocks in my previous instruction. I had never used Self-Selected Reading, but I was excited about having a block of time for my students to read each day. I knew that this was important, but could never find time for it in my schedule. My real weakness was the Writing Block. I had never really been trained to teach writing, and the Writer's Workshop information I had seen overwhelmed me! How could I get each child to do a rough draft, edit, and publish a piece each week?

As I began to search the Internet, I discovered the Four-Blocks mailring on *Teachers.Net*. What a wonderful resource for me! Teachers from around the country immediately answered questions I asked as I began to plan my instruction. There were a few aspects of the model that worried me as I planned. One was giving up my reading groups, particularly not listening to every child read every day. I really worried that I wouldn't know how my kids were progressing if I couldn't hear them read each day. After expressing my fears on the mailring, one person responded to me, "What makes you think you have to hear them every day for them to improve?"

That really made an impression on me! I realized that I needed to let go of some control. I finally decided to try the model in its pure form. If at any time I wasn't satisfied with how my students were doing, I could always go back to what I had been doing. But, I had been so unhappy with what I was doing that I was really ready for a change. All summer I planned and read, getting lots of support from teachers on the mailring, particularly Deb and Laura. Finally, I felt I could do no more until school started. I was so excited about beginning the new school year, and I couldn't wait for the students to come. I felt like a first-year teacher all over again! Even my colleagues at work commented on my excitement and enthusiasm. They wondered what had happened to me!

How I Began Using the Four-Blocks

I began the first day of school with all Four-Blocks. For the Working with Words Block, we began the names activities. We did a "Getting to Know You" chart with Kelly, a memorable student from a memorable group of students. After we interviewed her and wrote about her, her chart was displayed in the room, and we read it several times. Kelly's name was the first word added to our Word Wall.

We began our Self-Selected Reading Block with a read-aloud, and I modeled the three ways to read (read the pictures, tell a familiar story, or read the words). The children loved looking through the books in the book baskets.

For our first Guided Reading lesson, we read the big book, *Whose Mouse Are You?* in a shared reading format. The kids picked up on the repetitive lines quickly.

Writing was the scary time for me that day, but I shared the three ways the students could write (draw a picture, write some words, or write a sentence). The students didn't seem to notice my nervousness, and began to draw, scribble, and write with excitement.

What amazed me those first few weeks was how much more time I had for math, social studies, and science. I did my language arts and math instruction in the morning. In the afternoons, I had time (and energy) to get in social studies and science, which I had a great deal of difficulty doing in previous years. The first few weeks, however, were exhausting! (Come to think of it, the first few weeks of a school year are always exhausting!) The planning was time-consuming, but I had fewer papers to grade, so it balanced out.

I had warned the parents that I was trying a new program, and I told them we would not be doing reams of workbook pages, but lots of real reading and writing. Most of the parents knew me from the nine years I had taught at Davis Elementary, and they were willing to trust me. I think my enthusiasm won them over. I made it clear to them that if they had any concerns that their child wasn't making sufficient progress, they could let me know. I also gave them a standing invitation to come see the Four-Blocks in action. At least half a dozen of them took me up on the offer. Within a few weeks, I was getting rave reviews from parents about the reading progress their children were making and the enthusiasm their children had for school. I am pleased to say there was not one complaint all year from any parent about how I was teaching. Parents are happy when their children are learning and happy!

Sharing My Success

The reading consultant made several trips to my classroom throughout the year, observing and giving support. She, too, was amazed at what she saw my students doing. Our Title I teacher at school began to do some workshops on the Four-Blocks in our area, and filmed my classroom doing many of the activities from the Working with Words Block. When our teacher training center, RESA, got a copy of the tape, they began showing it to groups of administrators who were implementing Reading First, a Georgia program to improve reading instruction. Before long, principals were sending teachers to my classroom to observe my teaching. Other teachers in the area from the mailring also came to observe. One dedicated teacher even came one day during her spring break!

Learning More and Working on Writing

With the framework in place and clearly working, I was eager to learn more. In October, I was fortunate to be able to hear Richard Allington speak in Rome, GA. I bought *Classrooms That Work* and began to read about many of the theories behind the Four-Blocks™ framework. In November, several other teachers from my school and I went to Atlanta to hear Dottie Hall. What a wonderful day we had! She clarified many of the questions I had, and I left that day feeling even more confident in what I was doing.

I did realize, however, that I needed to strengthen the Writing Block in my classroom. I felt great about Working with Words and Self-Selected Reading, and felt Guided Reading was going pretty well, but I knew my real weakness was in the Writing Block.

I had modeled writing and had even felt that a few of my minilessons had really helped the children move along in their writing. One of those was a lesson I taught in late September. I had noticed that many of my students were writing short, choppy sentences. Their pieces didn't have much life or detail. No matter how often we talked in conference, it just didn't seem to help. I used an event from my life in a story to impress on them how details make a difference in a story.

• •

The previous day, we first-grade teachers had gone to Trenton to a workshop, and we had all gone out to lunch together. As I began my minilesson, I told my class that I would tell them about how the three of us had a wonderful lunch in Trenton. They really seemed interested in what I would write. I wrote two sentences on the board:

We went to Trenton to eat. It was fun.

I put my pen down and said, "How do you like my story?" You can imagine the uproar. Many began asking questions about where we ate and what we ate. I said, "Do you think I could answer your questions in my story to make it better?" Of course, they all agreed. So, I made a list of their questions and added the answers to my story:

We went to Trenton to eat. It was fun. We went to the Crabtree Café. Mrs. Tierce and I had chicken salad sandwiches, white chili, and a wonderful cookie for dessert. The meal was delicious! After lunch, we came back to school to finish our work. It was great to be able to eat lunch at a real restaurant.

We reread both pieces, and I asked them which one they liked better. They all agreed that the second example was better. From that day forward, we always took time when students shared their first drafts to let classmates ask a few questions. We talked about how they could continue their story the next day, adding the information their friends wanted to know. I began to see immediate improvement in their writing.

Although I had a few "light bulb moments" like this, I still felt the Writing Block was my weakness. At a workshop, I saw a book available called *Craft Lessons*. I bought this book and began to use some of the ideas. We did the "cut and paste" stories, several lessons on "new ways to write about old topics," and several other good lessons. When teachers on the mailring began asking questions about the Writing Block, I answered by telling them about my struggle with writing and the resources I had found to help me. I also shared some of my successful minilessons.

As January approached, I eagerly looked forward to the Leadership Conference in Clemmons, North Carolina. I felt excitement at being able to hear the speakers and meet the teachers on the mailring. Imagine my surprise when Dottie contacted me, told me that she had noticed all my good writing minilessons, and

Four-Blocks™ Finds Its Way

· **·to Georgia**

asked me to conduct a round-table discussion on writing at the Leadership Conference! My weakness in teaching had become a strength! I was nervous about it, but I must admit it went well and was warmly received by the teachers. I shared some of my minilessons and brought some samples of my children's writing. The teachers were amazed at the progress my children had made in their writing—and it was only mid-January!

I left the Leadership Conference revitalized! I had talked with teachers from all over the country who worked under unbelievable pressure and constraints, but still managed to help children be successful. Another real highlight was being able to spend time with fellow mailringers like Laura, Deb, Marti, and Joyce. I enjoyed all the speakers immensely, especially Jim Cunningham (Pat's husband). Jim talked about writing, and I was confirmed in what I was doing and got some new ideas to add to my growing repertoire! I was amazed by how approachable Dottie and Pat were. They weren't "famous people"—they were caring educators, just like me! How affirming it was for me to realize that there are so many people out there who are working every day to improve instructional methods.

My Assessment

I can honestly say that Four-Blocks restored my enthusiasm and love for teaching. I developed a real bond with my students, and more importantly, I knew their strengths and weaknesses in ways I had never known before. I was amazed at what all my students accomplished! My bright students were excited, motivated, and performing beyond my wildest dreams! My slow learners had accomplished so much! One little girl, who struggled at the beginning of the year, left reading on grade level! Although I had a few who didn't make such gigantic leaps, they all made progress, and they all left feeling confident, happy, and successful as readers and writers. (The school year has started as I edit this, and the second grade teachers are amazed at what these students can do!)

Looking Forward To Next Year

This summer, I taught Four-Blocks workshops around North Georgia, sharing how Four-Blocks changed my classroom. Those 13 days were exhausting but rewarding! I felt that Four-Blocks was too good to keep to myself and wanted teachers all over Georgia to know about it. Of the teachers I have worked with, nearly 100 have committed to try Four-Blocks. Many of these teachers have years of experience, but they realize that Four-Blocks answers so many of the questions teachers have been asking for years. It puts the "Reading Wars" to rest. All of the four major approaches to teaching reading are valid, useful ways to teach. Why not use them all?

I wonder how Four-Blocks will play out this year in my own classroom. Although last year was my most successful teaching year, and I am confident in the Four-Blocks™ framework, I still worry a little. "Had last year been a fluke? Was last year's group of students one of those dream classes? Was it the students or the framework?"

I have just started the year with my new group, and they are a different class. We have not jumped ahead quite as fast as we did last year. We have spent much more time this year on procedures for each block. Many of my students this year have difficulty with concepts such as tracking print. Many of my students have difficulty sharing after Writing and Self-Selected Reading. Some will not speak out loud in front of the class, and just show their book or writing journal page. I have spent a great deal of time modeling, and they are beginning to catch on.

We have begun the Word Wall, and they love the chanting and cheering we do. Each child eagerly anticipates their day as "Special Student," and they take their folder of our student stories home to share with their parents. Through the read-aloud at Self-Selected Reading time and the shared stories we read during the Guided Reading Block, they have become excited and enthusiastic about reading. *Junie B. Jones* is already a favorite, and they love the *Black Lagoon* series. After just a few short weeks, I see them becoming enthusiastic about books. So, I am sure Four-Blocks will be successful for me this year—although I wish we were moving along a little faster than we are!

Four-Blocks has restored my enthusiasm, and reminded me of why I decided to teach. I wanted to make a difference and help children develop a love of reading and a love of learning. Four-Blocks gives me the tools I need to accomplish those goals. It is exciting to see the model spreading in my school, in my state, and around the country and world. I can say it has changed me, and I can't imagine ever teaching any other way!

My "High-Risk" Students
Love Reading Real Books ●●●●●●●●●●●●●●●●●●●●●●●●●●●●●●●

by Deb Smith (with Dottie Hall)

I, like many other teachers, met Deb Smith vicariously "on line," listening to her answer questions and post lessons in response to other teacher's questions on the Teachers.Net mailring. This led to "really meeting" Deb at a seminar I did in Chicago in 1999 and again later at the Four-Blocks™ Leadership Conference in January, 2000. In April, I did a Four-Blocks seminar in Grand Rapids, Michigan and stayed an extra day so I could visit Deb's classroom. Michigan has a "schools of choice" plan, and children are bused from the Benton Harbor School District to the Colomba School District, where Deb teaches. Deb had 20 second-grade students in her class, 18 of whom were on free lunch, and two who were on reduced price lunch. Five of her students were classified as "special education students" with a wide variety of disabilities (one autistic, one hearing impaired and learning disabled, two educational mentally impaired and ADHD, one with cerebral palsy and learning disabled). Gates-McGinitie scores at the beginning of the school year indicated that two children were on grade level—2.0; five were on a kindergarten level; the remaining 13 had grade level scores between 1.1 and 1.4. As a second-grade teacher, she had her work cut out for her. What I saw that day helped me to understand that all over the country, there were teachers like Deb using Four-Blocks with "at-risk" children and finding success. These teachers on the Web were actually practicing what they preached! This is Deb's story:

Do you recognize these students? On the first day of second grade, Jackson strolls into school acting cool. He spells his name, recognizes his letters, knows most of his sounds (although vowels are difficult), and reads eight of the 120 second-grade Word Wall words. Will Jackson let down his guard to learn the skills he needs to read?

Ashleigh meanders into the classroom knowing how to decode lots of words. She scores below grade level in comprehension. She fills pages with writing that doesn't really say anything. Will Ashleigh learn to think about her reading and writing?

Andrew entered kindergarten reading. He loves school, and he loves to read. He comprehends what he reads. He uses his knowledge of sounds to figure out unknown words. How will this second-grade classroom meet his intellectual needs?

How I Discovered the Four-Blocks™

In 1989, when I began my teaching career, the big push was toward whole language and thematic teaching. Teaching phonics was frowned upon. To meet the expectations of my district, I developed thematic units linking comprehension and writing while incorporating fiction and nonfiction books. My high readers soared; my middle readers had wonderful comprehension skills, but lousy decoding strategies; and my lowest readers left second grade practically not reading. I was working really hard, but something was still missing.

In May of 1998, while finishing my Masters degree in reading, I began my journey to Four-Blocks. I enrolled in a reading research class. The professor announced that there would only be one assignment. Having two young children at home, I thought "Whew!" He asked us to write down a list of everything we believed was linked to literacy in our classrooms. Since I teach second grade, everything I teach is connected to literacy. My list was incredibly long. It included comprehension, decoding, reading strategies, reading to children, children reading books of their own choosing, and much more. I looked over at the eighth-grade science teacher sitting next to me. He had three items on his list. I thought, "Bad teacher!" Well, the professor collected our lists, copied them, and returned them. The only assignment was to find research — pro and con — for everything on our list! My mouth dropped open! Little did I know that I had just received the hardest and the BEST assignment of my graduate career. After weeks of researching, I wrote a balanced literacy plan that I would implement in my classroom. Someone in the class asked if I had read *Classrooms That Work*. I hadn't, so I bought it and began reading.

I had used Writer's Workshop for ten years, so I already knew that students need to write daily. I knew that the children needed direct instruction with comprehension. I also knew that children needed to read lots of books to make up for missing "lap time" at home. After reading *Classrooms That Work*, I knew what was missing. The chapter on Working with Words changed my teaching. I bought *Phonics They Use* next. Between these two books, I had FINALLY read something that I could understand about phonics. I didn't have to try and teach rules I didn't remember or sounds I couldn't hear. Next, I bought *Month-by-Month Phonics for Second Grade* and began teaching phonics holding this book tightly in my fist.

I started a Word Wall with five words. We clapped and cheered Word Wall words. The kids loved it! We started Making Words, Guess the Covered Word, and

24

Rounding Up the Rhymes—all the first week. If the *Month-by-Month* book suggested an activity, I did it. The fourth block was now in place. I had a multilevel, workable approach for phonics instruction.

I went on a search for every article Pat Cunningham or Dottie Hall had written. One article made a reference to a Web site: *http://www.teachers.net* (and later *http://www.readinglady.com*). I went to the Web site, joined the Four-Blocks mailring, and began to learn. I read every message, checking my E-mail several times a day. When others on the mailring asked questions, I read the books searching for answers. I did not give my opinion. Instead, I looked for answers in the books. I kept going back to the original sources—books and journal articles. Between the questions, the debates, and the answers I found on the Four-Blocks mailrings, I became very knowledgeable in Four-Blocks methods. In the summer of 1999, I went to hear Dottie Hall in Oak Lawn, Illinois. That day reaffirmed what I had been reading and trying in my classroom.

The structure of Four-Blocks really appealed to me. Previously, I had a tendency to teach the components of a balanced program throughout the week, but didn't teach all four blocks every day. I worried that the children would balk at not having time to finish an assignment. I had to learn to break my lessons down into smaller chunks. I did the rereading suggested for Guided Reading and was surprised to discover that the children enjoyed reading the same text for a new purpose the next day. The children seemed to enjoy the faster pace, and the fact that "nothing lasts too long." The shorter blocks of time weren't a problem for my children. It was a management issue for me!

The Four-Blocks mailrings have been a source of pride for me. Many teachers receive no formal Four-Blocks training; there is a great need for opportunities to learn and share. I don't believe that I would have seen the growth I saw in my students if it were not for the Four-Blocks™ framework, as well as the guidance and support my fellow Four-Blocks teachers provided on the Internet. The mailrings provide the best ideas and encouragement, while promoting practices that are consistent with the philosophy of Four-Blocks. There are many wonderful conversations about reading, learning, and teaching among the participants.

I do all the blocks every day, but Self-Selected Reading is my favorite block. The philosophy is simple. You read to kids, you let them read, and you give them time to discuss the books they are reading. As I discuss these three components, I will link a low student (Jackson), middle student (Ashleigh), and high student

(Andrew) to the discussion. (These are real children, but the names are pseud-onyms.) Since many of my children have long bus rides on overcrowded buses, I begin my morning with the Self-Selected Reading Block.

Getting the Day Off to a Good Start

Many of my children have long bus rides. When they arrive at school, they eat breakfast. They come to my room at different times. I have set up a Daily News routine which allows me to touch base with each child and meet our school dis-trict requirement for Daily Oral Language. (The children relate much better to writing and editing their own "news" than they do to sentences which have noth-ing to do with them.) The children enter the classroom and immediately write two or three sentences about what they did the night before. I call this their "Daily News." As each child finishes, she/he brings the News to me for an editing lesson. After completing their Daily News and their quick edit with me, each child chooses between five and eight books from the many book baskets spread around the room.

After approximately 15-20 minutes, all the children have written their Daily News, had some one-on-one time with me, chosen 5-8 books, and are ready to begin our Four-Blocks day. After the long, noisy and cramped bus ride, the quiet and calm atmosphere of reading aloud to the students combined with the children reading is a wonderful way to start the day.

Reading Aloud to Children

To open the Self-Selected Reading Block, I gather the children close to me. They sit at my feet as cozily as possible in a classroom. I try to imitate the setting of bedtime stories and routines of my childhood for those who were not so fortu-nate. I usually choose three different books for my read-aloud time—a chapter book, a nonfiction book related to our class theme, and an "everyone book"—a simple, small (usually 8-16 pages) predictable pattern book. I don't call these books "easy" books. I call them "everyone books," so everyone will feel comfort-able reading these easier books. I read and "bless" at least one "everyone book" daily.

I begin the read-aloud portion of Self-Selected Reading with a chapter book. To model metacognition (thinking about your thinking), I use a think-aloud tech-nique as I read the book. To prepare for this, I read the chapter in advance, record my thoughts on sticky notes, and attach these notes to the pages of the book. I tell the class that my thoughts will change as I know more events in the story.

Here is an example of the think-aloud technique based on the book, *My Father's Dragon*. A boy is running away from a mean mother who beats him for feeding a cat warm milk. He is packing a knapsack with a variety of items, including chewing gum, two dozen lollipops, a package of rubber bands, toothpaste, and more. After reading the items, I wonder aloud about the weird collection he packs in the backpack. To anticipate another chapter titled, "My Father Meets Some Tigers," I wonder aloud if the tigers will eat the boy. Then, I tack on this comment; "No, that can't happen since this is only chapter five, and there are ten chapters in all!" This is obvious to adults, but not to children.

In addition to this general think-aloud, I also use OWL—Observe, Wonder, and Link to your life. I teach the OWL strategy during Guided Reading. This is the procedure I use to teach OWL. The children sit in a circle. Holding a single copy of the book, I look at one page of the book and make one observation, always starting this observation with the words, "I observe" or "I notice." Then, one by one, the children pass the book around making "I observe" or "I notice" statements. The children are allowed to page through the book, making an observation about any page. When all students have had a turn, the book is returned to me. I then turn to the page about which I made my observation and make an "I wonder" statement. Once again, the book is passed around and the children each make an "I wonder" statement. Then, we read the book. When we finish reading, I make a statement linking the book to my life, and the children share links to their own lives.

Having taught OWL during Guided Reading, the children and I make "I observe or I notice," "I wonder," and "I link to my life" comments during Self-Selected Reading. Using *Owl Moon* as an example of the OWL technique, I observe that a man and his child are walking in the snow. I wonder why they are out in the middle of the night. I read the story to the class. The dad is taking his daughter out to listen for the owls. She is finally old enough to go. I link this to my life with this story:

> My mom and dad have four children. My dad has always worked a lot of hours. Every Saturday, he would take one of the four children with him on errands and to the bakery for donuts. I remember how special it was for me to spend one-on-one time with my dad. *Owl Moon* links to my life because the dad is spending special time with his child, like I did with my dad.

The children then share links from *Owl Moon* to their lives. The links begin with very basic comments, such as "I walked in the snow" or "I have a dad." The links deepen as the children practice.

Ashleigh is good at decoding, but is struggling with comprehension. She often chooses the chapter book I have read aloud for her own reading. In our conferences, I discovered that she liked to think about her thoughts while rereading what I modeled in my think-aloud or OWL statements. She loved placing sticky notes in the book to remind her of where she paid attention to her thinking.

Next, I share a few pages of a nonfiction book. While studying bats and owls in October, I read parts of the book, *Bats*. I don't read the whole book in one sitting. Instead, I read a few pages. The children love to finish a book I've begun during their Self-Selected Reading time.

Since we are learning about bats this month, we are also reading about bats during Guided Reading. We start a KWL chart during Guided Reading. Children love choosing books about bats for Self-Selected Reading and adding to the facts on our KWL chart. I have baskets of informational books related to each topic we study, and I include in these baskets the books I read to them, books we read during Guided Reading Book Club groups, and other theme-related books. Andrew often chooses these nonfiction books and uses his Self-Selected Reading time to greatly expand his knowledge of our current theme topic.

I close the read-aloud time each day by reading an "everyone book." I find that my struggling readers need me to celebrate their books every single day. They are eager and willing to read the book that the teacher reads first. After reading the "everyone book," I always ask one of my struggling readers if he/she wants that book. I try to have multiple copies of these books so that all the struggling readers can choose it if they like! After I read aloud from *Little Critter's This is My School*, I asked Jackson if he'd like to read this book during Self-Selected Reading time today. I then pulled out the book basket with a variety of Mercer Mayer books in it and found several copies of *Little Critter's This is My School* and handed them to children who wanted them. My children love rereading stories they just heard. Can you remember what your toddler's favorite book was? I can. My son's favorite book was *There's A Wocket in My Pocket*.

Reading and Conferencing with the Children

After I read from the chapter book, the informational book, and the "everyone book," the children return to their seats where the 5-8 books they chose are waiting on their desks. While the children are reading books at their level, I am conferencing individually with my students. I use this time to move my students from where they are to the next stage. Jackson is working on incorporating reading strategies to build fluency and understanding. Ashleigh is working on thinking while she's reading to improve her comprehension. Andrew is expanding his intellect. In your classroom, how would you meet their diverse needs?

I sit next to Jackson's desk. He is reading the book I shared from the "everyone book" portion of the read-aloud, *Little Critter's This Is My School*. I ask him to continue reading from where he is.

"Mom gives me an apple for the _____."

He doesn't know the last word. I coach him to name the letters, and then ask him what would make sense in the sentence if we were doing Guess the Covered Word. Jackson rereads the sentence correctly, reading "teacher" for the word he didn't know.

A few pages later he is reading along and reads, "We put our _____ away." I coach him to look on the Word Wall for this word. He finds "things" on the Word Wall, reads it, and then rereads the sentence. He needs a lot of word coaching. I remind him to ask questions: "Does it make sense?" "Does it sound right?" "Does it look right?" I also remind him to use reading strategies: Is it a Word Wall word? Do I know a rhyming word? If we were doing Guess the Covered Word, what word would make sense and have all the correct beginning letters?

After he finishes reading, I ask him to make connections to his school. Although Jackson's primary focus is figuring out what the words are, I also ask comprehension questions to encourage him to think about his reading. I may ask questions like: "How is Little Critter's school the same as ours?" "How is Little Critter's school different?" Jackson is able to discuss both questions. I am seeing growth in his use of strategies. I remind myself to make sure he has a good word coach for a partner in the Guided Reading Block.

I move on to sit next to Ashleigh. She is reading *Clifford and the Grouchy Neighbors*. She begins reading aloud when I approach her. I listen to her read four pages. She is fluent. I wonder about her comprehension though, so I ask her to go to the beginning of the book and find places in the story where Clifford's size helps people. She opens to a two-page-spread that shows Clifford using a pipe to blow away a cat from the bird feeder. Ashleigh understands the book she is reading! Ashleigh's reading has improved, since she now stops and says something after each two-page-spread. It has slowed down her reading a little, but she is now forced to think about her reading. We call this "Say Something" and teach it during Guided Reading. When my children partner read, I often use "Say Something" to keep them thinking about what they are reading. If they can't think of anything to say, they need to go back and reread.

I walk over to Andrew. I kneel next to his chair. He sighs. I think he views my conferences as an interruption to his reading. Andrew is usually the last child to put away his books from the Self-Selected Reading Block. His mom mentions that she takes away flashlights at night and finds him sitting in the closet with his books. I simply ask him several comprehension questions, trying to engage him in a book chat. He answers correctly and grins. I quickly move on. He doesn't really need Self-Selected Reading since he also has this time at home. However, it is his favorite block. Andrew loves to read. How nice that we can provide such an enjoyable time for him at school!

Children Sharing Their Self-Selected Reading Books

The third component of the Self-Selected Reading Block is the opportunity to share what the students are reading in the classroom. When there are seven minutes remaining in our Self-Selected Reading Block, the children put books away for approximately two minutes. Then, I quickly model how to talk about a book. Today, I talk about *Junie B. Jones and the Stupid Smelly Bus.*

"I like this book because it is so silly. The teacher is always looking at the ceiling, rolling her eyes at Junie B. If you want to laugh, read this book!"

The children are sitting in groups of four or five, and they each quickly share something about a book they read today. Every child discusses his or her book for one minute every day. I circulate between the small groups, listening to the children's comments. If a group tries to engage me in their discussion, I smile and nod and move on. I want the children to talk to each other, not me.

Getting Books for Self-Selected Reading

To organize for Self-Selected Reading, I bought forty book baskets for $2 each from Wal-Mart®. These baskets are bigger than the books so the books can lay flat or stand on their sides. The children can dig through them without bending the books or knocking the baskets over. I have all kinds of baskets. Some baskets contain books by only one author. Theme- and topic-related books fill other baskets. I have one basket which contains only very easy books—reading recovery levels 1-4, and another with Scholastic emergent readers. I have three levels of Creative Teaching Press books, each in its own basket. Laminated copies of *Scholastic News* magazines fill one basket, laminated *Kid's Week* newspapers fill another. I have a *Zoo Book* magazines basket, a joke books basket, a poems basket, a basket full of "How to Draw" books, and others. I have a variety of levels in most baskets, but some baskets contain books on a particular level. I try to keep the baskets in the same place day to day, so the children know where their favorite baskets are located.

I introduce new authors monthly. I also introduce a new animal theme each week. I keep the old author or theme books out for a month or two, depending on the children's interest. The librarian always knows what my students are reading, since they often check out books linked to the author studies and themes.

I have collected books through book clubs (Trumpet, Scholastic, Carnival, Troll, etc.). One hint that has helped my book collection is bonus points. In the September book orders, the clubs will multiply your order by 20 points once you've spent $200. September is the only month in which I spend $200, but I get 4000 bonus points for that order! I then use these 4000 points throughout the year to purchase multiple copies of books. I usually earn roughly 500 books each year this way. I have also gone to numerous garage sales and used bookstores.

Collecting enough emergent level books needs to be a priority. I have lots of emergent readers now, but many teachers tell me that getting enough of these books is a real problem. I suggest that if teachers would share, everyone would have more. If four teachers shared and bought sets of emergent readers from four different companies, each teacher could have one set of emergent readers for each grading period. At the end of each grading period, each set of emergent readers would rotate to another classroom. Of course, every child must be taught to take care of the books, and teachers must be responsible for seeing that this happens.

Finding Success with the Four-Blocks™ Framework

As the year ends, all the children are reading. Jackson enjoys reading second-grade favorites, including *Clifford* and *Franklin* books. He writes and correctly spells the second-grade Word Wall words in his writing. Ashleigh retells the stories she reads during Self-Selected Reading. She answers comprehension questions and has even written a chapter book about her life. Andrew reads science books, expanding his wide knowledge base.

Do you remember my beginning reading scores? On the Gates-McGinitie post-test, my two students labeled EMI made 0.9 years growth. They are not reading on grade level, but they are reading and have made tremendous progress. One child scored 2.5. Fifteen students scored between 2.9 and 3.5. My top two students scored 5.1 and 7.1. That is amazing at my school! The best result of Four-Blocks is that the children all view themselves as readers.

Looking Forward to Next Year

As I write this, I am also preparing my second-grade classroom for the 2000-2001 school year. I have spent the summer vacationing with my family, being a mother to my own two elementary-age students, and conducting a number of Four-Blocks workshops for teachers all over the country. I have enjoyed all of these "jobs," and Four-Blocks keeps me busy, both on the mailrings and on the road. Working with teachers is as rewarding as working with students! I look forward to another school year where I will continue to teach Four-Blocks in my second-grade classroom, and continue to talk about the Four-Blocks on the mailring and in person, with schools and school systems that I can fit into my teaching schedule. Life is busy, but life is good!

Four-Blocks™ and Writing— Right from the Start ·

by Denise Boger (with Dottie Hall)

Having worked with Denise Boger for ten years, Pat and I were thrilled when she agreed to tell her story. Denise has a very "special" story to tell. Denise was hired at Clemmons Elementary the same year that Four-Blocks™ began. She was one of the first teachers to learn how to do Four-Blocks from Margaret Defee, the Four-Blocks pilot teacher. Denise watched lessons modeled in Margaret's classroom and learned from Margaret how to do Writer's Workshop. Today, Denise is the teacher in room 33, the room Margaret used to teach in and the room where Four-Blocks began. She often has student teachers from Wake Forest University, sometimes in first grade, sometimes in second grade, for she is a looping teacher and has been for a number of years. Denise is also a teacher who opens her classroom to visitors—more than we can count! Denise is a quiet, effective, wonderful Four-Blocks teacher. This is Denise's story of how Four-Blocks was born and why Writing is her favorite block:

Four-Blocks™ has changed my teaching methods and effectiveness so much that it kept me from changing careers! The fall of 1980 found me in a first-grade classroom doing my student teaching. The children were wonderful, and I adored them! But, the days and nights were boring to me and very busy. During the day, we gave our first-grade students seatwork while we worked with small groups. At night, we graded the seatwork, drew, colored, and cut out items for learning centers for the children to do when they finished their seatwork! I thought I had gone into teaching because I wanted to help children grow to love learning and to feel good about themselves! Maybe I was being too idealistic, but this was not what was happening in my student-teaching classroom. Maybe planning a wedding while student teaching was discoloring my view! Having my own classroom would be better! In the fall of 1981, I had my own second-grade classroom and found myself doing the same kinds of things! For three years I taught, thinking each year that the next one would be better! It wasn't.

How I Found Clemmons Elementary, Margaret Defee, and Four-Blocks™

After the birth of my second child, I was ready to just stay home and "teach" my own children, but finances would not allow that. I vowed, "I'll go back to teaching if I get a job at Clemmons where I can get home to my own children as soon as possible." I knew very little about Clemmons Elementary except that it was close to my house, and everyone said that it was difficult to get a teaching position there. Feeling the way I did, I was certain that I would never get a teaching job at Clemmons. That's when I met Margaret Defee, the pilot teacher for Four-Blocks. The principal at that time was Daisy Chambers, and she invited Margaret to help with my interview. As they say, "The rest is history." I got the job, and I have been at Clemmons Elementary ever since!

Margaret became both a mentor and friend. While Margaret and I were preparing for our students to arrive that year, she began to discuss her daily schedule with me. There were two parts of her scheduled day that were new and very interesting to me. Those two parts were Writer's Workshop and Self-Selected Reading. I became curious and excited when she explained what went on during these two blocks of time. She also told me about Guided Reading and Working with Words, and how doing all four of these approaches provided children a more balanced reading program. Of course, Four-Blocks did not have a name at that time. It was just being born!

Getting Started—Following Margaret's Lead

I followed Margaret's lead from the beginning. I learned from her how to do all the blocks, but Writing was the one I knew the least about. Margaret was "a pro" at Writer's Workshop, so she told me what to do, and I did it!

I began Writer's Workshop each day with a minilesson. I called the children up to the floor and did a short (no more than ten-minute) minilesson on whatever I needed to teach—how to write, how to choose a topic, how to spell words, capital letters, periods, question marks, how to publish, and so forth. The minilesson was followed by a 20-minute writing time in which the children wrote on topics of their own choice. The idea was that the children would write more about topics they knew—topics from their own world—rather than topics in which they had little or no interest.

After writing, one table of children would share something that they had written in the "Author's Chair." The "audience" (those children who were not sharing on that day) would ask questions and make comments.

Margaret told me how she would model questions for the children during Author's Chair. I did the same, and soon the children were asking wonderful questions! First graders were asking, "How did you get the idea for your writing?" and

"What was the topic of your writing?" They asked about the main idea, the setting, and the main characters! They asked whether the writing was fiction or nonfiction, realistic or fantasy. I was amazed at how much these children were writing, and how much they were learning.

Writer's Workshop came just before lunch every day. I would watch the clock until it was time for writing—my favorite time of the day. Those 40 minutes would just fly by!

Once I learned about the Four-Blocks, I enjoyed teaching all four of them. I now felt like a "real teacher," not someone who stands and dispenses information only to have it given back to me on paper, so that I could take it home and spend my nights reading and correcting papers to see who understood the information I had dispensed! I was now actually involved in hands-on teaching and working with the children, including all kinds of learning styles, helping all children feel good about themselves. I observed children that were able to grow and be challenged according to their own abilities. The result was that all children were moving ahead in their literacy learning. I liked it that all the children were making progress, and I attributed this progress to the fact that they were not labeled as being members of the "top" or "bottom" reading groups. All four blocks worked together to accomplish this wonderful learning environment.

Today, 11 years later, I am still teaching Four-Blocks. I loop with my children from first to second grade and enjoy teaching all the blocks, but the Writing Block remains my personal favorite. Teachers who visit my classroom are always impressed with how well and willingly all my children write, and they want to know everything about what I do in Writing. I will try to share with you what I share with my visitors.

Minilessons During the Writing Block

Each Writing Block still begins with a ten-minute minilesson. During first grade, I start out by modeling how children write. I let them know that whatever they do (drawing, driting, emergent writing, or conventional writing) will be accepted in my classroom. For my minilessons, I use the overhead and write short pieces with only a few sentences each day. I stretch out words and write the sounds I hear. It only takes a week or two of this before you hear the beautiful sounds of children stretching out words during writing time. The wonderful thing about this activity is that from that point on, chunking words and sounding them out when they are reading comes so much easier and faster for the students. It becomes obvious that children truly not only learn to write by writing, but also learn to read.

Once we start adding words to the Word Wall, I model how to use the Word Wall and "read the room" to spell words that are displayed in the room. It becomes a "no-no" to spell words incorrectly if they are on the Word Wall. After a few times of modeling looking on the Word Wall for a word, I will invariably stretch out a word that is already on the Word Wall. Immediately, I hear, "Uh, uh, Mrs. Boger, that word is on the Word Wall. You shouldn't have spelled that one wrong." This is so neat! They read to write, write to read, and write to spell!

The minilessons get more complex as the children become better writers. During my minilessons, I cover such skills as choosing a topic, staying on the topic, grammar, punctuation, sequence, how to edit, how to publish, choosing a setting, adding on to a piece, run-on sentences, and any other topic that I need to teach. I teach these minilessons either because these skills are part of our required curriculum, or because I have observed students' writing and see a need to cover a particular skill. In second grade, I include minilessons on stating the main idea, summarizing, using descriptive words, adding details, and other more advanced writing skills.

The minilesson can be a how-to lesson in which I model how to write a fable, a fairy tale, an autobiography, a biography, a report, a letter, a funny story, a scary story, a realistic story, or a poem. Sometimes, my minilesson is just reading a story or a series of stories by one author or on one topic and helping the children notice details about the author's style or the type of book. Science and social studies can be integrated into the writing lesson by way of the minilesson, also. I might read a book related to a science or social studies topic and model how to summarize that information into a report.

I teach writing every day and do a minilesson every day. I have most of my children for 360 days—that's a lot of minilessons! I have the time and opportunity to teach my first- and second-graders everything there is to know about how to write—from picky mechanical details to sophisticated writer's craft. And I do!

Writing and Conferences

The minilesson is followed by 20 minutes of writing time. The rule during Writer's Workshop is that children write. When they finish one piece, they start another. On any given day, some children will be writing new pieces, others will be working on pieces they have already started, and some are choosing a piece they want to publish. (I let them choose a piece to publish when they have written three to five good pieces.) While they write, I conference with children who have chosen pieces, helping them revise and edit. These revised and edited pieces then are published and become real books. The children see themselves as real authors!

Children do not publish every piece they write, and I do not correct the pieces they are not going to publish. This was one thing that first attracted me to Writer's Workshop. I did not have to correct every piece that every child wrote! And when I do correct a piece, it is in a one-on-one conference where the children learn how to revise and edit as we do this together. I don't do all the work; I help the children and teach them how to revise and edit.

The children edit their stories first by using an Editor's Checklist, which they keep in their working writing folders. We begin the checklist in first grade and gradually add things to check for. Some of the first things we add to our checklist and check for are: name, date, title, and five good thoughts. As the children grow in their writing, we add to the checklist. The students learn to circle words for which they need to check the spelling; to check their writing for beginning capitals and ending punctuation; to check that their piece has a beginning, middle, and end; and that sentences are complete thoughts and stay on the topic. After I teach a skill several times, I add it to our Editor's Checklist. The students help me edit my writing during the minilessons, and then they are expected to do this on their own.

After they have edited their own writing, they often ask a peer-editor to help them edit. Some children are better writers than others. Some children can edit better than others. We work on writing, revising, and editing all year long. I do not expect everyone to edit well immediately, but I know that with constant modeling, they will all get better. Before anything is published, I do a final edit.

Sharing in the Author's Chair

The 20-minute writing time is followed by 10 minutes of sharing time. This is another time where it is obvious that the children are writing to read and reading to write! One fifth of the children share each day, so that each child shares one day each week. They read either a piece of writing they are working on, or a book they have published. Then, "the audience" gives positive comments (a must!) and asks questions. I model higher-level thinking questions, and soon the children pick up on this and begin asking the same kinds of questions themselves.

One good question children ask is, "How did you get the idea for this writing?" This helps those children who are more hesitant about coming up with ideas on their own. The teacher models and encourages children to write on subjects they know a lot about, rather than on specific topics or story starters they may know little or nothing about. This not only keeps the children writing, but it also boosts their self-esteem as they share writing that has personal value to them.

Publishing

Most visitors marvel at both the writing and publishing of young children in the Four-Blocks classrooms at Clemmons. They often ask, "How do you do it?" and "Where do you get the books?" Children write daily, so publishing flows naturally as they finish several pieces and choose one to revise, edit, and publish. We do not edit and publish the first month of first grade, but some children are ready to start soon after that. Because writing is naturally multilevel, I let the children show me when they are ready to publish. When most of my class has published a book, I help those who haven't published yet to publish one. Some children publish four or five books each year, some publish 20 or more!

We have wonderful parent volunteers at Clemmons who make blank books for the teachers. The books are made by cutting packages of duplicator paper in half and using half-sheets of 8" x 12" colored index cards as the front and back covers. The books we use to publish in first grade have eight pages. Those pages include: a title page, a dedication page, five lined pages with a space to draw at the top of the page, and a page where the teacher writes "About the Author" as the child dictates something about himself or herself. The books we make later in the year and in second grade need more space for writing, so we add more lines to the pages and more pages to the book. The books are "bound" with a commercial book binding machine (some teachers at other schools staple them together), and we keep a supply of books in various colors in our classrooms. When a child is ready to do a final copy, he or she has a book that is ready to write in. Sometimes children type their final copy on the computer, cut the sentences apart, and paste them on the pages. After the book is written, the children illustrate their books. We have a publishing table where I keep crayons, magic markers, correction fluid, scissors, and all the materials the children need to illustrate and finish their books.

Visitors often ask me how we have time to publish all the books. The publishing—editing, revising, copying or typing into the skeleton book, and illustrating—

all happen in that 20 minutes of writing time that we have each day. When a child has three to five good pieces, chooses one to publish, edits using the checklist, revises and edits with me, and then publishes, that child is not writing any new first drafts on those days. Once the piece is published, the child starts producing first drafts again, and the cycle begins all over. During the daily 20 minutes of writing time, different children are at different stages of the writing process.

Preparing for State Mandated Writing Tests in the Upper Grades

At our school, we loop grades one and two. In other words, we keep the same children through first and second grades. There has been more emphasis on writing in the past few years because of state mandated writing tests than there was ten years ago when I began doing Writing with my class. Although the state tests are in the upper grades, there is more emphasis, focus, and accountability, even in first and second grades. With the Writing Block in place, the writing tests do not pose a problem for us. The basics of good writing are taught every day throughout first and second grade. Near the end of second grade, I can introduce narrative writing during the minilesson. I use some of my minilessons to teach how to respond to a given prompt or topic and carry it through from beginning to end. I do some minilessons in which I show examples of good writing and how to make writing better. During our sharing time, the children hear each other's writing and they get more feedback on how to improve.

Assessing Writing

I believe that keeping writing samples is the best way for a teacher to assess a student's writing development over time. Record keeping and work samples are a cinch during the Writing Block. The children keep a log of the pieces they have written. They keep pieces they are working on in a working folder. They also have a permanent folder in which they keep rough copies of pieces they have published and pieces they have decided not to work on anymore. I look for progress in all my writers, from emergent to those writing well above grade level. I expect to see progress over time, and I usually do. I look at their first drafts to assess their writing development, including meaning, vocabulary, grammar, and spelling. I have these samples available to share with parents when they want to know how their children's writing is being evaluated.

First- and second-graders absolutely love Writer's Workshop. They ask, "Why can't we have writing?" when the schedule has to be changed around for one reason or another. Believe it or not, I have had children who choose to skip playtime on a day when something is going to have to be left out, rather than miss writing time! When this happened the first few times, I was just as bedazzled as you probably are, but it's true!

Writing is the only one of the Four-Blocks in which I must set a timer to stop both the children and myself, so that we get everything else covered! I remember one day back when I was working in the Writing Block, and Margaret Defee walked in and said to me as I was working at the publishing table, "You've got to stop. You could do this all day!" That was as true then, when I was first learning Writer's Workshop, as it is today. Writer's Workshop is most definitely a valuable building block in the construction of successful and effective readers and writers—a must today in our world of global communications! A must for me as a teacher!

Looking Forward to Next Year

What will I be doing next year? That's easy! I will be a first-grade Four-Blocks teacher in Room 33 at Clemmons Elementary School. I look forward to watching another group of first-graders learn to read and write using the Four-Blocks™ framework. Next year, I will take them on to second grade and see my work pay off as all my children become fluent and avid readers and writers!

The Road to Change: Solving the Dilemma of Guided Reading

by Laura M. Kump (with Dottie Hall)

"Neophytelm" was a name that kept appearing on the Four-Blocks™ mailring during the 1998-99 school year. Who was this person? How did she come to use this name tag? From her postings, I learned that she taught first grade at P.S. 18 in New York City. I would find out the answers to my other questions the following summer as I traveled the country. The first time I met Laura Kump (and her husband and three school-age children) was in Philadelphia in July, 1999. In August, when I was working for a school system in Connecticut, Laura came again (with her family), and I got a chance to spend some time with her. That is when Laura told me the story of her name tag (her principal dubbed her "neophyte" because she was a new teacher) and her Four-Blocks story. Listening to Laura's story convinced me, and later convinced Pat, that we should write the book Guided Reading the Four-Blocks™ Way. *Laura started her own Web site that fall, and the "readinglady" became well-known to teachers who surf the Web. This is Laura's story:*

My journey to implementing the Four-Blocks™ framework has continuously pushed me to develop as an educator. I came to teaching later in life and had a Master's degree and my Reading Specialist certificate when I was hired for my first job at Public School 18 on Staten Island. P.S. 18 is an inner-city, Title I school with a very transient population. Our students consistently score poorly on standardized testing. In the 1997-1998 school year, merely 30% of our students attained minimum competency levels on state tests. As a Reading Specialist, I was hired to work with students identified as being most "at risk" of not becoming literate. My job was to push into the classroom and work with the classroom teachers to set up leveled Guided Reading groups to teach these students to read. I set about this task and worked very hard, yet was extremely disappointed with the results. There was a mere 1% increase in overall test results, and far worse, the children still were not able to read.

The following school year, I made the decision to return to the classroom and try the leveled groups approach in my own classroom. My class consisted of 24 first-graders, most of whom were significantly lacking in language development, phonemic awareness, and writing abilities. Unfortunately, the leveled groups approach did not work for me any better in my own classroom than it had when I was helping other classroom teachers to implement it. Management was a huge issue. I set up my literacy centers and trained my children in how to use them. They were, however, unable to complete their center work without my guidance, and my groups were constantly interrupted.

Meanwhile, I had been reading *Classrooms That Work* and other books and articles by Pat Cunningham. What I read blended with my belief that all children are unique, and as such, all bring something different and special to the classroom. The Four-Blocks™ framework, outlined in *Classrooms That Work*, acknowledged that all children learn differently, and provided a model for teaching with four different blocks: Guided Reading, Writing, Self-Selected Reading, and Working with Words. This framework outlined a systematic, multilevel approach to teaching literacy and provided the balance I sought. I decided to abandon the leveled groups and experiment with the Four-Blocks approach.

Once I began using Four-Blocks as my organizing framework, I did it pretty much "by the book." Assessments given in October and May demonstrated that my students had made significant gains during the school year. My students far surpassed my expectations. They were excited, motivated, and best of all—reading and writing!

Guided Reading with the Focus on Comprehension

Reflecting back on that year I taught first grade, it's quite clear that the most striking transformation in my teaching was the delivery of instruction during Guided Reading. My training as a Reading Specialist was with the guided reading format outlined in *Guided Reading: Good First Teaching for Children*. When I was hired as a Reading Specialist, this was the format I was asked to follow. Accordingly, I set up reading groups, placing children based on their levels and needs. While the children in the group were reading together, they were not really interacting with each other as they read. During this time, the remainder of the students were in literacy center activities and expected to work independently. The main problem we experienced with this format was that many students' skills and levels were so low they really didn't have the ability to work independently in centers. We constantly struggled with management issues during this time. In addition, the time for each group was so short that we couldn't do good before and after reading activities that teach children how to comprehend.

When I made the switch to Four-Blocks Guided Reading, my students were placed in mixed ability groups, and started reading, discussing, and learning together. I began Guided Reading every day with a whole group minilesson, in which a comprehension strategy was taught. The children were then given a purpose to read for, and they read the text in some type of flexible grouping format. The conclusion of the block involved the whole group coming together to share and discuss what they had learned from their reading. This approach was far more effective in that all children were actively involved in the learning process and the actual time spent reading was substantially increased. I found it easier to manage because the children were so involved with the text and each other. Most importantly, I was teaching comprehension strategies and developing their knowledge and language every day.

Ellin Keene discusses literacy teaching in her book *Mosaic of Thought*. She states,

> *We have found many classrooms where there was a great deal of direct instruction, but it focused on random strings of unrelated skills. The skills instruction and comprehension tools did not teach children how to comprehend.*

This is not the case in a Four-Blocks classroom, as far greater attention and time are being devoted to comprehension instruction. Keene further says that,

> *If reading is about mind journeys, teaching reading is about outfitting the travelers, modeling how to use the map, demonstrating the key and the legend, supporting the travelers as they lose their way and take circuitous routes, until, ultimately, it's the child and the map together and they are off on their own.*

We teach children how to read; we even teach them how to make sense of what they read. But are we really creating independent readers? How can we best enable our students to go off on their own? The answer is to equip them with the tools they will need to navigate through text. This is my ultimate goal as I plan and teach Guided Reading lessons.

Guided Reading Lessons

Guided Reading lessons include a before reading activity, which should be directly related to during reading, and after reading activities. For example, if your before reading activity is to make predictions—"What do you think will happen one Monday morning?"—the during reading purpose is to find out what happens one Monday morning, and the after reading activity is to revisit the predictions and discuss and perhaps chart what actually happened one Monday morning. This gives a nice flow and sequence to the block, connecting the activity and giving relevance to the skills being taught.

An example of a Guided Reading lesson using this format with the book *Angel Child: Dragon Child* follows. This book is about a Vietnamese child, Ut, trying to adjust to life in the United States without her mother. Ut is treated badly by her peers because she looks different. This is a wonderful story about accepting differences in others.

Day One: Focus–Vocabulary

Before Reading

Students are introduced to five key vocabulary words (brave, fuss, hoping, cruel-hearted, screeched) using RIVET. What you do is make a blank line to represent each letter of the word. Then, one by one, you begin writing the letters in each blank until the word is revealed to the students. You then can talk about the meaning of the word. Be selective about the words you choose, as you don't want to take away opportunities for the children to decode and use strategies to read unknown words. Generally, I try to select words whose meaning would be essential to know in order to comprehend the story. The activity was given the name RIVET by Pat Cunningham because the children are riveted to the chart trying to figure out the word as you write the letters.

During Reading

Everyone reads the first few pages to locate the vocabulary words introduced in RIVET in the text. Students read with partners, and using sticky notes, mark the pages in the text on which they found the words.

After Reading

The class meets on the rug to discuss where they found the words. Volunteers read aloud the paragraphs where the words were found, and word meanings are discussed based on the context.

Day 2: Focus–Generating Questions

Before Reading

The teacher reads part of the text aloud and does a think-aloud, "When I read that Ut's mother didn't come to America, I wondered why she didn't come." The teacher writes on the chart:

Why didn't Ut's mother come to America with the family? She then asks students what they wondered after reading the first few pages of the story, and charts several of their questions:

"Why was Raymond so mean to Ut?"

"Why did the children think Ut's clothes were pajamas?"

During Reading

Students are told to finish reading the story in playschool groups to see if the questions are answered. Each student is given one sticky note. On the sticky notes, students write down any additional questions they have, then place the sticky notes in the book.

After Reading

Students meet on the rug to discuss the questions on the chart and to add new questions to it.

Day Three: Focus–Coding Questions

Before Reading

Revisit the questions that were charted, beginning with the teacher's question:

"Why didn't Ut's mother come to America with the family?" Read the question and ask students if they found the answer to this question in their reading. Add students' answer to the chart:

"She didn't come because they didn't have enough money." Ask students how they knew this, and help them to notice that the answer was directly stated in the text. Indicate this information on the chart by placing an "A" next to the answer for "author answered." Repeat this process with another question on the chart.

During Reading

Ask students to reread the text in the same groups as Day 2. Prior to reading the text, they should reread the questions on the chart. As they read, they should look for questions which have a direct answer in the text and put an "A" next to these.

After Reading

Children reconvene with the teacher to share their findings. More answers to questions are written on the chart with an "A" next to them, indicating that they were directly found in the text.

Day Four: Focus–Making Inferences

Before Reading

Revisit the chart and notice that not all questions were coded with an "A." Explain that authors don't always give us explicit answers in the text. Sometimes, we as readers have to use the clues the author gives us and combine that with what we already know to figure out the answers ourselves. Do an example.

"Why did Raymond make fun of Ut?"

Write the children's response on the chart under the question.

Raymond made fun of Ut because she was from a different country, and he didn't understand her ways.

Ask students where they found this answer. Ask them if the author said those words in the text. When they realize that the author didn't, code this answer "I" for inference. Explain that while there were clues in the text, the author never directly stated the answer. Explain that this is an inference they made as they read the story.

During Reading

Do Everyone Read To... in partners to find clues in the story for the remaining questions on the chart. When they find a clue and make an inference, the students write it on a sticky note and place it in the book on the passage that helped them do so.

After Reading

The group finishes coding the chart and discusses the inferences they made. Attention is given to the clues they used in the text, as well as connections they made that helped them to make the inferences.

These four Guided Reading lessons flowed not only during each day, but also throughout the week. One lesson built upon another as the students worked their way through this book. In this way, the difficult task of teaching inference was broken down into manageable pieces that students could handle. This outline called for four days to be spent on the book, as the text was a bit more complex. The fifth day of the week would be spent on something easier, maybe a fable with a moral about kindness, or a poem like this one:

A Real Bouquet

(Author Unknown)

Everybody has two eyes,
Bright as stars they shine.
But their color may not be
Just the same as mine.

Brown or blue, gray or green,
What difference does it make?
As long as you can see the sun
Shining when you wake.

Some folks' hair is very black;
Some have blonde or brown.
Whatever color it may be,
It's a pretty crown.

Flowers have so many shades,
And I'm sure you know,
Many lovely gardens
Where such flowers grow.

Children in this great big world
Are flowers in a way.
Some are light, some are dark,
Like a real bouquet.

Did you ever stop to think
How awful it would be,
If everybody looked the same,
Who would know you from me?

Day Five: Focus—Text-to-Self and Text-to-Text Connections

Before Reading

Write the poem on chart paper and read it aloud to the class. Reread the poem accenting the natural rhythm and flow of it. Invite students to chime in and join you by pausing at rhyming words. Pause and model a think-aloud by saying, "This poem reminds me of my friend Barbara. When we were little, Barbara used to get teased a lot because she had an accent. She was born down South and spoke differently than the rest of us."

Remind students that good readers think about how text relates to their own lives and that this helps them understand their reading. Remind them that we refer to this kind of connection as a "text-to-self" connection.

> "I made a 'text-to-self' connection when I thought of my friend
> Barbara, and this connection helped me understand the poem better."

Remind students that in addition to text-to-self connections, we sometimes connect something we read in one text to something we read in another text.

During Reading

Use a choral reading format in which different groups read different verses of the poem. Have it read several times, changing which group reads which verse. As the children are reading and listening to the other groups read, ask them to think of any text-to-self or text-to-text connections they can make.

After Reading

Lead children in a discussion of their connections. Remind children of your connection and how it helped you comprehend.

> "I made a text-to-self connection when reading this poem because it
> reminded me of my friend Barbara. Maybe the author wanted me to
> see how Barbara must have felt about being teased. What connections
> did you make when you were reading?"

Discuss students' connections and have them articulate how they think it helped them understand the poem. In addition to text-to-self connections, someone will most likely make a text-to-text connection between *A Real Bouquet* and *Angel Child:Dragon Child*. Ask them how knowing about that story helped them to comprehend this poem. These responses will also serve as a quick assessment for the theme presented during the week.

GUIDED READING BLOCK PLANNING SHEET

<u>**Text Used**</u>: _____

<u>**Before Reading**</u>: (10-15 minutes)

Comprehension Minilesson Focus: _____

_____

_____

Purpose for Reading: _____

_____

<u>**During Reading**</u>: (15-20 minutes)

_____

_____

_____

Format: _____

<u>**After Reading**</u>: (10-15 minutes) ·

_____

_____

_____

Varying the Amount of Support

During Guided Reading, the support that is provided to students includes a balance of teacher direction and peer interaction. Here are some of the different grouping options I have used to provide varying levels of support for my students:

• Whole Class

Shared Reading, Echo Reading, Choral Reading, Readers' Theatre, or ERT....

• Book Club Groups

Four or five different books that are related by some theme are read in small groups. Students get to preview books and choose which club they'd like to belong to. All students receive the same minilesson and will have the same purpose for reading, but apply that concept to varying texts. One of the texts is always easier than the rest, and one is harder.

- Playschool Groups
  Four or five children read together, with one child "playing teacher."
- Partner Reading
  Two students read together and support each other.
- Individual Reading
- Teacher meets with flexible group while other children are reading in partners or individually.

Success Leads to More Change

The first-graders that walked through my door that first day were very different from the ones that were to leave in June. They were now confident readers and writers and very much prepared for the challenges that lay ahead. My administrator decided to implement a looping program in first and second grade, and asked if I would consider staying with these children for a second year. With his support, my class and I embarked upon the next phase in our literacy quest. September found us together again in second grade, picking up right where we left off. With the strong foundation that was laid in first grade, I began to refine and further develop their reading and writing.

At the end of the second year, we compared assessments done on this pilot class and those done on students in traditional classrooms. We found that the children who were taught using the Four-Blocks™ framework far exceeded those taught in traditional classroom settings. End-of-year writing scores were higher, as was growth over the two-year period in reading and phonemic awareness.

As my students continue to develop as readers and writers, my interest and enthusiasm grows. This was the driving force that led me to create my Web site—*Readinglady.com*. It is my hope that through this site I can help improve the literacy instruction that goes on each day in classrooms across the country. There are many teachers in classrooms struggling, as I was, trying to reach each student in their room. Through our questions and dialogue, we have become a close-knit community. We've formed mailrings to discuss Four-Blocks issues, such as *FourBlocksEarly@egroups.com* and *FourBlocksElementary@egroups.com*, and an online study group, *ProfReadingGroup@egroups.com*. It is our hope that if we continue to develop as educators, our students will continue to develop as readers and writers.

Looking Forward to Next Year

What initially attracted me to the Four-Blocks™ framework was the fact that it was not a "program," but rather a framework that outlined a balanced approach to teaching literacy, which works well with whatever "program" you are using. I think it works because it is practical and provides students with four different approaches to learning. When we teach using only one method, we risk not reaching all the students in our room. Further, without devoting ample time to literacy, we deprive our students of the practice they so desperately need. We can no longer assume that our students will go home and read; we now must provide this time daily in our instructional day.

My first group of students who looped with me from first to second grade and who used the Four-Blocks™ framework are now in third grade, off on their own with strong wings ready to fly. This year will find me with a new group of first-graders, eager to begin again. I will no longer be a "lone ranger" using Four-Blocks in my school, for the other teachers have decided (or have been encouraged) to use this framework to improve instruction at P.S. 18. The principal has bought the basic books for all the teachers, and I will be helping them to implement the model in their classrooms.

What saddens me most as an educator is the acceptance, and even expectation, that some children will not become literate. Reading has been my passion since I was a very small child. I could not fathom my life without books, and to think that this was what lay ahead for many of my students was totally unacceptable to me. I truly believe we can break this cycle of failure when we teach ALL children to read. Literacy is the greatest gift we can ever give, and the Four-Blocks™ framework has allowed me to give it to my students.

Implementing the Four-Blocks™ in Third Grade:
Guided Reading and Written Responses •••••••••••••••••••
by Diane Zueck (with Dottie Hall)

Four-Blocks™ started in one first-grade classroom. It quickly spread to other first- and second-grade classrooms. Second-grade teachers have even said it is "perfect" for their students. In most second-grade classes, no Building Blocks™ activities are needed at the beginning of the year as in first grade classes, and no adaptations are needed for time as in the upper grades. Second-grade students can do all the "during" reading formats with little or no trouble. Second-grade teachers can use all the Working with Words activities successfully with their students. Third grade is not such an easy fit. In some third-grade classes, the students still need the Four-Blocks and still need to give equal amounts of time to each of the blocks because many of them are still learning to read. In other third grades, most students read and write at or above grade level and need to spend bigger blocks of time reading and writing and less time on words. It is impossible to know how closely a third-grade teacher should stick to the Four-Blocks™ framework until you know how well the children read and write. Diane is one of those third-grade teachers who used the Four-Blocks to greatly improve her students' reading and writing skills. Instead of teaching the test, or spending the year practicing for the test, Diane adapted her reading and writing lessons to make sure all students would be familiar with the kinds of reading and writing they would be asked to do on the state-mandated test. This is Diane's story:

Before explaining how I implemented the Four-Blocks™ framework, I would like to share "why" I decided to implement Four-Blocks. I am a latecomer to the teaching profession, but I feel teaching is what I should have been doing many years ago. When I first began teaching, I relied heavily on teacher's manuals, workbooks, and worksheets. I also taught the way my predecessor had been teaching before I was hired for her position. After all, I inherited her materials, and that made it easy. However, I knew even then that I didn't want to be a carbon copy of her because I had my own ideas and teaching style. I made some changes, added some new lessons, and felt I was teaching in a whole new way. In reality, I was still very textbook/workbook-dependent. I didn't feel as though I knew my students' reading abilities or weaknesses. I didn't know how to help them grow to become better readers. I still had this nagging feeling that there must be a better way. I knew I wanted to move away from so much dependence on the teacher's manual, but I didn't know how.

As I began my fifth year of teaching third grade, I grew very restless with what I had been doing in the past. At the same time, I made a conscious decision to focus on reading and writing. I was still accountable for teaching all the other subjects, but in my mind, I knew reading was the key to unlock the other subjects for my students. I also made a commitment to help my third-grade students become more fluent readers.

How I Found the Four-Blocks™

One night in a chat room on the Internet, I met a teacher from Alabama. She asked me if I had ever accessed the web site, *Teachers.Net*. I immediately typed in the URL, went to the site, and registered for the third-grade mailring. It was from that mailring that I began to hear about the Four-Blocks™ framework. I, of course, registered for the Four-Blocks mailring, too. I lurked for a long time, soaking in information about Four-Blocks. I read the books by Pat Cunningham, Dottie Hall, and Cheryl Sigmon. I read Cheryl's articles posted on the *Teachers.Net* Web site. As I read, I had a million questions. One day, feeling brave, I posted some questions to the ring. The responses and encouragement I received were wonderful. It gave me the confidence to try Four-Blocks without any formal training.

Starting with Guided Reading

I decided to start with the Guided Reading Block. I was so unhappy with the way I had been teaching reading (using a strictly teacher-directed, round-robin approach), and I knew this was the area I wanted to change first. In November 1998, I taught my first Guided Reading lesson the Four-Blocks way. After I taught the minilesson, I used the partner reading format to have my students read the text. I could immediately see an increase in enthusiasm for reading. The students were actually discussing the focus question with each other and exchanging ideas before writing in their journals. This was not what would have happened if I had told them to round-robin read the selection and then do page 20 in their workbook! I could also see how much more of their time was spent reading using the partner reading format instead of listening to others read (or, more likely, not listening!). I was sold!

I began to use the Four-Blocks approach to Guided Reading for all the reading lessons after that successful experience. I did encounter problems along the way, but many of them were management problems. I had to establish a set of expectations for Guided Reading and the new formats recommended by Four-Blocks. I again turned to the mailring for help. And again, I found the answers from teachers using Four-Blocks in their classrooms. In the beginning, I relied on the basal the school district provides for my Guided Reading lessons. I still use the basal as the backbone of my Guided Reading Block, but I also include trade books, *Weekly Reader*, poetry, songs, the science and social studies textbooks, and articles I have found on the Internet that are related to a theme we are studying. I fine-tuned my Guided Reading Block until I felt it was running effectively. Then it was time to add another block.

Adding Self-Selected Reading

While implementing the Guided Reading Block, I began to collect trade books for the self-selected reading baskets. I sent home book club order forms with the students. From their orders, I managed to collect enough bonus points to order many books on a variety of reading levels and topics for our classroom library. I purchased five plastic baskets that would be rotated once each week, and placed a variety of reading materials in them. I had been doing Sustained-Silent Reading with fair results, but switching to Self-Selected Reading the Four-Blocks way added a whole new dimension to silent reading. I began reading aloud to the students daily and noticed that they were much more motivated to read after my read-aloud. They loved sitting in the "Book Talk" chair to share their books. These two components have made all the difference in the world with silent reading. Once the routines for this block were firmly established and understood, I began to conference with students. I have gained so much from these conferences that I could never have gained from just listening to them round-robin read.

Getting Writer's Workshop Started

It was mid-February before I added the Writing Block. We had been doing a lot of writing to prepare for the Illinois Standards Assessment Test, given to third-graders in February. These writing lessons were always focused on writing to a prompt. After the state assessments, I began to do the Writing Block using a "Writer's Workshop" approach. Right away, I could see that the children enjoyed being able to write on topics that were of interest to them. I began to see a lot more variety in writing styles, and the students' interest in writing grew by leaps and bounds. Again, the sharing portion of the Writing Block made a huge difference in helping the students grow as writers and readers. I made a list of the language skills I am required to teach third-graders, and these have become the basis of some of the minilessons I teach at the beginning of each writing period.

Finally Adding Working with Words

In the spring of 1999, I was able to observe a school that was implementing the Four-Blocks™ Literacy Model. Being able to observe these teachers was a great help to confirm in my mind that I was on the right track, and also to inspire me in continuing to improve what I was doing. The last block I added was the Working with Words Block. I had been preparing the lessons for this block from *Month-by-Month Phonics for Third Grade* as I implemented the other three blocks. The preparation did take a considerable amount of time since I made my own letter cards for the students to manipulate for Making Words. Once I added the Working With Words Block, everything fell into place. I could see that I was reaching each child in my classroom in the way that each needed in order to learn to read. Adding this last block completed the model.

Guided Reading in Third Grade

Guided Reading was the first block I implemented because I was so unhappy with what I had been doing. I worked hard on using a variety of activities and formats, and adapting Guided Reading for third grade. I would like to share some of what I have learned with you.

In third grade, we begin the year with choral reading of poetry. We do some shared reading, but much less than they do in first and second grades. We use partner reading, playschool groups, Three-Ring Circus, ERT..., and book club groups frequently throughout the year.

As I began my second year of doing Four-Blocks in third grade, I developed a Guided Reading lesson plan template to help plan each reading lesson.

Title of Story, Author, Illustrator

Day 1

Before Reading:

Background:

Preview and Prediction:

Vocabulary:

Minilesson:

Focus Question and Purpose:

Format for During Reading:

After Reading:

Day 2

Repeat above plan as many times as necessary to complete the selection.

The more I taught Guided Reading using the Four-Blocks™ model, the more I began to see the importance of the before and after reading activities. There are many things to be accomplished before reading, and I don't do everything every day or spend equal amounts of time on each. We usually read every day during Guided Reading. At the beginning of a long selection, however, I sometimes spend a day building background knowledge. Then, we begin the other activities on the second day. For example, with the story *Through Grandpa's Eyes*, I spend the whole first day building background.

The question about the length of third-grade stories was a common one on the mailring. Rarely could a third-grade selection be completed in one day. I began to break the selections into manageable parts or sections. I would paper-clip the part of the selection that was not to be read, so when students reached the paper clip, they knew to stop reading. I did before reading activities each day, and then the children read the section in whatever format I had chosen. Most days, we did the after reading activities at the end of the Guided Reading time, but for long sections, we sometimes did the after reading activities at the beginning of Guided Reading on the following day. Here is my Guided Reading lesson plan for *Through Grandpa's Eyes*.

Sample Guided Reading Lesson

Book, Author: *Through Grandpa's Eyes* by Patricia MacLachlan

DAY 1

Background:

Ask students to think about their grandparents. What kinds of things do they do together? Do they talk about things? Share things? Help each other? Learn from them?

Explain that for the next few days the class is going to read a story about a boy whose grandpa is blind. But, Grandpa does not feel sorry for himself and neither does his grandson.

To build background, use the whole GR time. Blindfold half the class and let the other half guide the blindfolded students down the hall. Tell students to switch roles and repeat the activity. Then, blindfold the first group again. Place three different kinds of food on a plate, and have the blindfolded student try to guess what they are eating. Reverse roles and repeat. As a whole group, discuss students' feelings and reactions during both roles—as the blind person and the guide.

DAY 2

Prediction: Students should write the date and the title of the story in their journals. Have them make a prediction of what the story is about. Tell them to use what they already know about grandparents and blind people.

Vocabulary: Use Guess the Covered Word to introduce the new words (exercises, marigolds).

Minilesson:

When we read a story, we can often understand the story better if we think about things in the story that are different and things that are the same. This is called Compare/Contrast. Define compare/contrast for students. Using a large Venn Diagram, explain that the middle section will be the things that are the same – comparisons. The other two sections are for the things that are different – contrasts. Explain that each day, information will be added to the Venn diagram.

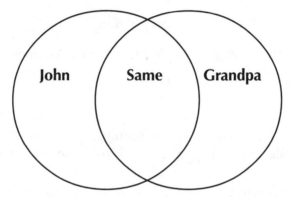

Focus and Purpose:

Write the date and title, *Through Grandpa's Eyes,* at the top of a journal page. As students read today, have them think about things John and Grandpa do together—these are the things that are the same in the story—and list them in their journals. During the discussion, add these to the Venn diagram, and also add the way the boy and his grandpa do them differently.
Format: read pp. 151 – 155 (Three-Ring Circus)
After Reading: Have students contribute ideas and work together as a class to fill in the Venn Diagram. Discuss compare/contrast as they help fill in the contrast sections.

DAY 3

Background: Review the Venn Diagram and share responses.
Vocabulary: dollop, sculpt, imitating
Minilesson: Ask students if thinking about how things in the story are the same and how they are different helped them to understand the story better.

Focus and Purpose: Continue thinking about compare/contrast and filling in the Venn Diagram. Have students continue to add to their lists of things Grandpa and John do together, and to think about how the two characters must do them differently. Tell students to use sticky notes to mark passages that describe the differences and be ready to help fill in the Venn Diagram. Let students choose a sentence starter to respond to in their journals.

Format: read pp. 156-158 (Playschool Groups)

After Reading: Continue the Venn Diagram from the previous day. Have students share responses from their journals.

DAY 4

Background: Review the diagram from yesterday, and share responses.

Vocabulary: promptly, Braille, sternly

Minilesson: Today, students will be answering a prompted response question as a group. **Here is the prompt:**

> In a paragraph, compare and contrast John and Grandpa. What do they do the same, and what do they do that is different? Use many examples from the story.

> Tell students to use the information on the Venn Diagram to help them write a response to the question.

Focus and Purpose:

Have students add to the list of things John and Grandpa do together to help finish the Venn Diagram and write the paragraph.

Give each child three Wikki-Sticks®. Have students place them under examples of things John and Grandpa do together (the same) and things they do their own way (the differences).

Format: Finish the story. (Partner Reading)

After Reading: Complete Venn Diagram. Work together to write paragraph.

The following sample is a shared writing response:

John and his grandpa do many of the same things. They have to do things in a different way because Grandpa is blind. They both wake up with the sun. The sun gets in John's eyes. It warms Grandpa's face. They both exercise. Grandpa doesn't fall over even though he can't see. John falls over when he closes his eyes. They eat breakfast. John can see the food on his plate. Grandpa's plate is like a clock. Grandpa knows the food by their smells. John knows the food by the way it looks.

John and Grandpa both play the cello. John needs music and a music stand to play music. Grandpa plays by ear.

John and Grandpa go for a walk. John knows the direction of the wind because he can see the trees blowing. Grandpa knows the direction of the wind by the way it blows his hair. John and Grandpa read. John reads print. Grandpa reads Braille. John knows the birds because he can see their feathers. Grandpa knows the birds by their song. They do many things together, but in their own way.

Reading Response Journals

In early November, the students began a Reading Response Journal. After the students read, I often had them respond in this journal. I told the students that it is important to be able to say the words when reading, but it is also important to "think" about what has just been read and respond in some way. To create their journals, the students used spiral notebooks on which I had them write "Reading Response Journal" with a permanent marker. They could not use this notebook for anything else. (This creates a sense of importance.)

Writing a response in a journal is just one of many ways in which children can respond to what they have read. I use written response frequently, however, because the state assessment in Illinois requires that third-graders be able to do this. I modeled many, many times how to write a good reader's response to a selection before I actually required students to do it on their own. I have often observed the students looking back at previous responses they have written.

Reading response in a journal can take two forms: open response, where children freely respond as they wish, or prompted, where the teacher provides a question or statement to which the students write a response. I use both forms. In a prompted response, I look for specific features. This is necessary in order to prepare students for the state assessment. In a prompted response, I model how to turn the question around into a response. For example, the question might be: "How do the children in the story feel about Miss Rumpius? How do you know?" To turn it around, say "I think the children in the story like Miss Rumpius because they listen to her stories. They also help her pick the lupines. They have smiles on their faces, too, so I think they enjoy being with her. My grandma tells me stories, and I really love that." I tell them that in order for them to be complete in their responses, they really need to write more than one sentence. The responses are shared during the after reading portion of Guided Reading, or the next day if we don't have time that day.

What I Look For in a Good Reader's Response:

1. Turns the question around into a **topic sentence**
2. Addresses the question (answers all parts of the question)
3. Finds and uses specific details from the story for support
4. Makes connections and inferences to answer the question
5. Uses correct sentence structure and punctuation

As the year progressed and ways to respond became internalized, I then introduced open-ended response sheets. I have two—one for story text and one for expository text. These two sheets are stapled to the inside front cover of students' journals. They are then free to choose a sentence starter or make one up of their own. I still look for the same features in their responses.

Story sentence starters:

1. I wonder what this means....
2. I really don't understand this part....
3. I really like/dislike this idea because....
4. This character reminds me of somebody I know because....
5. This character reminds me of myself because....
6. This character is like (name of character) in (title of book) because....
7. I think this setting is important because....
8. This scene reminds me of a similar scene in (title of book) because....
9. I like/dislike this writing because....
10. This part is very realistic/unrealistic because....
11. I think the relationship between _____and _____ is interesting because....
12. This section makes me think about, because....
13. I like/dislike (name of character) because....
14. This situation reminds me of a similar situation in my own life. It happened when....
15. The character I most admire is _____ because....
16. If I were (name of character) at this point, I would....
17. I began to think of....
18. I love the way....
19. I can't believe....
20. I wonder why....
21. I noticed....

22. I think....
23. If I were....
24. I'm not sure....
25. My favorite character is_____. He/she is my favorite because....
26. I like the way the author....
27. When I don't know a word, I....
28. I felt sad when....
29. I wish that....
30. This made me think of....
31. I was surprised....
32. It seems like....
33. I'm not sure....
34. Some of the illustrations.....
35. This story teaches....
36. I began to think of....

Expository starters:

1. What fact did you enjoy learning about most?
2. What information did you learn that you would like to share with someone else?
3. Would you like to read more books about this topic? Why? What else would you like to find out?
4. What pictures or illustrations did you find interesting? Tell me about them.
5. Is this book like any other book you have read? If so, how are they alike? How are they different? Which one did you like better? Why?
6. What kind of research do you think the author had to do to write the book?
7. What questions would you want to ask the author if you ever met him/her?
8. What more do you want to know about the topic? How will you find out more about it?
9. Would the book be different if it had been written 10 years ago? 100 years ago?
10. By reading and investigating, what did you discover that can help you outside of school?

I also introduced double entry journals at this point. We still used the same Reading Response Journal. To do a double entry journal, I had the kids divide a page lengthwise down the middle. On the left side, they wrote the label—Summary. On the right side, they wrote the label—Opinion. I called these a Summary and Opinion Response. On the Summary side, students wrote a brief summary of the story using only two or three sentences. On the Opinion side, they wrote a response of their choice. I told them to respond to something interesting, funny, sad, exciting, weird, confusing, or something that they could connect to themselves, other text, or the world. Students really liked the Summary and Opinion responses much better than the ones I prompted them with. I saw deeper and more meaningful responses using the double entry journals.

The Right Reading Format Is Important

It is very important when planning Guided Reading lessons to consider which reading format to use. I decide by judging the difficulty of the selection and the level of my students. With a more difficult selection, I use the Three-Ring Circus format so I can read with and support some of my struggling students. (I always include a few more able students in my group along with most of my struggling readers). Playschool groups are a favorite of the students, and I often use this format with informational text. With playschool groups, choosing a good "teacher" is crucial to the success of the reading format. We use partner reading frequently. I usually partner my more capable students with students who are reading on or almost on grade level. I partner my struggling students with students reading on grade level who are helpful and supportive.

We use book club groups when we are studying a particular genre (mysteries, biographies, tall tales) and when we are doing author studies. The children enjoy them, but I am limited how many sets of books I can acquire.

When planning a Guided Reading lesson, it is important to vary the before and after reading activities and the formats. Children become bored with doing exactly the same thing each time they read. Even though I use written response quite often, I also use other activities for responding to reading. A list of these activities is posted on my Web site *http://scribers.midwest.net/cazueck.*

Looking Forward to Next Year

I believe in Four-Blocks with all my heart. I witnessed huge leaps in the students' enthusiasm for reading. I saw their reading abilities grow as a result of their enthusiasm. These students became active learners; a class of involved readers and writers on a daily basis.

After teaching third grade for six years, I decided to make a change when a kindergarten position opened up. So, I am teaching kindergarten this year! I am using the Building Blocks™ framework. The first day of school was a real challenge, but the children were so eager to learn. In just the short amount of time I have been using Building Blocks™, I can see how it blends into Four-Blocks. My little ones are already fascinated with the printed word—observing writing, learning letter sounds, and writing in the writing center. I can only imagine how far Building Blocks™ will take them by the end of the year, and I will be learning right along with them.

How I Adapted Four-Blocks™ for My Third-Grade Class

By Lynn Mellis (with Pat Cunningham)

Making Guided Reading multilevel is one of the greatest challenges in the Four-Blocks™ framework. Guided Reading is the place where we teach comprehension skills and strategies and help children build background knowledge, language, and concepts. The selections we read during Guided Reading are too easy for some children and too difficult for other children. We accommodate this somewhat by reading two selections each week, one grade level and one easier, and by rereading selections to build fluency. We give children as much support as needed to get through the selections, and we expect our average readers to be fluent on the last reading of the average selection and our struggling readers to be fluent on the last reading of the easier selection. (Above-average children learn comprehension skills and strategies and build background knowledge and vocabulary, but do most of their on-level reading during Self-Selected Reading.)

This works well in first grade and early in second grade when the differences in reading levels between average and struggling readers is not too great, and the selections are short enough to permit rereading. From third grade on, however, this "grade level and easier with rereading" solution doesn't work as well. The struggling children, many of whom move in from schools not doing Four-Blocks™, often read at beginning levels and "dipping down" a little during Guided Reading still does not provide them with instructional level reading. Selections are longer, and rereading entire selections is not an option. Novels and informational chapter books take a few weeks to read and shouldn't be constantly interrupted by "easy reading." This is the problem Lynn Mellis faced with her third-grade class. The solution she came up with is nothing short of brilliant! Here is Lynn's story:

I teach third grade at College Park Elementary in Berkeley County, South Carolina. I have taught for 10 years, all of it third grade, and for the past four years have used the Four-Blocks™ framework which Berkeley County mandated. It has been a massive undertaking for our school district, training teachers and moving them out of their comfort zones, but it is a priority for our district to be sure that all children get the best instruction available. When the framework was first presented to me, I was enthused to feel that, finally, here was a framework that fits my teaching style. My first love is as a math teacher, and I love the hands-on, activity-oriented method of teaching. I felt that I had reached a level of competency with my teaching of math, but that my language arts program needed more focus, and the timing was right to make some major shifts in how I approached the teaching of reading and writing. I liked the balance in the Four-Blocks™ framework, and I especially liked the fact that Four-Blocks sanctioned a daily Self-Selected Reading time, during which the teacher's goal is to have conversations with children about books they choose. I also liked the analogy approach to decoding because I know that is how I decode new words. Four-Blocks had just enough structure—and just enough freedom—for me to decide I was going to do everything I could to make it work for me and my children.

College Park Elementary is a large school with over 800 students and has a wide range of children. Thirty-nine percent of our children qualify for free/reduced lunch. Approximately 30% of our children are living in single parent homes. Twenty-three percent of our children are African-American.

In the 1999-2000 school year, I had 20 children in my class. Early in the school year, I gave all the children the Basic Reading Inventory to determine their instructional reading levels. According to this inventory, five children were reading at grade level, three children were reading above grade level, and twelve children were reading below grade level.

I began the year with a lot of confidence. This was my fourth year using the Four-Blocks™ framework, and I felt like I had a good handle on each block. I used *Month-by-Month Phonics for Third Grade* to guide our work in the Working with Words Block and got our Writer's Workshop started. I got my Self-Selected Reading Block up and running and scheduled my conferences with the children. I scheduled three days of Guided Reading for grade-level selections and two days for easier selections. I also devised a rotation schedule for the blocks, so that children who were pulled out would not miss the same block every day.

How My Rotation Scheduling Works

My children were pulled out for ACE, speech, compensatory help in math/reading, and exceptional children. Our building administrator worked hard to coordinate schedules, but of course, they didn't all go at the same time! I decided that by rotating my blocks daily, the children wouldn't consistently miss the same block. (This also helped my chronically-late children who would have missed the same block every morning.) Since we were rereading selections during Guided Reading, a child might miss one of the readings, but would be included for the others and would know what we were doing and be included in the comprehension instruction. Some children would miss Self-Selected Reading one day, but they would be there for the other days. I also staggered which Working with Words activities I did on which days, making sure I didn't always do Making Words on Monday and Using Words You Know on Tuesday, so that children didn't always miss the same activity. I scheduled each block for 40 minutes and stacked them up so that my morning schedule looked like this:

7:35-8:15	Four-Blocks
8:15-8:55	Four-Blocks
8:55-9:35	Four-Blocks
9:35-10:15	Four-Blocks

If I started with Working with Words on Monday, then I started with Guided Reading on Tuesday, Self-Selected Reading on Wednesday, Writing on Thursday, and Working with Words again on Friday, Guided Reading the following Monday, etc.

I also believe that children have different learning styles. My rotation puts each block in both early morning and late morning time frames so those slow to wake up get some time each week with each block in their preferred learning time. (I am also one of those people who dump the schedule regularly to present a new math skill in early morning one day, late morning the second time I introduce it, and later switch it with social studies to practice in the afternoon. Sometimes that is all that it takes to make it click.)

How I Adapted Guided Reading and Self-Selected Reading To Fit My Class

By Thanksgiving, I only had four children still reading below grade level, one of whom had just moved to our area. We had begun reading novels and chapter books, and many of the children resented having to interrupt their reading for the two days of easier reading. I began to think about how I could provide my four struggling readers with some comprehension instruction in materials at their level without using the 3 days/2 days format.

I decided to extend my Self-Selected Reading time by 10 minutes each day and include some individual comprehension instruction with two of my struggling readers each day using their Self-Selected Reading book. (I found these 10 minutes by eliminating my bathroom break, letting children go on an as needed basis.) So every day, I met with two of my struggling readers individually at the beginning of Self-Selected Reading, and then I had conferences with two or three of my other children.

To prepare for my instruction with my struggling readers, I went through their Self-Selected Reading folder and planned a lesson based on their "next read" book. (My children are required to keep their book in progress and their "next read" in a folder that is centrally stored, when not in use.) I would skim their "next read," deciding on a comprehension purpose and choosing three difficult words. Willy, for example, had picked *Alexander and the Terrible, Horrible, No Good, Very Bad Day*, which is perfect for feelings and characterization, collecting details, and sequencing events. I chose three words (cereal, Australia, invisible) to introduce during our picture walk.

As a before reading activity, Willy and I would picture walk the book, and I would point out these three difficult words and coach him to decode them. Sometimes, I would point out how the word had a pattern like one of our Word Wall words or cover a few words with sticky notes to create a "Guess the Covered Word" activity. Picture walking the book was very helpful to all my struggling readers, who often don't look for problems and solutions in a story or pay attention to sequence or details. Just picture walking a book and noting that there are five distinctly different people in the pictures went a long way towards story understanding.

Next, I would establish a comprehension focus by helping him set a purpose for reading. For *Alexander*, I might ask Willy to name all the places that Alexander went that day and the problem he had at each place. I would point out ahead of time that the story had repetition of certain words, so Willy wouldn't waste precious time and energy decoding the same words over and over. We would end this first meeting with the two of us partner reading a few pages to get him started in the book.

The second meeting that week with Willy would be a normal conference in which we would have a conversation about the book, emphasizing the parts he liked and letting him read some parts he had chosen to me. In addition, I always followed up on the comprehension purpose. "What different places did Alexander go, and what problem did he have in each?"

If I have a few minutes, I try to slip in some small activity that works on comprehension. I might put together some sentences on the story and have the child put them in the right sequence. Once in a while, we play "said is dead" with a few pages. (The kids love this game. We read aloud and when we come to the word "said," we substitute another word such as cried, exclaimed, wept, groaned, etc. I do it so the children find meaning in the way the sentence was spoken. I got the idea after reading *The Boxcar Children*, where the word said is literally worn out. This has transferred into our writing with great results.)

I have trouble deciding how much instruction to do with my struggling readers on their Self-Selected Reading books. I don't want to do so much that they aren't reading for enjoyment and fun just like all the other children do during this block, and I always let them select the book for which I plan the lesson. I don't do elaborate comprehension lessons, such as graphic organizers, which I do with the whole class (including my struggling readers) during Guided Reading. I do, however, like to find opportunities for my struggling readers to relate comprehension skills we are working on with the whole class to their Self-Selected Reading books. I then "let them out" of the rereading portion of Guided Reading that day to do something special with one of their previously read Self-Selected Reading books. The "getting out" is a big deal to the kids, and they love it when I give them one of their previous SSR books with the mandate that they do the graphic organizer on whatever comprehension focus the class was working on to show everyone how it works with lots of different books.

I will use Willy again as the example. The whole class was doing a graphic organizer on the mood of *Owl Moon*, but Willy was lost as we did this because the mood-setting language was not language that was in his spoken vocabulary. He would, however, be able to reread *Alexander* and find the mood of that story and write words to describe how Alexander felt. When the group was dismissed to reread *Owl Moon* and find the mood-setting words, I would get with Willy and give him his "special" job, doing the same thing, but with *Alexander* instead.

When the whole class reconvenes to discuss the mood of *Owl Moon*, Willy can make some connections as he listens to what the others are saying, because he has done the same activity with a simpler book. Next, he gets to share his graphic organizer with his mood words from *Alexander*. It is wonderful transfer for all the kids, and we complete the lesson with a great discussion of how the *Alexander* mood is different from the *Owl Moon* mood.

How I Adapted Four-Blocks™
for My Third-Grade Class •

This sounds complicated, but it really isn't. It only takes a few minutes to plan each lesson, and I am usually only planning one for each day. (I meet with two children individually each day, but the second meeting doesn't require the planning that the first meeting–in which I introduce the book–does.) When I plan, I decide on a comprehension purpose that fits the book and which the whole class has already worked on. When I meet with the child prior to his initial reading of the material, I first ask the child why he or she chose the book. Next, we picture walk the book, and introduce the three difficult words. If the purpose for reading hasn't come out in the picture walk, I link it at the end. It is important to be sure that the child clearly understands the purpose for reading. We partner read a couple of pages before ending the meeting. When possible, I have the child reread the Self-Selected Reading book as an additional example of the comprehension purpose the whole class is reading for.

My struggling readers have responded very well to their individual time and to the times when I "let them out" to do something special with one of their books. I think the key to managing this is in meeting with the strugglers both before and after they read their Self-Selected Reading book. I set the stage for their reading, and then have a chance to follow up individually to see how it went, to make course corrections, do a follow-up activity, and reinforce their successes.

How My Children Have Grown as Readers and Writers This Year

My children came to me with a significant population reading below level. The end-of-the-year Informal Reading Inventory results indicated that nine children were reading above grade level, seven were reading on grade level, and four were reading below grade level. These four, while not yet on grade level, have each made a year's growth in reading, more than they have made in any of their other years in school. In addition, all four of my struggling readers were able to pass the vocabulary from most of the third-grade level Harcourt Brace Unit Tests, and all of them passed some of the comprehension skills tests that come with the unit.

The most significant indicator of their growth and love of reading is the wear and tear on my novels—wherein in previous years, it was picture books that got the most use. My Scholastic/Troll book orders are up significantly over previous years, indicating that parents are supporting their children's desire to read. The children are also choosing more mature books when they order. My fondest memory of this past year is the giggling from Ryan and Erica during Self-Selected Reading. I looked up to chastise them, and they were giggling because their books were funny! They understood what the author was communicating, and I was over-whelmed by their successes in reading.

I can also look at writing and see significant growth, despite my concerns that it is not my strongest block as a teacher. During the early part of the year, simply getting sentences capitalized and remembering ending punctuation was an ac-complishment for many of the children. Very few children would voluntarily write more than a single paragraph, and several children were still writing in a list for-mat. I followed the suggestions from the Four-Blocks™ framework and did daily minilessons in which I modeled all aspects of writing. I also used many ideas from the writing chapter of *Classrooms That Work*. Graphic organizers, paragraph frames, and character webs for descriptive writing were particularly helpful in teaching my students how to organize their paragraphs.

The children all enjoyed our daily opportunities for them to share their writing with the class. This sparked great enthusiasm for writing, especially when the sharing was followed by "two stars and a wish." The writer, after sharing, would call on two classmates for "stars," or positive comments, about what they had written. Then, the writer would call one classmate who could give one "wish"—a suggestion for a revision in the writing.

By mid-year, I was seeing paragraphs that consistently had a main idea that was supported by appropriate detail from almost all my children, almost all the time. More importantly, writing for a number of children was becoming a trea-sured time. I gave each child a sheet with a checklist of writing skills on which they were working. They loved it when they showed they could consistently use that skill in their writing, and we could place a check in the mastery column.

By the end of the year, most of the children could research a simple topic, select several "big ideas" that they wanted to share with the group, and construct paragraphs that supported the topic sentence. They were consistent in producing good descriptive paragraphs and were able to persuade me, in writing, to serve ice cream one Friday!

Looking Forward to Next Year

Every year brings with it a different set of challenges, and I think that is one of the many things that makes teaching such an exciting and rewarding career. Again this year, I will administer to each child an Informal Reading Inventory to determine their reading levels. I will also get some beginning-of-the-year writing samples to determine where to focus my early writing minilessons. Last year, I found these two pieces of information to be invaluable as I chose appropriate reading material and decided which strategies to focus my teaching on.

I have been fortunate enough to have a grant proposal funded to buy class sets of nonfiction books that tie in with my science and social studies units. This will also allow me to incorporate more content area into Guided Reading and provide an opportunity for literature to be more relevant.

I am also initiating a home-school connection reading program in which parents listen to children retell what they have read and share a little bit of that in writing with me. I piloted this idea with my summer school parents this summer, and all of them were supportive in jotting down a couple of lines telling me what their children had shared with them after completing their nightly reading. The children were more motivated to read since they were going to be able to share it with their parents, and the parents were more involved in what their children were learning. One mother told me that she "learned an awful lot about sound" after her son shared his *Magic Schoolbus* book with her.

I learned from my summer school experience that if you provide simple and quick ways for parents to be involved in their child's learning, they will embrace the opportunity. This experience has led me to think about ways to engage the children in writing at home without overloading the family schedule. Although I improved my teaching of writing greatly last year, I still am not completely satisfied with what we have accomplished. I am planning to have children complete simple graphic organizers related to their writing topic with their parents. Having sufficient background is critical in successful writing, and I think that the conversations with parents will help provide that background information. Filling in graphic organizers with ideas will allow parents to support writing efforts in a comfortable format of words and phrases, with no emphasis on writing conventions. This will save some class time, get children and their parents talking about what they are learning, and hopefully, allow children to write more fluently and with less frustration.

Since I first began using the Four-Blocks™ framework, I have developed an enthusiasm for language arts that rivals my interest in mathematics. The format is so varied that you can teach all aspects of reading and writing every day and not feel locked into one single approach. The games and activities are interesting, and instead of a scripted lesson, there is plenty of room for an individual teacher's personal delivery method to shine through. I think people who choose to be teachers are, by nature, creative. Once you grasp the basic principles of the framework, you can design imaginative lessons that suit your own teaching style while still keeping the framework intact.

When I am asked for advice by teachers new to the framework, I tell them to go slowly, but to persevere. I also suggest that they find some teachers who are experienced in the model. If there is no local support, there is wonderful support for Four-Blocks teachers on the Internet. I often find teachers having difficulty deciding where an activity they have done for a long time fits in the framework. I suggest that they look at the goals of each block, and they will find that most meaningful activities fit somewhere. What Four-Blocks teachers do have to give up is the isolated skill worksheets which aren't multilevel and don't transfer to real reading and writing! I also suggest that they keep good records of children's progress. These records not only provide proof of your success, but they allow you to reflect on your teaching in order to evaluate and modify various aspects of your presentation of the framework. Finally, I tell teachers that it takes of lot of planning and preparation when you first implement the Four-Blocks™ framework, but you will grow tremendously as a teaching professional. For me, it has been and continues to be a most exciting journey.

The Little Engine That Could
and the Giant Roller Coaster •

By Marti Plumtree (with Dottie Hall)

I first met Marti at a workshop I was doing in southern California in the summer of 1999. During the break, Marti came up to me and explained that she had heard Pat Cunningham speak and was trying the Four-Blocks™ framework with her students. After the workshop, I noticed Marti contributing ideas to the Teachers.Net *mailring. After Cheryl wrote her column on "Story Bits", many teachers on the mailring were discussing how they could use this idea. Marti took the "Story Bits" idea and ran with it. She came up with practical ideas for implementing it in her classroom and a Response Form for parents. Here is Marti's story of how she became a Four-Blocks™ teacher and how to do "Story Bits" which, because we also read informational books, we now call "Souvenirs":*

Pat Cunningham says that the character in literature she is most like is the Little Red Hen. I have taught for 25 years, and I'm most like the Little Engine That Could. Instead of tracks, I have been chugging along on a giant roller coaster, in search of an educational program that would not only help all children learn how to read and write, but also help them become lifelong readers and learners.

I have taught structured and scripted programs, such as DISTAR, and programs without much structure, such as whole language. When one program didn't work, the district would change to another, or worse yet, send us to an inservice to "add that missing piece," or to "plug in the holes." Up one side of the roller coaster and down the other! In the last 25 years, there have been more programs and more pieces to fill-in-the-gaps than I can count. Yet for all of this effort, money, time and training, many children struggled, and in my opinion, they struggled needlessly. The children got lost in the shuffle between the book companies and the politicians. I believe some practices have turned more children off to reading than have turned them on.

Like the Little Engine That Could, I chugged on, searching for something that would work for everyone. At one time, I thought that the missing piece was a structured phonics program. Like most teachers, I had tried bits and pieces of many phonics programs, not to mention all the workbooks, worksheets, black line masters, games, and activities that I had amassed over the years. With lots of skill and drill, most of the time, most of the children could learn the phonics rules.

They could recite them, but often didn't apply them to their reading or writing. Equally frustrating for me as a teacher was watching young children "read" but not be able to understand what they had read. I felt my language arts program at its best was fragmented.

My First Attempt at a Balanced Literacy Program

In 1995, I got involved in ELIC (Early Literacy Inservice Course) sponsored by Rigby. ELIC stressed a balanced literacy program, including Writer's Workshop, Reader's Workshop, Shared Reading, Guided Reading, sustained silent reading, and phonics. I replaced my literature anthology with leveled books for guided reading. I became the coordinator between my school literacy team and the district literacy team. I helped develop the literacy lab. I pushed to have all books leveled for grouping purposes.

I was trying to do it all, but scheduling was a nightmare! Every day I tried to do shared reading, sustained silent reading, Writer's Workshop, Reader's Workshop, phonics, and five leveled reading groups. Of course, I had to find time for math, social studies, science, physical education, and all the "extras." My ESL children and children with special education needs all needed extra attention. I didn't see my "struggling readers" advancing very much.

How Phonics Led Me to Four-Blocks™

While at a staff development meeting, I was introduced to Making Words. This activity intrigued me, so I got the original article from *The Reading Teacher*. After reading this article on Making Words, I quickly made up some of the lessons. I shared one of these lessons with a special education teacher. After he had completed the lesson with some upper-grade students, he told me that in the process of manipulating the letters, one fourth-grade boy declared, "I didn't know that you could make all these words with the same letters!" This insight brought both of us to tears. About a month later at a district reading workshop, I saw the book, *Making Words*. I bought a copy of the book, ran down to Office Depot, and had them copy the letters at the back to make one set of Making Words letters for each of my thirty-two children.

The next book I found was *Phonics They Use*. In this book, Pat Cunningham described how certain traditional techniques and rules didn't work and that patterns were more predictable and understandable to young learners. In addition to

Making Words, she described other phonics activities that seemed much more appropriate for my children. I decided to give these activities a try in my classroom.

In September, 1997, I found myself doing leveled reading groups, Pat Cunningham's phonics activities, and all the other components of a balanced language arts program. In February 1998, I attended a seminar entitled, "Phonics They Use" with Pat Cunningham. That day changed forever the way I taught. Besides learning how to make phonics more usable to the young learner, I was introduced to the idea of "Four-Blocks." Somehow, I knew this multimethod, multilevel framework for reading and writing made sense! Maybe this was the link I was looking for.

I waited very impatiently in the fall of 1998 for the publication of *Month-by-Month Phonics for Second Grade*. In the meantime, I purchased the Four-Blocks video and *Implementing the 4-Blocks™ Literacy Model*. I also joined the Four-Blocks mailring at *Teachers.Net*. Through the mailring, I met teachers like Laura Kump and Deb Smith. I also read Cheryl Sigmon's Four-Blocks columns and tried many of her ideas. The mailring and Cheryl's articles kept me in motion.

In late October, my *Month-by-Month Phonics for Second Grade* arrived. I was already using many of the activities, but this book stressed transfer and making sure the activities were multilevel. I "tweaked" my activities to make them more multilevel and emphasized transfer. My children responded much better and began using phonics as they were reading and writing. I was delighted! I did my 30 minutes of phonics instruction each day and was meeting the needs of all my students. But, I was still struggling with getting in all of the components of a language arts program and having five guided reading groups every day. I began to think, "If the Working with Words Block was working so well and was so multilevel, maybe this whole Four-Blocks approach is what I need." I was doing Writer's Workshop and felt the Writing Block was in place. I changed my sustained silent reading to Self-Selected Reading by making sure to include teacher read-alouds and conferencing with my children. During the conferences, I made sure children knew how to select books on their level.

In January, 1999, I received the book *The Teacher's Guide to the Four-Blocks™*, and I began "playing" with the Guided Reading Block. Even with the book, I was still not sure about what to do with all the before, during, and after reading strategies. I was still not convinced that this block could meets the needs of all my students as well as my five leveled reading groups. In February, Pat presented a seminar on the Four-Blocks in San Francisco. Although I live and teach in southern California, my school district allowed me to attend the seminar miles away in northern California, as long as I paid my own expenses. This was the first time I had heard the Four-Blocks presentation. After coming back from the seminar, I continued to do the other three blocks, implementing some of the new ideas I got at the seminar. Part of me wanted to do Guided Reading the way Pat described it, but I was apprehensive about the change. In the spring, I went to see Cheryl Sigmon and decided that I must stop playing around and do Guided Reading the Four-Blocks way. In the fall of 1999, I abandoned ability groups and got the Guided Reading Block up and running.

Souvenirs (aka Story Bits)

After doing an incentive reading program for years and making sure that the class got the reward that was offered, I began to tire of the process. It did not seem to have a lot of positive impact on the majority of the kids. The process was a chore for me, the kids, the parent helper, and the parents on the home front. The children did not seem to be developing a desire to read. I had been playing with the idea of not participating in the Pizza Hut® reading program again. Yet I knew I had become famous as the teacher who had the pizza party every year. Then, Cheryl wrote Article 27—"Motivational Reading Programs: The Good, The Bad, and The Ugly." In this article, Cheryl questioned the use of rewards for reading and suggested that children needed to learn to love to read and to read for enjoyment and information—not so that they could get rewarded. Her article put into words the concerns I had been feeling, and I became convinced it was time for a change.

In August, Cheryl wrote Article 33, "Summer Planning, Home-School Connections: A Bit of a Story" and Article 34, "More Summer Planning, Story Bits—the Sequel." In these articles, she described how you could motivate children to enjoy and retell books by giving them something to remember the book by—a story bit. For example, for *Alexander Who Used To Be Rich Last Sunday*, the story bit was a penny. For *The Popcorn Book*, the story bit was a popcorn kernel. (Stories have characters, settings, problems, and solutions. *The Popcorn Book* is not a story. Children get confused when we call all books "stories," so the name has been changed from story bits to souvenirs.)

I began to think about how to make souvenirs manageable in my classroom. I went to the 99¢ Cent Store, and bought juvenile gift bags with a handle for each of my students. Then, I made a sign, "My Souvenir Collection Bag," and taped a copy of the sign to each bag. I told the kids to put their bags on a hanger in their closets or in another safe place and to put each souvenir in the bag. "By the end of the year," I promised, "you will have a great collection of souvenirs from the books we have read this year." (A great book to read to kids to introduce this concept is *Souvenirs*.)

I developed a parent response form because I wanted something tangible to see how the children and their parents were responding to this new way of interacting with books. The responses were informative, positive, didn't require any record keeping, and were not graded. I learned so much about my families and how they discuss things. Many of my parents commented on how much they got out of the book.

Souvenir Response Form

Child's Name: _____

Parent's Name: _____

Date: _____

    This year, your child will be bringing home a souvenir each week. The souvenir will be a reminder for your child of a book we have read. Please ask your child to tell you about the book. This sharing experience will help your child's literacy development and will provide a warm and special time for you to talk about books. I think you and your child will be surprised at all the souvenirs they will have collected by the end of the school year.

    Please take 5-10 minutes tonight to have your child tell you a little about the book. If the book is a story, your child will tell you about the setting, the characters, the plot, the problem, and the solution. If it is an informational book, your child will tell you what new things were learned.

    Please record a few of your child's thoughts about the book. Then, have your child place the souvenir in the bag. Tomorrow, return only this response form, which I will keep and give back to you in June. What a wonderful collection you will have!

Book Title: _____

Souvenir: _____

My Child's Thoughts: _____

_____

_____

_____

I gave my children one souvenir every week, and I kept it simple. I elicited the children's ideas for souvenirs. I included a mix of fiction and informational books, as well as some simple and more complex books. The children enjoyed all the books and souvenirs, but some of the most successful ones were:

The Crayon Box That Talked—(Souvenir - a crayon) Responses from parents were great for this book. Parents felt compelled to tell me what they thought as well as what their child had learned.

Spider's Web—(Souvenir - a spider pattern the kids traced onto black paper) This is an informational book about how and why spiders build their webs. It is simple, but factual. To my surprise, the children retained incredible amounts of information. The parents were also impressed with how much the children had learned.

'Round and 'Round the Money Goes—(Souvenir - a penny) Again, the responses were great, and I could really tell the children's comprehension was good and that parents had spent quite a lot of time with their children interacting about this book.

More Than Anything Else—(Souvenir - application for a public library card) This is a story about George Washington Carver (the peanut man), telling how much he wanted to learn to read. The kids really enjoyed this book.

Even Steven and Odd Todd—(Souvenir - a 3"x3" piece of white construction paper which the children complete by putting two dots and the number 2 on one side, and on the other side, three dots and the number 3) The children seemed to especially enjoy the souvenirs that they had a part in making.

As the weeks went on, the children began to really look forward to their weekly souvenir. My ESL children and parents responded particularly enthusiastically to the souvenirs. One time, one of my ESL children asked to take the book home that went with the souvenir so that her parents could read and translate the book.

The principal came into my room one afternoon as the children were preparing their souvenirs. She inquired about it, so I explained. She was impressed enough that she took some of the souvenirs and parent responses to her principals' meeting. The other principals wanted a copy for their schools. Great PR!

The Little Engine That Could
and the Giant Roller Coaster ●

Looking Forward to Next Year

I finally feel I am in control of my language arts program. Each day as I finish each block, I truly feel that I have touched all the children in my second-grade classroom. I finally know that I am getting it all in. When I hear of a new activity or idea, I ask myself, "Where does it belong in the Four-Blocks?" The Four-Blocks is a framework that has pulled together the best of the best practices. My children's end-of-the-year reading achievement scores have risen. My parents and students are happier, and I feel like I am teaching all my children to read and write.

During the last three years, my principal has been supportive. Although our district is encouraging ability grouping, she has allowed me to develop and continue to use Four-Blocks. I have involved her in all aspects of the process and have invited her into my room to observe the framework and the strategies in action. We have hired three new teachers for next year, and my principal has bought *The Teacher's Guide to the Four-Blocks*™, *Guided Reading the Four-Blocks*™ *Way*, and their grade level's *Month-by-Month Phonics* book for them. I am going to work with them, and hopefully, I won't be the "lone ranger" at my school anymore.

I am also networking with other Four-Blocks teachers in Southern California. I hosted a Four-Blocks party in the cafetorium of my school, and we are meeting soon to discuss Guided Reading. I still feel like the Little Engine That Could, but I have changed my "I think I can" to "I know I can," and I have gotten off the roller coaster!

Implementing the Four-Blocks™ in a Rural School Setting: From Discovery to Block Parties •

By Angie Lewis and DeLinda Youngblood (with Dottie Hall)

Creative, clever teachers often find the Four-Blocks™ as they search for ways to improve their reading instruction. Angie Lewis and DeLinda Youngblood were two such teachers. Both worked for Raccoon Consolidated School District #1, which serves a small, rural community between Centralia and Salem, Illinois. The K-8 facility currently educates 265 students. Primary grades have two classes at each grade level with an average of 16 students each. Angie was teaching first grade, and DeLinda was teaching second grade. These two teachers were not happy with what was happening in their classrooms, so they began to search for a solution to the problem. While attending a workshop on phonemic awareness, they heard about someone named Pat Cunningham and something called "Four-Blocks." Having heard about this multilevel framework, they returned to their classrooms with a new mission—to find out all they could about the Four-Blocks. They set out to read everything that was available. At that time, there was no Teacher's Guide to the Four-Blocks™, but they found additional support on the Internet. DeLinda and Angie held the first "Block Party" and added the "Block Party" to the list of things that Four-Blocks teachers do! Here is their story:

As first- and second-grade teachers, we were very frustrated with our reading program, especially the phonics piece. We found our high-achieving students were bored with phonics, and our struggling students were frustrated. We heard about an intensive phonics program that was supposed to be really good, so we called up the company and asked if we could pilot their program. The company sent us their materials, and we began using their phonics program with our first- and second-grade classes. Once again, we noticed that our high-level students were bored with these repetitive activities, and our struggling students were frustrated. After several months of following the teacher's manuals and trying this program, we decided that these materials were definitely not the solution. We knew we needed to continue our search for more appropriate materials to use to teach our children. We pulled materials from here and there to make it through the remainder of the year. We wanted to have some fun teaching, but we also wanted to see some growth in all the students, regardless of their ability level. Phonics was the "in" thing in education, so the next year we began using a new workbook in phonics. We did not like that phonics workbook any better! Again, the new phonics workbook was boring for the children who already knew their letters and sounds, boring for those who did not understand the jargon used in the teacher's manual, and boring for the teachers who had to use the teacher's manual, too! So, the search began again to find something that would be beneficial for ALL the students in our classes.

Finding Four-Blocks™ at a Phonemic Awareness Workshop

In July of 1998, we attended a workshop on Phonemic Awareness in Chicago. During the workshop, the presenter demonstrated how to use a Word Wall. She kept referring to the book *Classrooms That Work* and a lady named Pat Cunningham. We listened intently, soaking in every word. We could not believe that we had never heard of anything that the presenter was speaking about. After the workshop, we went up to the presenter and began asking all kinds of questions on how to find out more about the Four-Blocks™ framework she had mentioned. She told us what books to buy to help us get started. We immediately went to the bookstore and bought *Classrooms That Work* and *Phonics They Use*.

We frantically read these new books on the ride home. We realized right away that the Four-Blocks made sense. In fact, we found ourselves saying over and over, "This just makes so much sense!" as we continued to read and ride. When we got home from our trip, Angie went straight to her computer, looked up Four-Blocks on the Internet, and began reading and printing everything she could find. It was like we had come across a buried treasure. We both agreed that we wanted to use this approach when we started off our new school year.

When the 1998-99 school year started, we began using the Four-Blocks™ framework. The children liked the activities, especially the phonics activities in the Working with Words Block. We liked the activities, and we shared our successes with other teachers at our school. We took the Four-Blocks information to our superintendent, Glen Bryant, and told him we were using this framework with our classes this school year. Having come from a reading background, he was very impressed with the whole concept of a "balanced literacy" program and encouraged us to continue with this approach.

Implementing the Four-Blocks™

So, with the books *Classrooms That Work, Phonics They Use, Making Words,* and *Month-by-Month Phonics for First Grade* (*Month-by-Month Phonics for Second Grade* was not available for DeLinda until November!), and with the support of teachers on the mailring, we continued using the Four-Blocks™ model. Since both of us were new to the Four-Blocks, it was like the blind leading the blind, but we hung in there and tried to give each other as much support as possible. We were searching for other teachers in our area that had heard of Four-Blocks, but no one knew what we were talking about! We were so excited about the results we were seeing in our classrooms, and the fun we were having teaching. But, we were just not sure that we were doing it right. We wanted to see the Four-Blocks in action. We wanted to have a "real" talk with someone who was doing the Four-Blocks. This led us to search for Pat Cunningham's phone number, and then to call her. I asked if she knew where we could get some training or visit a classroom doing the Four-Blocks. She told us we would have to come to North Carolina if we wanted to do both. She explained that she and Dottie Hall were having their annual Four-Blocks Conference in January. We learned that if we went to North Carolina a day earlier, Dottie could arrange for us to visit the school where the program was first piloted years ago, and we could watch kindergarten, first, and second-grade teachers who had been using this approach for a number of years. Our kindergarten teachers, Angie Hart and Angie Watkins, wanted to find out about the kindergarten part of the program—Building Blocks™. It sounded like the perfect opportunity, but where to find the money? We went right to our superintendent, Glen Bryant. Glen was so impressed with what he was seeing in our classrooms that he agreed to not only fund our visit, but to come along with us!

In January of 1999, seven of us flew down to North Carolina. The team consisted of two kindergarten teachers, two first-grade teachers, two second-grade teachers, and the superintendent. On Friday, we had the opportunity to see Four-Blocks in action at Clemmons Elementary. On Saturday, we went to the annual Four-Blocks Conference where we attended sessions, asked questions, and networked with other teachers implementing the framework. The *Teacher's Guide to the Four-Blocks™* had just been published and each participant was given a book; so we now had a more complete description of the Four-Blocks and the activities for each block. We also got a chance to meet and talk with the people who changed the way we taught——Pat Cunningham and Dottie Hall.

Implementing the Four-Blocks™ in a Rural School Setting: From Discovery to Block Parties •

The trip to North Carolina convinced us we were on the right path. Our superintendent made a further commitment for more training that spring and summer with Cheryl Sigmon. We started the next school year once again with Four-Blocks activities that we enjoyed teaching. Our children enjoyed the reading, writing, and phonics instruction as much as we enjoyed teaching it.

Hosting Visitors and Helping Others

After our visit to North Carolina, we began to have requests from teachers in neighboring districts to come visit our classrooms. Soon, monthly visits were established. Teachers arrived between 8:30 and 9:00 a.m. for a continental breakfast and a short introduction to the program, delivered by either the superintendent or the principal. Teachers were split into three groups and taken to the classrooms to observe two of the blocks. The groups switched classrooms at 10:00 a.m. to observe the other two blocks. Lunch was served in the library, and Raccoon teachers joined the visitors to answer questions. After lunch, round-table discussions about each of the blocks assisted the visitors in understanding the delivery system. Each participant received a complimentary book for their classroom and a handout packet. Approximately 360 teachers visited Raccoon School through the observation program that first year.

Two questions most groups of visitors asked were, "Does everyone in your building do the Four-Blocks ?" and "Why aren't we observing in all the classrooms?" We have learned that implementation of any new idea creates a situation in which there is a group of individuals who immediately jump on the bandwagon (us!) and a group of individuals who need to be persuaded and given assistance to get on board. Four-Blocks implementation has been no different. Administrators and teachers proficient in Four-Blocks have acted as coaches by providing modeling and becoming mentors to those not yet comfortable with the new techniques.

Continuing to Grow with Four-Blocks™

For our Four-Blocks teachers at Raccoon, we began an after-school study group as additional support. The meetings ran for 45 minutes after school, with drinks and snacks provided. Participants in these after-school study groups requested to study *Classrooms That Work* and Cheryl Sigmon's articles on *Teachers.Net*. In these meetings, teachers had opportunities to brainstorm, ask questions, and form a cohesive team. We soon noticed teachers were talking the same language and solving common classroom problems.

In January, 2000, we returned to North Carolina to attend the first Four-Blocks Leadership Conference. We learned many new ideas about how to help others implement Four-Blocks, both in the sessions and in our "after-hours" meetings in the lounge with Four-Blockers from all over the country.

The one new thing we learned to add to our own classroom repertoires was how to add "Coaching Groups" to our Four-Blocks instruction. When we returned to our schools, we each began doing some small coaching groups in which we coached children to use what they were learning during the Working with Words Block as they were actually reading. On some days, during the Guided Reading Block, we called together a heterogeneous group of four or five students to read with us while the others were reading with partners. We explained to the children that they were going to learn how to be "word coaches" and could then coach each other on how to figure out hard words. We set some ground rules: everyone would read a page to themselves first, and then one child would read the page aloud. When the reader was reading and came to a hard word, the word coach would coach them through the steps of figuring out the word. Everyone except the reader and the word coach were to pretend to be invisible, but to pay attention to the coaching because soon, they would all qualify as word coaches. In the first lessons, the teacher would be the word coach. As the children learned how to coach, they became the coaches, and the child reading a page aloud got to pick his/her word coach. We taught the children four steps, and once they understood these, displayed them on a poster as reminders.

How to Figure Out a Hard Word*

1. Put your finger on the word and say all the letters.
2. Use the letter and the picture clues.
3. Look for a rhyme you know.
4. Keep your finger on the word, finish the sentence, and pretend the hard word is the covered word.

(*From *Guided Reading the Four-Blocks™ Way*)

The students quickly picked up on these techniques, and we began letting each reader pick another child to be the word coach. It was amazing how well they did, and how much they liked doing it. Just for fun, we gave the student coaches' shirts to help set the mood!

A Block Party!

During that school year, we also developed an evening event to support local teachers implementing the Four-Blocks™ Literacy Model. DeLinda contacted the Regional Office of Education and several local merchants for financial assistance. The State Board of Education Office in Mt. Vernon, Illinois provided publicity and support. First, we thought of atmosphere. To set the party mood we decorated with helium balloons in primary colors. Plates and napkins in these festive colors were arranged throughout the room. Down the middles of the tables we had grouped crayons and colored paper clips. The tables were divided into four groups, one each for kindergarten, first, second, and third grades. We had invited our local teacher supply store to set up in the lobby, so teachers had time to browse and shop. Since it was in the evening and several teachers drove for over two hours before arriving at our school, we provided refreshments. Pizza, popcorn, cookies, and pop provided the desired relaxed atmosphere for an after-school "party." That got us off to a great start!

After the introduction, teachers were divided into grade-level groups for a tour of classrooms so that others could see how we had set up our Four-Blocks classrooms. Everyone enjoyed seeing other teachers' Word Walls, letters in blue pocket charts for Making Words lessons, crates of books for Self-Selected Reading, editors' checklists, partner reading rules, etc. Teachers then met back in the library for grade-level group discussions. Each group had a facilitator who was very knowledgeable in that particular grade level. Each facilitator's responsibility was to give a quick overview, one block at a time, and then to answer questions that the group might have. It was so exciting to have teachers sharing the different ways that they had found success, and how they had overcome obstacles. Teachers enjoyed networking with the other teachers in the area who were trying and enjoying Four-Blocks activities with their students.

After all four blocks had been discussed, we came back together as whole group. At that point, each facilitator gave a summary of that group's discussions.

Then, it was time for door prizes, and everyone got to choose a free book for their Self-Selected Reading tubs. The local bookstore donated teacher materials for the door prizes, and several book companies donated the books. It was a great idea, and what a party! The event became known affectionately as "The Block Party."

Looking Forward to Next Year

The 2000-2001 school year finds DeLinda on a "leave of absence" from Raccoon School System. She is presenting workshops to schools and school systems in her area that are interested in Four-Blocks training and implementation. Angie is teaching first grade at Raccoon School and seeing that all these valuable Four-Blocks projects are continued. Angie also does Four-Blocks workshops when her teaching schedule permits. We are both having a wonderful year, and are sharing the new things we learn with each other and many others around the state and the country.

Looping with My Class from K-2, Doing Building Blocks™ and Four Blocks™ • • • • • • • • • • • • • • •

by Kurt Nilsson (with Pat Cunningham)

Kurt's census form was one of the first to be returned, and I read his responses with great interest. Many Four-Blocks™ teachers reported looping with their class to the next grade, but Kurt had taken his class of children through three years of school—kindergarten, first grade, and second grade. His class clearly contained a lot of "at-risk for reading failure" children, as almost all children qualified for free/reduced lunch and approximately one third were English Language Learners. The school also had high mobility, with children moving in and out throughout the year. In answer to the census question: "How do you know Four-Blocks is working for you?" Kurt answered, "I feel more successful at reaching all of my students and can document their growth with our RESULTS assessments." I wanted to know more about how Kurt taught these children for three years and to see the RESULTS data. I e-mailed Kurt and asked him to tell me more. When I got his additional information and data, I wanted to share it with other teachers—particularly teachers with many children for whom learning to read is a struggle. Kurt's census response piqued my curiosity and was one of the sparks that eventually led us to the idea of writing this book. Here is Kurt's true story of children he spent three years with. I hope you will be as inspired by it as I was.

I discovered Four-Blocks™ (and Building Blocks™) three years ago as I was beginning with a new group of kindergarteners, whom I would keep for three years. I teach at Wyandotte Avenue School in Butte County, a rural area north of Sacramento. Approximately 30% of our children are English Language Learners and 98% qualify for free/reduced price lunch. We are a year-round school. The children come for three months and then are off for three weeks. We begin the school year the Monday after July 4th. My track is in session for July and August, and then off for September. Our next session is from October until the beginning of Christmas vacation. We begin again at the beginning of February, and go until the end of April. We have the month of May off, and finish the school year with a one-month session in June.

Our school has high mobility. Of the 19 students that I ended my loop with, 12 had been with me since the first day of kindergarten, four came in first grade,

88   © Carson-Dellosa CD-2411

and three came in second grade. There have been many others who came and left, but none for very long. One of the real advantages of a looping class is the way the teacher and kids become a family. Adding a new kid to a looping class is an adjustment for the class as well as the new student. After several new students came, I began to sense that my new students were feeling like "stepkids." I initiated "new kid" meetings where we discussed as a class how we would incorporate this new person into the class and who would be the "new kid helper" to assist with all the procedures.

Kindergarten

I relied heavily on the just published *Month-by-Month Reading and Writing for Kindergarten* as a way to organize and sequence my instruction. I began by convincing my students that they could read and write. Because I had many English Language Learners who did not speak English yet, we spent a lot of time playing with the letters in their names. I also made sure that the students began associating their name with its "special place" on the Word Wall. I had many reluctant writers in the beginning, but they seemed comforted when I told them to "watch what I did" (modeled writing), "have a go," and "see what comes out of your pencil." Nine times out of ten, what each student made come out of his or her pencil was more than I had expected, so we both got excited about writing.

I also began the year with *Zoo-Phonics*, but I only used it to associate the letter shapes and sounds. I adapted an idea from our math program to give my students a fun, daily drill session on letters and sounds. Our math program relies on daily 5-10 minute skills warm-ups. I wanted to use this idea with the "Building Blocks" of phonemic awareness and letters and sounds. All my kids needed daily practice with these two blocks. So, by August, I instituted a time of the day called "Brain Snacks." Each day, we would have a "math snack" to reinforce skills like numeral writing, connecting numbers to quantities, etc., and a "word snack" of letter sounds, or blending and rhyming activities. We also had an "art snack" of discussing an art print so that I could integrate some oral language into this time of the day. The entire brain snack only took 20 minutes, but I believe this daily practice paid off big in improving the students' skills in speaking, writing, blending, rhyming words, and phonics.

Looping with My Class from K-2, Doing Building Blocks™ and Four Blocks™ •••••••••••••••••••••••••••

As the school year went on, my day evolved into a schedule which fit the needs of a class with so many English Language Learners:

1. Opening—Attendance, Flag Salute

2. Calendar

3. Math Snack, Art Snack, Word Snack

4. Rug Time—Guided Reading, Print Concepts, Literature

5. Recess

6. Workshops:

   A. Reading Center (This time evolved into small-group reading in easy books.)

   B. Writing Center (This time evolved into a small-group version of the first-grade Writing Block. I posted one word each week until we had the "Kindergarten 10—I, a, is, the, to, go, have, has, we, are.")

   C. Math Center

   D. Thematic Studies Center (Social Studies, Science, Health, and Fine Arts)

   E. Plan-Do-Review (Student-initiated activities)

By the end of kindergarten, my students generally knew all their letters and sounds. Most ELL children could read a Level 2 book (Reading Recovery Levels). Most native English speakers could read on Level 4. They could all write on their own topic using inventive spelling and the 10 Word Wall words. By the end of kindergarten, most of my ELL children had moved ahead dramatically in their ability to communicate in English.

First Grade

For first grade, I tried to implement the Four-Blocks as they were written in the books I bought or borrowed. I did all the blocks in the morning. Late in the day, I met with different children so that I could monitor their reading growth with leveled texts. Knowing the reading levels of my struggling readers helped me decide what level of text was needed for my Thursday and Friday Guided Reading selection.

I began my day with the Guided Reading Block, and used our literature series for Monday, Tuesday, and Wednesday. This was my "on-grade-level" reading for the week. I used all the comprehension activities found in the manual for that selection and worked hard to help the children develop comprehension and language. Our literature series is grouped by themes, so on Thursday and Friday I would pull a text set from our leveled reading resources that tied to the theme. This text was usually at my lowest readers' instructional level, and I would repeat the comprehension activities that we had practiced on Monday, Tuesday, and Wednesday. What I found was that Thursday was a big "Ah-ha" day because our comprehension strategy for the week (like telling the major events from the beginning, middle, and end of a story) became a cinch when it was applied to the easier reading on Thursday and Friday.

For the Working with Words Block I did everything "by the book." Each week I would add five high-frequency words, one of which was designated the "Rhyme Time Word of the Week." These words went home in my weekly newsletter, and parents were told that the students would be tested Friday on the five words, and on how well they could use the Rhyme Time Word to generate new words. My spelling tests on Fridays looked like this (the underlined parts are what the students wrote):

1. <u>is</u>
2. <u>am</u>
3. <u>I</u>
4. <u>was</u>
5. <u>at</u>
6. at rhymes with <u>cat</u>
7. at rhymes with <u>sat</u>
8. at rhymes with <u>flat</u>

In addition to Word Wall, I did all the other activities—Making Words, Guess the Covered Word, etc.—described for first grade.

For Writing and Self-Selected Reading, I followed the basic time schedule and format, and made adjustments throughout the year according to student needs. (I also attended a workshop Pat did in Sacramento, which cleared up some of my confusion about these two blocks.)

Looping with My Class from K-2, Doing Building Blocks™ and Four Blocks™ • • • • • • • • • • • • • • • • • •

In the fall, I also began an after-school ESL class for my English Language Learners. My school district had just purchased a kit for me to use. I asked the ELL parents if their students could stay for an hour after school to work on speaking English. Most were glad to have their children get this additional help.

Early in first grade, I received a new student. Jamie (pseudonym) came from another school and had been qualified for special education with a 70 IQ and fetal alcohol exposure. I was told that I should not expect much from Jamie academically. When he first came, he did absolutely nothing. He was cute and entertaining to the other kids and found a million ways to get out of doing his work. He could write his name, copy letters, and produce a few letter sounds. His phonemic awareness was pretty good; he could rhyme and do some blending. I was so shocked that such a clever, active kid had been to kindergarten and had so few reading skills that I requested to have his IQ test redone. It came back with the same score. When I told our school psychologist about what I saw as his potential, she explained that at his level, he could develop into a reader, just at a much slower rate. I decided that this little boy would be a good candidate for the "systematic, multilevel" approach to reading instruction that Four-Blocks provides.

I am not a fan of standardized tests, but I do rely heavily on running records to monitor the growth of my children—especially my struggling readers. At the end of first grade, 13 of my 20 students were reading at their appropriate exit first-grade level. The goal for first-graders at that time was Level 12 for ELL students and Level 16 for "English Only" students. Seven students were not reading at the level expected, three of these were reading at Level 7, and four were at Level 3. None of the children reading at Level 3 had been with me since the first day of kindergarten. All the children who had been with me for two years were at least at Level 7, and most were at Level 16.

Second Grade

As I began the year with my second-graders, my school district joined the California RESULTS project. The district also became very strict on accountability and "all students meeting standards." Even though 13 of my students had met the standards in place at the end of first grade, the bar had been raised and only two students met the standards at the beginning of second grade. Eighteen of my 20 students were at risk of retention. This included my special ed. student, all my English Language Learners, and all but two of my English speakers. None of my class could read the beginning second grade text passage with the appropriate fluency and accuracy. Only one of my students could pass the reading comprehension test for beginning second grade level. Only two of my students could read the required 280 (out of 300) sight words from the high-frequency word test. My children had made tremendous progress with me during kindergarten and first grade, but it didn't look like it was going to be enough.

After looking at the data and realizing the distance we would have to go during second grade, I reread *Classrooms That Work* and *Implementing the 4-Blocks™ Literacy Model* and started carefully putting in place everything I read on the Four-Blocks mailring.

Comprehension and fluency became a daily focus in the Guided Reading Block. We charted stories weekly. I used a story map for fiction and a different chart for informational text. On Mondays, we would read for comprehension and begin our chart, which we completed on Tuesdays. On Wednesdays, we would do retellings based on the information recorded on the chart. Later in the year, I began having students retell the week's stories in writing once we had orally retold it .

I also assigned homework called "bookmark reading," in which the students would reread the grade level text at home, and then place special bookmarks (labeled "This page describes the main character, "This page describes the setting," etc.) on the correct pages of the text.

For Working with Words, I continued using my Word Wall and Making Words activities. We "Rounded up the Rhymes" and "Guessed the Covered Word" in every text selection that fit. I began including some word-sorting activities from the book *Words Their Way* in students' afternoon literacy centers or as homework. This correlated very well with the word sorting we do after Making Words and gave students some additional practice.

Late in the year, my school purchased the Read Naturally program, and some of my children left my class for a short time during math to work on fluency with this program. Read Naturally is a program in which kids practice reading a grade level text (mostly informational) for fluency. Students do a "cold" reading first and graph their correct words per minute. Then, they listen to a fluent reading at a listening center and practice reading fluently, both with the tape and to themselves. Then, they do a second solo reading of the same text and chart their fluency rate.

Looping with My Class from K-2,
Doing Building Blocks™ and Four Blocks™ •

Jamie was beginning to make progress in his reading, and so I arranged to keep Jamie with me instead of sending him to his pullout special ed. class. With the consent of his mother and his Resource teacher, Jamie remained in the classroom for all four blocks. I got a copy of his IEP and tried to tailor my Thursday and Friday easier Guided Reading to meet more of his needs. For a short time, Jamie got a "double dose" of Guided Reading—one with me and one with the first-grade class next door.

At the end of the school year, only one student was retained (which I will regret forever). The rest passed second-grade standards, with some of my ELL students just on the cusp of passing—close enough for me to argue that, due to language status, they should be moved on. But, it's Jamie that I am most proud of. In second grade, he went from reading at Level 1 to Level 9, learned 70 sight words, and now attacks literature and complex reading with reading strategies rather than avoidance behaviors. Jamie was moved on with the rest of the students to third grade. The student who was retained had been with me since mid-first grade, had many emotional problems, and had not made much progress. I doubt that he will make a lot of progress spending another year in second grade!

Looking Forward to Next Year

As I edit this final draft, I have started with a new group of kids. Because of a change in staffing, my loop is now grades 1-2. I am starting my new loop with a monthly focus for the Four-Blocks tied to standards. My first month was all about print concepts, and 19 of my 20 students showed mastery of these. The second month's focus was about letters and sounds. The results of these assessments were very good, too. Unlike three years ago when I was determined to do Building Blocks™/Four-Blocks and hoped it would work, I am fully confident this time around. It is hard work each day for me and the children, but I know they will all learn to read! Four-Blocks™ is a "systematic, multilevel" framework through which I can teach ALL my children to read—including my English Language Learners and special education students!

I Finally Found It!

by Patrick Young (with Dottie Hall)

I have heard it said by school administrators that beginning teachers often have trouble teaching reading, especially phonics, because they did not receive the necessary training in their undergraduate courses. I never really thought that was true, because I had worked with student teachers at Wake Forest University for years. After hearing Patrick's story, I rethought this. I think there is something to be said for experience, but I think that teachers should be trained so that teaching reading is both pleasant and profitable. I met Patrick at a seminar I did in Atlanta in the fall of 1999. He had taught kindergarten for two years before he moved to first grade. When I met him, he was struggling to put into practice what he had been taught in order to teach first grade. Once he heard about the Four-Blocks™, he implemented the framework after just a one-day workshop! Although he worked through this alone in his school, he found that his first-grade students were learning more and enjoying the activities. I next heard from Patrick in June, 2000, when he sent me an E-mail to tell me about his year and ask if I knew any first-grade teachers in his area who used the Four-Blocks so he could visit their classrooms. Patrick Young's story is similar to many of the "young" teachers who find the Four-Blocks. This is Patrick's story:

As I begin my second year in first grade, I finally feel as if I found it! Even though I knew how kids learned, I couldn't find a program, book, strategy, or combination that would fit into my philosophy of teaching. It was like being lost with so many ways to turn, but just going in circles. There was, of course, the "programs" that my county had adopted, which were okay if you could pick and choose; but nothing really said, "Voilà"! That "voilà" did occur in the fall of 1999. But before I get to the "voilà," I need to explain where I came from in terms of teaching reading.

The Problems

I'll begin with the way I taught Guided Reading in first grade at the beginning of last year. I was doing Guided Reading in the newly-termed "flexible grouping" style. The problem was that the groups weren't flexible and didn't change that much, and the children didn't make that much growth. I was doing all the work, and the children were basically passive learners. Also, the children were "labeled" like in the old days with the "Eagles" and "Buzzards." Of course, I didn't use those names or any names at all. I just called together groups who were on or near the same reading level. The students knew who were the slow learners and the high achievers in the class. This didn't help the self-confidence of my struggling readers. The children in the lowest-leveled group definitely lacked motivation the most.

To add to the dilemma I had with grouping was another problem—planning worthwhile literacy centers. The rest of the class had to have something to do while I read with the Guided Reading groups. It seemed like I spent more time managing the rest of the class than I did teaching my Guided Reading group. Most of the work completed in the literacy centers by the other children was basically busywork, as much as I hate to admit it now. Also, I spent a considerable amount of time planning, making, and explaining the literacy centers.

Another problem I had was with teaching phonics. Whole language was emphasized in my undergraduate courses, so I had a problem right off with teaching phonics. I understood that children had to know their sounds, but I also knew the sounds changed depending on the surroundings. I used a phonics program in my classroom because the county required it, and I was new to teaching first grade. I have to say that I was disappointed with the results as a whole. The biggest problem was that I didn't see the children doing the transfer from the phonics lessons to their reading and writing.

How I Found the Four-Blocks™ Model

It was one regular, hectic day at school, and I had received yet another workshop brochure. (They seemed to appear in my mailbox at least once a day.) It wasn't by itself, but covered up with a bunch of other miscellaneous paperwork that didn't have any direct correlation to the instruction or the children in my classroom. After I recycled ten or so papers in the recycle bin, I found a flyer on "Four-Blocks™." It was just a few seconds away from hitting the recycle bin when I saw the words, "Originally developed in first grade!" I was especially excited about this because I'm used to seeing K-2 on these brochures. I don't generally get much out of those workshops. I like workshops that will directly affect me as a first-grade teacher. I was so thrilled, I practically ran to my principal's office to see if I could go. (No kidding!) The workshop was for the Four-Blocks™ Literacy Model. I did not know at the time that this was the "it" I had been searching for over the last three years.

In my district, teachers get to go to one workshop a year where both the substitute teacher and the conference are paid for out of schools funds. The Four-Blocks workshop was to be my day. Our Learner Support Strategist heard that I was going and showed me her copy of *The Teacher's Guide to the Four-Blocks*™. I borrowed it and read a little of it before I went. I woke up the day of the workshop with an exciting new feeling for teaching. With the horrible traffic in the Atlanta area, it took me an hour and a half to get there; normally it would take about 45 minutes. I was lucky to get there just before the workshop began. I had to sit at almost the very back of a large crowd, which was disappointing to say the least. When the presenter, Dottie Hall, began to talk about her background and the program, I forgot about the long drive and bad seat I had and began writing notes as fast as my hand would go. As we broke for lunch, I ran into a friend from college who had gone through the teacher education program with me. I ate lunch with her and her team. I thought it was a great idea that the school sent a team so they could all hear the same things about the Four-Blocks and could discuss the ideas and activities when they got back. I had come alone and was expected to talk about the program to my team when I got back.

After we returned from lunch, we finished the rest of the workshop. I was so interested that I just had to go and meet Dr. Hall. She was packing up as fast as she could because she had to catch a plane, but was nice enough to talk with me a few minutes. I told her I wanted to implement the Four-Blocks when I returned to my classroom. She asked me if I had the book, *Month-by-Month Phonics for First Grade*, and I told her, "No." She said with that book and *The Teacher's Guide to the Four-Blocks*™ (which we received at the workshop), I would have the help I needed to implement the Four-Blocks in my first-grade classroom. She asked for my address, and I received an autographed copy of the book a few days later. I just couldn't believe it, an author sending me a book!

I helped Dr. Hall pack up, and I talked with her all the way to the front of the hotel where a cab was waiting for her. (Generally, I'm racing for my car when a workshop is over. I have even been known to leave the workshop before lunch if I feel it really doesn't pertain to me.) I wanted to start the model the very next day, but I didn't know where to start since the model was quite a bit different from my current schedule. Should I change everything at once or just a little at a time?

I Finally Found It! •

My Solution Begins with Working with Words

I decided to begin with the Working with Words Block first since I had *Month-by-Month Phonics for First Grade,* and the book was organized so well that it didn't require too much planning or adjustment to start off. I started with the "Getting to Know You" activity. The kids really liked having charts written all about them. The best part was it kept their interest so they wanted to read it, and they could read it after a few days of choral reading. I was amazed that so many of my non-readers were able to read these charts after repeated readings. The children would practically fight over who got the chart tablet to read during my D.E.A.R. (Drop Everything And Read) time because it was about them and their classmates, and it was something they knew they could read.

Although the children loved the names activities and the charts, I realized when I was halfway through the class that the charts were too long (six sentences). Another mistake I made with the charts was tearing off the pieces of paper, which made them hard to organize. Next year, I am going to write fewer sentences and leave them on the chart tablet. I am also going to type each story and add each child's picture, and then duplicate these so that every child has every story to take home to read with their families.

Next, I began Making Words, using some lessons from the *Month-by-Month* book and some from *Making More Words.* This ended up being an organizational problem for me. I started by using some class sets of letters I had from our phonics program. Each child got a set of cards in a resealable plastic bag to keep in their desk. I would write down the letters on the board that we were going to use that day, and the children would get out the corresponding cards. This worked okay for a day or two, but then the kids began losing cards, or they didn't have enough when the final words had two of the same letters in them. I solved this by making copies of the "Making Words Homework Sheet" reproducible at the back of the book, *The Teacher's Guide to the Four-Blocks*™. Each morning when the children arrived at school, they had to write the letters on their sheets, cut the letters apart, and put them in their plastic bags.

Even with the organizational problems I dealt with when I started the Making Words lessons, I still saw all my students making progress and using what they were learning in their reading and writing. This made me feel it was worth it, since I didn't see this transfer with the phonics program I used previously.

After a month of doing the Making Words lessons, I started adding in some Guess the Covered Word and Rounding Up the Rhymes lessons, which the class enjoyed.

One major mistake I made during the Working with Words Block was having a Word Wall, not doing a Word Wall. Since we were well into the year by the time I got started, I put all the words up on my Word Wall and skipped all those activities that go along with this part of the block. Even though I referred to the words every day when I did Writer's Workshop, I didn't feel the Word Wall was used as it should have been. What a mistake! I will correct that next year. Not only will I have a Word Wall, I will do the recommended activities from the beginning.

Self-Selected Reading

The second block I added was the Self-Selected Reading Block. I basically thought this was the same as D.E.A.R. until I got to the part of how the teacher interacted with the students. Previously, I just sat at my desk or walked around the room while the students were reading. I didn't read a book to them before they read, nor did I have any students share after they read.

I began reading a book to them each day, and I modeled the three different types of reading first-graders can do—reading the pictures, telling the story, reading the words. The best part was that when I got done reading a book, everyone wanted to read that book. As the children read, I conferenced with a few students. I could tell the children really enjoyed this one-on-one time we spent together discussing a book.

The problems I had with this block at the beginning were the time wasted by the students choosing and returning books, and the noise level of the children reading in the classroom. Once I began using baskets of books, with a variety of levels and types of literature in them, it solved the problem of too much time spent choosing and returning books. The children had the baskets on their tables, and they had to choose from only that basket for the week. The baskets were rotated the next week until all the baskets had been at all the tables.

Writing

My next block to work on was the Writing Block. I felt as though I had this block down the best of all since I already knew about Writer's Workshop, but I had been making some mistakes. I never would have thought to start so early in the year on writing until I read about "writing." I also learned how to help students choose a topic, what to do when they couldn't spell a word, how to add to a piece, how to use the Editor's Checklist, and how to publish. I had been modeling how to write, but I learned that I could model all the different things they needed to learn.

I have heard some teachers don't like to do writing minilessons, but I really enjoyed doing them. I wrote about whatever was going on in my life or something I knew the kids were interested in (Pokemon®, at the time). I have to say that I thought I did well at modeling how to stretch out words, referencing the room for words, rereading what was written after each sentence, and brainstorming a list of topics—which we left on a big piece of chart paper at the front of the room.

Guided Reading

Guided Reading was by far the hardest block for me to handle. The biggest problem I had from the start was how to get class sets of books, or even half class sets, for partner reading. The literature series we currently had seemed to be too hard to read, and the selections were mainly fiction and not very interesting. I went searching for old reading texts our school may have had in storage, but came up short since our school was only three years old at the time. Then, I tried to see if our county warehouse had a surplus of books. I came up short again. I finally found some teachers on my team with some old basals. I mostly did echo and choral reading with the class sets and shared reading with the big books. I did some partner reading with these resources, but did not get to the other formats for Four-Blocks, such as Three-Ring Circus, book club groups, ERT…, or sticky-note reading. I was quite discouraged that I did not have all the materials I needed for this block, especially when it was the one block I wanted to make work the most. However, I did use predictions, KWL's, graphic organizers, story maps, doing the book, etc., when I could with the materials I had available.

Looking Forward to Next Year

Just after school ended, I began to think about what I needed so that I could do the Four-Blocks more efficiently. I also wanted to see the Four-Blocks in action, so I went on the mailring and asked for any Four-Blocks teachers in my area to e-mail me. All the teachers in our area were already out of school, but I made some contacts and hope to visit them this fall. I also got the new book, *Guided Reading The Four-Blocks™ Way*.

As this chapter is being finished, I'm into the second week of a new school year. I purchased a Word Wall at a local school supply store and plan to "do" the Word Wall this year. The first words I put on the Word Wall were the kids' names. We add one name a day after we do the activities from the August section of *Month-by-Month Phonics for First Grade*. My kids really enjoy these "Getting to Know You" activities because they are in the limelight. I have added a little special touch to the occasion by making this the time when my "student of the day" also gets recognized. The student of the day gets to wear a crown for the day and has special jobs to do all day long. The kids really love this! I plan to follow closely the activities outlined in *Month-by-Month Phonics for First Grade* for the remainder of the year.

I follow the Working with Words Block with Guided Reading. I am using lots of nursery rhymes and traditional songs. (I got this idea from *Guided Reading the Four-Blocks™ Way.*) This is another time when all the children feel successful, because all of the children in my class can read the rhymes and songs after some practice. I write the rhymes and traditional songs we do together, duplicate them, and put them into a book for the first graders to "read." The children love taking home a book so early in the school year that they all can read.

I also have a lot of big books for shared reading. I continue to look for class sets of books as I move into partner reading and the other formats.

I am just beginning the Self-Selected Reading Block. At the beginning of this block, I read a book or two, depending on length. I've found this time to be critical for promoting those short, easy-to-read books which are crucial for beginning readers to use in order to practice reading and to develop confidence and fluency. I can't say I totally enjoy reading those books, but I sure try to put on a show and act like I do.

I am now using crates of books on all different reading levels which rotate to the different tables. One crate sits by each "table," which is actually four desks put together. I make sure that each crate has all different types of literature to read from, including fiction, nonfiction, poetry, *Scholastic News*, etc.

One problem I've run into in the past (which still haunts me about this block) is the amount of books it requires. My children read about three books a day per child, so I am always on the lookout for more books! Thank goodness the children will revisit books and can read and enjoy them more than once during the week. I have found it true that the boys do like informational books. I am currently trying to go to as many garage sales as possible to find more books at cheap prices. I am also going to send out the Scholastic Book Club orders this year, and I am asking parents for any old books they may have at home. I have also asked parents to be on the lookout for books for our classroom throughout the school year. You can never have enough books!

I am just getting the Writing Block started. I have reread The Writing Block chapter in *The Teacher's Guide to the Four-Blocks™*, and I'm all set to go. I will use an overhead projector with a lined transparency, similar to the paper the children are going to write on, as I model for my class. I think that using an overhead projector will work better for me because I am facing the children. I am more aware now of who is paying attention to the minilesson than I was last year, when I wrote on the board and my back was to the students.

My goal for this year is to have at least one parent volunteer per block. From the looks of my volunteer sign-up sheet, I may not be that lucky! I would really like to have one parent during the Writing Block to help with conferences, as the children need so much one-on-one attention during this time. I am hoping this extra help will come from one of my parents who happens to have taught first grade before. I know parents are on your side when they see the wonderful things you are doing!

I have great plans for this year and this class. I am still the only first-grade teacher at my school doing Four-Blocks, but one second- and one third-grade teacher are trying it this year. Getting Four-Blocks up and running well took a lot of work and worry, but it's worth it because of the success I see for different children each day. I'm glad I finally found it!

My First Year of Teaching: First Grade and Four-Blocks™ •

by Marsha Boylan (with Pat Cunningham)

Most teachers have vivid memories of their first year of teaching. No matter how prepared, smart, hard-working, and concerned you are, the first year is a shock. (I am reminded of the old saying, "Love is blind, but the first year of marriage is a real eye-opener!") Imagine being a first-year teacher and implementing Four-Blocks™ at the same time. That is exactly what Marsha did. Here is her story, and her plans for getting a running start on her second year of teaching:

I began my teaching career on Sept. 7, 1999, at Dort Elementary School in Roseville, Michigan. I had 20 first-graders. At the beginning of the school year, I had one student who was reading at approximately a Reading Recovery Level 8 and one other student who was reading at approximately a Reading Recovery Level 4. The remaining 16 students were non-readers, including four students who did not know all of their letter sounds. My classroom consisted of 13 girls and seven boys.

Our school district uses the reading/language arts program developed by MacMillan/McGraw-Hill. The first six books in the series are individual trade books and then the program switches to reading anthologies. Although I was satisfied with the literature selection overall, the teacher's guide provides so many possibilities of what can be taught that, as a new teacher, I was completely overwhelmed. My mentor explained that it was not possible to cover all of the material in a one-week period, so I needed to be selective. This is where I had trouble, selecting activities which would most support my students' emerging reading and writing abilities. I tried the workbooks that came with the series and found them to be out-of-context and completely hands-off activities. Four-Blocks™ guided me to re-structure the skills and strategies lessons suggested in each chapter into a format which made sense and connected my entire language arts program.

How I Found Four-Blocks

On February 1, I went to a one-day seminar on the Four-Blocks given by Pat Cunningham. I was already using ideas from *Phonics They Use* and *Month-by-Month Phonics for First Grade,* and I was eager to meet the author and see what else I could learn. As Pat was describing the Four-Blocks, it was like a 300-watt lightbulb came on in my head. I realized that my language arts program was "some of this and some of that" and had no real direction. Pat made so much sense that I went home and read *The Teacher's Guide to the Four-Blocks™* cover to cover <u>twice</u>. Six days later, I completely changed my language arts program, and I haven't looked back!

My Schedule

Due to the specials (art, music, gym, library, etc.) which are held in the morning, I found it necessary to schedule my Four-Blocks in the afternoon. I was a little wary, but I had no choice because I wanted and needed uninterrupted time to move from one block to the other. I felt that the transfer would be most evident to my students, and it does seem to have worked out that way. Here is how my schedule worked.

Right after lunch, I read aloud to the children, and then the children had their Self-Selected Reading time. I conferenced with four students each day. To end the Self-Selected Reading Block, one student would read aloud to the class from a book he or she had chosen.

Next, we would do our Working with Words Block, beginning with the Word Wall and then moving into the second activity. In February, I started using the activities suggested and described in T*he Teacher's Guide to Four-Blocks™*, which I received at Pat's seminar. We used the Making Words activity every Thursday, and I sent home a homework sheet with the same letters used in class. (This really helped the students who wanted to make words of their own during the lesson.) We also used Rounding Up the Rhymes, Using Words You Know, and Guess the Covered Word. My students favorite Working with Words activity was Guess the Covered Word.

Next came our Guided Reading Block, which was my weakest block. The other first-grade teacher in my building uses the leveled-reading-group style of Guided Reading. I could see some advantages to that, but I wanted to stay true to Four-Blocks, and I couldn't do the leveled groups and still have time for the other blocks. I also knew that the before and after reading activities were where I was teaching comprehension, and I couldn't do that if I had 15-minute groups. Once again, I used *The Teacher's Guide to Four-Blocks™* as a guide when teaching Guided Reading. I used shared reading, choral reading, echo reading, independent reading, and partner reading. Except for playschool groups and book clubs, I used all of the reading groupings suggested. For materials, I used our literature anthology, poetry, and our *Weekly Reader*.

The last block each day was Writing, which soon became the favorite block for many of my students. (Some of the students would love to write all afternoon and just skip the other blocks!) I started out conferencing with certain students on certain days, and ended the year editing with students who needed to edit. There was never enough time for editing, however, because the students who love to write can "produce" so much and would like to edit with me every other day!

I feel the Writing Block was the most successful in my classroom. I received many compliments from teachers regarding the writing they saw from my students. I had been doing journal writing since September, and at the end of the year, I gave my students their September journals and had them compare that writing to their most current pieces. They were amazed (and so was I) at how much they had grown. Some of their comments were:

"This didn't even make sense."
"I didn't even know how to spell like." (She had spelled it lak - which I thought
    was great in September!)
"I can't read what this says."

On the next-to-the-last day of school, I had a substitute and to make life simpler, I had her write a prompt on the board:

On my summer vacation, I will . . .

The sub of course didn't edit with the students (and we don't edit everything we write anyway). Not only was the content excellent, but their mechanics were really in place, too. The students shared their pieces on Thursday morning (our last day of school), and their first draft writing was phenomenal! Comparing their September and June writing and these excellent first-draft samples was proof-positive of how well they all were writing.

Their Reading Progress

At my school, we give running records in January, March, and June to determine progress. We use the DRA—Developmental Reading Assessment, which I think does a fairly good job of assessing comprehension as well as fluency.

Here are my students' Reading Recovery Levels in January, March and June.

Level	# of Students at that Level		
	January	March	June
24+	1	7	9
20	0	1	3
18	0	0	1
16	0	1	2
14	0	4	1
12	0	1	1
9	2	1	0
8	3	1	0
7	2	0	0
5	7	1	0
4	0	0	1
3	1	2	1
2	2	0	0
1	2	0	0

Total # Students (20 in January, 19 in March and June)

I am very worried about two of my students (a boy and a girl), who only read at Level 3 or 4 in June. I wonder if they would have made more progress if I had started Four-Blocks at the beginning of the year. Fortunately, both students will be attending a summer program that is focused entirely on reading and writing. I understand that the teacher is excellent and has seen progress with students in similar circumstances. So, I hope they can make some more progress.

Looking Forward to Next Year

All in all, I think I had a good first year of teaching. I just wish I had started out knowing what I know now! Since I am a recent graduate myself, I share the Four-Blocks™ framework with anyone I know that is graduating and looking for a position. Not only was it something for me to grab onto, it was user-friendly, and most importantly, a balanced program for my students.

Next year, I will begin implementing Four-Blocks immediately. I am so happy I began Four-Blocks when I did last year, because not only did it positively affect my students' reading and writing, it gave me time to experiment with the model so that now I feel much more comfortable beginning the year with Four-Blocks. I went to a seminar this summer in which Cheryl Sigmon really outlined how Guided Reading should be conducted. Guided Reading was my weakest block, and I will start the year with a clearer concept of what I am trying to accomplish in this block. Our school has many sets of leveled readers, and I plan to put these to good use with the book club format. I think my students will love this! Having completed my first year of teaching has given me much more confidence as a teacher, and with the solid support of the Four-Blocks™ Model, I can't wait to see the growth in my students next year.

My First Year of Teaching: Second Grade and Four-Blocks™ •••

by Kelley Kennedy (with Pat Cunningham)

Each year, I do some large seminars in different parts of the country in which I do an overview of the Four-Blocks™. There is a lot to cover and I only have one day, so I tell everyone to fasten their seatbelts as we go through all Four-Blocks. Some days, I look out at my audience near the end of a long day and wonder what sense they have made of the day. I often worry about the "same-age-as-my-son-looking" teachers and hope they were not too overwhelmed and have learned some things they can take back to their classrooms. As I read Kelley Kennedy's responses on our Four-Blocks census, I realized that she, at least, had not been overwhelmed! Here is Kelley's story:

In my first year of teaching, I taught second grade at Creekside Elementary in Franklin, Indiana. We gave the Gates-McGinitie Reading Test early in the year, and my students had a wide range of reading levels, with about half still reading at early first-grade levels and about one third reading at third-grade level or above. My approach to reading was pretty traditional. I used the stories from our basal at the beginning of the year, and (I'm sorry to say) did a lot of round-robin reading. I didn't use ability grouping, but I did allow a "high" group of kids to read a difficult chapter book while the rest of the class worked with on-level material. I would cover the story in the basal (round robin/oral question style), and then I would spend a couple of days doing activities that related to the stories. This is where I incorporated some of my writing. For example, we wrote recipes for friendship pizza after reading *Little Nino's Pizzeria*. Students also wrote in a daily journal during morning work, responding to a question I wrote on the chalkboard.

In October, I went to Pat Cunningham's Four-Blocks™ conference in Indianapolis. A master teacher who I observed early in the year was kind enough to share the registration form with me. I was very impressed and energized by the conference. I came home, read *The Teacher's Guide to the Four-Blocks™*, and subscribed to the *fourblocksearly@onelist* mailring. I also read all of Cheryl Sigmon's Four-Blocks columns at *www.teachers.net*. I began to change my reading program, slowly working towards the full Four-Blocks™ framework, which took me until January to get fully in place.

Working with Words

I began with the Working with Words Block, following pretty much the activities outlined in *Month-by-Month Phonics for Second Grade*. I got the Word Wall started, and as the year went on, added some fun ways to practice the words. We did push-ups while chanting Word Wall words on Friday. The students also liked to disco, box, and "volcano" their words. (These types of chants are just a few of the many ideas I got from the teacher mailring.) My students all loved Be a Mind Reader, an On-the-Back activity we did every Friday. I knew I was doing something right when the kids would always say, "It's a word on the Word Wall" in unison with me when I gave the first clue.

For the second portion of the Working with Words block, Guess the Covered Word and Reading/Writing Rhymes were the students' favorites. Being typically silly second-graders, they loved writing silly rhymes! They also enjoyed Making Words, and I enjoyed creating Making Words lessons to go with our themes and units. (I went to *www.easypeasy.com/anagrams* and typed in the word and got a list of all the possible words to choose from.) Some of the secret words for which I made lessons included Washington, tadpoles, butterflies, chrysalis, and evaporation. The kids really enjoyed figuring out the secret word. It made me feel so good when one particular student always figured out the secret word as soon as she saw the letters. She was "average" and didn't participate much in class, so this was a way for her to feel successful. Parents have also responded well to Making Words. I sent home the take-home sheet with the letters across the top for the same lesson we had done in class, and members of the whole family (siblings, parents, and grandparents) would get into figuring out the secret word and coming up with lots of other words that could be made with the letters. I like how this hands-on activity encouraged parental involvement solely by completing a meaningful activity. I love the Working with Words Block! It is the easiest for me to organize, and my students love the activities.

Self-Selected Reading

After hearing Pat speak and surveying my classroom library, I purchased many nonfiction books. (I'm convinced that some of my kids would not be readers now had they not been able to read informational books during Self-Selected Reading.) I was already reading aloud to my children every day. (I was doing some things the Four-Blocks way!) I added the time for the children to read books of their own choosing and began conferencing with them. For conferencing, I had my Monday kids, Tuesday kids, etc. It was quite difficult at first to fit in all of the conferences, but we all got faster and better-organized as the children learned the routines. I enjoyed listening to the kids read and talking with them during this time. It helped me to know what they were interested in, and I got to boost their confidence during this time as well.

Guided Reading

Guided Reading was (and is) the most difficult block for me. I tried to use a variety of materials—both levels and genres. I used the sets of books from the Pegasus reading series (*Frog and Toad Are Friends, Long Way to a New Land, My Little Island, The Chalk Box Kid*) during second semester. To make sure I was teaching my children how to comprehend informational text, I did some Guided Reading lessons with *Scholastic News* and used some Gail Gibbons' books and other informational books that integrated with our study of frogs, butterflies, and weather.

I love to use RIVET as a before reading activity. The children love to guess the words and then predict what will happen based on the words given. I often used sticky notes for kids to find information related to the purpose I set for them. I replaced my round-robin Reading with ERT… which the children saw as a puzzle to be solved. We did partner reading, and on some days, I used the Three-Ring Circus format in which some children read in partners, some by themselves, and some in a small group with me. I used the book club format only once, due to lack of books (but I plan to use it more next year).

Writing

The hardest part of the Writing Block was figuring out what to do for minilessons. I purchased *Craft Lessons*, which has wonderful ideas for minilessons. I also surfed for minilessons on the Internet and got some ideas from the mailrings. Minilessons are great because I can fit them to my kids' needs instead of teaching from a prescribed textbook.

I really enjoy conferencing with the kids. I like how I can teach them about different elements of the writing process at their developmental level. I generally conference with kids when they are ready to publish or stuck on a topic idea. Before kids conference with me, I have them complete a publishing checklist in which they must edit with a buddy before they come to me.

For author's chair, I let kids sign up for whatever day they choose. With this method, though, some kids have hardly shared this year. I don't want to force kids to share if they don't want to, but I think next year I will try to gently coax more students into sharing.

Students write their rough drafts in spiral notebooks, but I have also set up a box with one file folder for each student. In this folder, they can keep their publishing checklist, final draft paper, about the author pages, and dedication pages. This has kept them from losing their precious work.

Results

We give the Gates-McGinitie Reading Test at the beginning of the school year and again in March. On the March testing, 12 students were reading at third-grade level or above; four students were reading at grade level; six students were reading below grade level. All but two students grew at least one grade level this year. This is about the same as the other second-grade classes in my school. If I had started Four-Blocks at the beginning of the year (I didn't have all blocks up and running until late January), I'm sure that more of my kids would have shown more growth. I hope to be able to demonstrate this with next year's test scores.

What Was Most Difficult

The most difficult thing for me was the time constraint. Some days I had to skip a whole block, but I hope to never have to do this next year. We are required to go to the computer lab for two hours each week to work on a program that our district purchased to prepare kids for the third-grade state standardized test. I have also had to give my kids practice sheets with bubbles to fill in and other test-prep worksheets. Although it's important to teach test-taking skills, these activities cut into my Four-Blocks time more than I would have liked.

It was also difficult being the only teacher in the building using Four-Blocks. I felt that since I was new, my use of it wouldn't be taken seriously. I did have some teachers tell me that Four-Blocks is just another fad that will be gone in a few years. I know this is not true. It was hard to have no support with my Four-Blocks instruction; however, when I found Cheryl Sigmon's articles and the mailring, I found this missing support. What truly kept me going was reading and rereading of all of my resources (*The Teacher's Guide to Four-Blocks™*, *Month-by-Month Phonics for Second Grade*, *Classrooms That Work*, and *Phonics They Use*). By doing this, I have been constantly re-energized toward my goal of balanced literacy.

Looking Forward to Next Year

I almost can't wait for next year—my second year of teaching second grade and my first year to do Four-Blocks from day one! There are so many things I will do differently to benefit my kids next year, because I know so much more now!

In Guided Reading, I plan to use book clubs more often. I would also like to use more poetry, and plan on having a poem a day. I would like to have an "after lunch bunch" next year and show kids how to coach themselves when they get to a difficult word. (I'm also thinking about having a night session to teach my students' parents how to coach their kids in reading.) I also plan to do comprehension strategy lessons that I have read about in *Mosaic of Thought* and *Strategies That Work*. I would like to use running records periodically to track the reading growth of my students—particularly my struggling readers.

In Self-Selected Reading, I would like my kids to make news reports and commercials for the books they are presenting when they do the Reader's Chair. I would also love to have a "read-in" in which parents, other teachers, and administrators would read to kids after school in a slumber-party-type atmosphere.

I have done a lot of thinking about the Writing Block and have outlined some writing minilessons I want to use to organize my thinking. I even had the courage to post these on the Four-Blocks goodies page of *Teachers.Net*. I have gotten so many ideas from other teachers on the mailrings, and I was delighted that I finally had something to share with others! I want my students to do more publishing using the computer. I'm not sure how I will organize the conferencing. Some kids "slipped through the cracks" when they signed up for conferences. I think I am going to make sure I conference with every child at least once every other week.

Just like kids have a specific purpose in Guided Reading, Four-Blocks has given me a specific focus in my teaching. This organizational framework has been invaluable for a first-year teacher like me. I can't wait for next year!

How My ELL Children Learned to Read
with Four-Blocks™ •

by Cheryl Ristow (with Pat Cunningham)

How to teach reading to children whose first language is not English is a source of debate and contention everywhere. California has decreed that all children will have their beginning reading instruction in English. Easier said than done! Learning to read is hard enough when you recognize the words you have just decoded and have meanings for them. For children who are learning English as they learn to read, many words are new words, not just in their printed form, but also in their oral form. New words are really "NEW" words to children learning English as they learn to read. When the Four-Blocks™ census forms began to arrive, we were astonished by the number of teachers who have large numbers of English Language Learners in their classrooms. All these teachers reported that, while still a difficult task, they had more success teaching ELL children using the Four-Blocks™ framework than with more traditional methods. Cheryl Ristow is just one of the teachers who told us of her success with her English Language Learners and Four-Blocks. She tells a compelling story which we are delighted to share with you.

I teach first grade at Valencia Park School in Fullerton, California. Our school is in a blue collar section of Orange County where many families have settled after coming from other countries. Most of our children qualify for free/reduced price lunch. Title I is school-wide. Most of our children are English Language Learners.

When school started in the fall of 1999, I had twenty children. While I've had as many as five different languages spoken in my classroom, this year I had ten children who spoke three different languages—Spanish, Punjabi, and Tagalog. Five of these children spoke relatively fluent English, three spoke little English, and two were limited English speakers. Three students were not fluent in either English or their native language due to speech and language problems. These children received speech and language therapy twice weekly. All the children had many common words they didn't know meanings for and had difficulty understanding some English sentence patterns. Vocabulary for all students, both native English speakers and those speaking English as a second language, was limited.

While all the ELL students in my class had BICS—Basic Interpersonal Communication Skills (the ability to have a simple conversation), most of them did not have CALPS—Cognitive Acquired Language Proficiency Skills (the language of schools and learning). For example, a student with BICS could give an appropriate response to the request, "How are you today?" or "What color is the girl's dress?" However, they would be unable to respond to the statement, "Describe the main character in the story."

As part of our assessment procedures, I record the results of three running records a year. (The books we use for running records are from the Sunshine Assessment Guide.) In October, after the first assessment, I had 17 "U's" out of 20 students—the U stands for "Unable to read." The three who could read were at the "readiness" level. I had to tell many of the parents that their children were at risk of retention. Believe me when I say it was not a happy time!

Early in the Year

Because I had so many English Language Learners, I started the year using some of the Building Blocks™ ideas developed for kindergarten and activities from *Month-by-Month Phonics for First Grade*. We did a weekly predictable chart using a predictable pattern such as: My friend and I _____; A ____ is _____ (color word), etc. We read and reread the sentences every day. On Friday, each student got his or her own sentence to cut apart, rearrange, copy, and illustrate. We made these into class books which became the favorite books of many children for Self-Selected Reading.

The children also enjoyed being the "king" or "queen" of the day during the first few weeks of the school year. I let each child lead the cheer of his/her name by using a battery-operated toy megaphone. The megaphone changes the child's voice so that it sounds like a robot, or a monster, or they can talk normally. They are given the choice of how they want their voice to sound and are usually very excited to get to speak into the megaphone! After the letters in the child's name are cheered, we look at the name and compare it to the other names of the children who have previously been the "king" or "queen" of the day. Naming the alphabet letters and looking at them in the names is good review and practice for my ELL students, as well as the rest of the class. I then pass out drawing paper, and as I guide them through the correct procedure in printing the letters, they write the child's name at the tops of their papers. When they are through, they draw pictures of the chosen student. These drawings go home with the child of the day. The chosen child's drawing is labeled with his/her name and put on our names bulletin board. The children frequently refer to this board in the weeks and months ahead when they want to see how to spell a classmate's name.

After the pictures are finished, I lead the students through an interview of the chosen child. During the first day or two of school, we come up with five questions to ask each child. I have five groups of children in my class, and each group has their own color. I write the questions on a poster with the appropriate colors of markers, so that each group has a question. Each day during the interview, I have each group read their question as I point to the words on the poster. I write the chosen child's response on the overhead projector, and we read it over several times. I then have volunteers come to the overhead and circle words they know. By the fifteenth or sixteenth interview, it's amazing to me that almost everyone knows most of the words!

For the children who don't speak enough English to participate, I have a student translator (another first-grader) translate the question into the native language. The child's response, however, is written in English, since I don't read or write Spanish or any of the other languages that my children speak at home. I almost never have a child who speaks a language that no one else in the class speaks. We have a school policy to place completely non-English speaking students in a class where there is another child who is more fluent in English, but speaks the native language as well.

To give more help with English, I make and display large picture posters each month. These include words and pictures of seasonal and theme topics. These posters are a huge boost to the students' writing all year long and are crucial to their writing early in the year.

I also do lots of phonemic awareness activities. We sing, chant, act out—just about stand on our heads!—learning those letter sounds, rhymes, blending, and segmenting. We are fortunate to have Hallie Yopp, a phonemic awareness expert, as a resource for our district. A professor at California State University-Fullerton, she has written extensively on phonemic awareness and has held workshops for the teachers in the Fullerton School District. Many of the activities I use come from her book *Oo-pples and Boo-noo-noos: Songs and Activities for Phonemic Awareness*. I have also used activities from the *Phonemic Awareness: Songs & Rhymes* series. This series includes books for Fall, Winter, and Spring and all the books contain songs to teach beginning and ending consonant sounds, rhyming, blending, and segmenting. One of my favorites is "Fee, Fie, Fiddle-I-O." When we are learning, for example, the /t/ sound, we change the initial consonants so that it sounds like this: "Tee, Tie, Tiddle-I-O."

When learning the short vowel sounds, I use a poster I made with pictures of "Grandma and Grandpa." (This can be found in the book *Phonics Fundamentals*.) I elaborate and talk about Grandma and Grandpa when introducing the short vowel sounds. For instance, when introducing the sound of short "o", I have the students put their hands on their cheeks, and I tell them this is the way Grandma sounds and looks when she sees her new grandbaby. The "u" sound is what Grandpa says when he catches a basketball thrown at his stomach. The poster has pictures of Grandma and Grandpa acting these same things out. I refer to it often as we talk about it, and the kids begin to use it when they are trying to figure out which vowel to use in the words they are writing.

Whenever possible, I try to use pictures, songs, hand motions, or some other physical response to introduce letter sounds and other new concepts. These are good techniques for all learners, but they also give an added layer of support for my ELL students. Getting the children physically involved in singing a song about a new concept really seems to help them remember.

Working with Words

The phonemic awareness activities described above were used for the Working with Words Block at the beginning of the year. I also began our Word Wall, choosing words from Scholastic's *Literacy Place Phonics Book*. I am required to use this book as part of my language arts instructional program, so I use the 75 sight words listed in the book as a start to my Word Wall. One of the assessments our district requires is a spelling test of 25 basic sight words. I make sure these are the first 25 words on the wall so that when testing time comes in February, they are very familiar to the students. At the beginning of the year, I introduce new words only every other week so that we can do lots and lots of review and practice. When we are practicing, I always use the words in context or in a sentence frame. For example, when learning the word "like" I might say, "I like to eat cookies." I would then ask for someone to tell what he/she likes to eat—each time the word "like" is said, I or a student points to the word "like." These sentence frames often become the basis for a predictable chart (described earlier). During the Working with Words block, the students love to play Guess the Covered Word, Be a Mind Reader, WORDO, and Sentence Dictation (believe it or not!).

Writing

My children like all the blocks, but the Writing Block is their favorite. If we don't have time for it, then they let me know they are upset about missing it! I think my enthusiasm for this block has been a key to the students' success. I am so excited to feel successful as a writing teacher and to see their success! I have been known to yell, scream, and even dance around the room when one of the children shows real improvement in their writing. When the children see my reaction, they want it for themselves and strive to get it!

I start Writer's Workshop the first or second day of school. I talk to the students a lot about what their writing could look like. For some, there will be a picture and perhaps some pretend or "scribble" writing. I tell students that as long as they know what those scribbles say, that it is okay with me. I also tell them that some of them might be able to write a few letters, such as initial consonants. At this time I begin to teach the students that if they don't know how to write the whole word, they can write the first letter and then a dash. Of course, I also tell them that writing words is great, and it is what I hope to see from all of them eventually. I repeat these lessons over and over again as my minilessons before they begin their own writing. I emphasize that they can write in the way that feels most comfortable to them, as long as they know what their writing says! If they don't, I make them either start over or write something else. Even those children who are not fluent in English feel free to write at whatever level they can. I have had children write in their native language, and I accept that joyfully since I know that they have made the connection that what we talk about can be written down. Usually these children quickly transition to writing in English as their vocabulary and knowledge of our phonetic system grows. During these early days of the school year, I set the timer and have the students write for only five to seven minutes. While they write, I circulate to help and encourage as needed.

My school supplies us with as much lined newsprint as we want throughout the year. The paper comes in 12" x18" sheets with a blank "picture" part at the top and about 6 or 7 wide lines (with a mid-space) at the bottom. I cut this paper in half (9" x12") to use for Writer's Workshop. Early in the year, most of my children want a new sheet of paper each day and do not continue with anything they have started writing on an earlier day. I do encourage them to continue writing on a piece the next day, and as the year progresses, most of the children do save writing pieces to edit or continue with on another day. While I do talk about punctuation and capital letters during my minilessons at the beginning of the year, I don't start any formal sort of editing until January or February. Most of my class is not ready for it until then. Just getting some thoughts on paper is hard enough for them until midyear.

At the end of the first three to four weeks of school, I slowly begin to increase the amount of time being spent writing and begin doing different types of minilessons, although they are still very basic and simple. Some of these minilessons include where to begin writing on the paper, what to do at the end of the line, where to put your name and the date, and how to turn the paper over when you need more lines. These things seem pretty obvious, but these are the kinds of things the students don't know and need to learn! I model how to do beginning or temporary spelling in my minilessons daily, and gently nag/encourage them to do this as they write.

At the end of the writing time, I choose four children to share their writing by pulling four sticks from a jar. The children have the option of sharing or of passing. Most are pleased to share! I model asking a few questions of each writer. Then, each writer can choose someone whose hand is raised to ask a question.

I think the key to success in the Writing Block is doing it every day, doing lots and lots of modeling, celebrating the successes of the children (such as when someone passes from that scribble writing stage to writing some initial consonants), and not despairing! I had a child who drew what looked like the same stick figures and wrote "ABCDE" underneath them every day until Christmas. But in January, it finally began to "click," and he slowly began to write words. This was one of my boys who was not fluent in either English or Spanish. At the end of the year, while not on grade level by any means, he was able to write three readable sentences. He had made tremendous progress since September. At the same time that his writing began to improve, so did his reading.

One of the things I find to be very successful in getting the children to write is the use of picture posters mentioned earlier. For example, the September poster includes pictures of our school, myself, an apple (our first science/social studies topic), Johnny Appleseed, etc. All of these pictures are labeled with words. When I'm modeling writing for the children, I point to the words on the chart and ask the children to spell them as I write them down on my writing paper. I also begin to teach students to look around the room for color and number words, and I ask them to point the words out to me as I'm writing.

I find pictures to use on these posters from seasonal coloring books, computer clip art, old ditto books, etc. I also occasionally use photographs. It's important to choose just a few important words and pictures and label them in large, easy-to-read writing or with a computer font of about 150 points. I also make sure to post these charts where they can be seen easily by all of the children. I enlarge the pictures on the photocopier (if necessary), color them, and glue them to large pieces of butcher paper. When I take them down, I roll them up and save them for next year.

These posters were a good way for the ELL students to become familiar with symbols of seasonal traditions and holidays. Since each picture has a word or two attached (under the picture of the apple, I might also have the words "red" and "sweet"), and since we practice reading the posters often and also have felt, tasted, and smelled real apples, the students quickly learn what the picture says and have some idea of its meaning.

Guided Reading

Guided Reading was my weakest area. We use Scholastic's *Literacy Place*; and I do a lot of choral reading, echo reading, and partner reading with those stories. I use RIVET to introduce vocabulary words, and students' attention is indeed riveted to the words. This is the block I plan to change the most next year.

Self-Selected Reading

My students just love Self-Selected Reading time! And they are really reading! I did have to spend almost half the year getting them trained to really read instead of just chatting with their friends, but it has really paid off! By the end of the year, they were all reading for 20–30 minutes at a time. However, I didn't start the year by having them read for 20 minutes! Like writing, this is a block where I use a timer set for about five to seven minutes during the first few weeks of the school year. When most children could handle reading for that amount of time, I'd increase the time gradually.

At the start of the year, my book baskets have just a few books in them, and they are the easiest books I can find. These include alphabet books, number books, our class books made from predictable charts, the easiest phonics readers that came with *Literacy Place,* and books that go with whatever science or social studies topic we are presently doing. I also include Mother Goose rhymes and fairy tales my children can read by telling the story that goes with the pictures. As the children begin reading more and more, I add books and make the baskets more multilevel. And, if I have a student who is already reading at the beginning of the year, I make books available at his/her reading level.

My class sits in five groups with four children per group. Each group gets a book basket each day. In addition, each child has a number. I alternate having the children with odd or even numbers staying at their seats to read or going to different areas of the room. Spreading the students out all over the room helps to cut down on the "chattiness." However, if someone is having a particularly hard time, they have to sit in a certain corner and read to the wall for a few minutes. The children don't like this, and I usually don't have to do it very often.

I always start the Self-Selected Reading Block by reading to the class. I usually pick a book from one of the baskets, and I model the three ways to read (especially at the beginning of the year). Some books can be read by talking about the pictures and making up what it might say. Some books can be read by memory. ("I've heard this story of the Three Pigs before! I think I can tell just by looking at the pictures what is happening.") In some books, like the simple alphabet and number books and our class books, I can read it by reading the words. I tell the children that learning to read is hard work, and we need to practice. Self-Selected Reading time is when we do this. The students know that what we are doing during this time is serious, important work. They also know that I don't expect them to be able to read every word, and this gives them the comfort level to do what I ask. I circulate around the room during Self-Selected Reading time, reading with the students and reminding them that this is reading practice time, not chatting time.

Before long, the children start noticing that they can read a few words that we've learned through the Word Wall, and that they can decode some words from all the phonics instruction that's been going on. These little discoveries seem to thrill them and lead to more noticing, decoding, and trying to "figure it out." This is the time of day when I notice students using and trying out all the techniques we've practiced during the Working with Words and Guided Reading Blocks, such as skipping an unknown word, pretending it's the "covered word," and using the context and beginning letters to figure it out. As they are practicing all of these new skills, things begin to "gel" in their minds. The secret here—if there is one— is in setting up a non-threatening atmosphere, while at the same time keeping them on task. I don't conference with students at the beginning of the year. My goal is to keep their noses in the books (and not each other!). Once they understand this and have increased on-task reading time to 10-15 minutes (around December or January), then I can sit in the back of the room and start conferencing.

Communicating with Parents

Most of my parents work. Some have two or more jobs and work long hours. I have many parents who are illiterate or who attended only a few years of school. Each year, some of my parents are not fluent in English. It is hard for them to help. I try to keep my homework assignments simple enough for the student to complete without parental assistance. A typical nightly assignment would be one of the following: spelling practice, a math assignment, a phonics book page; or a science or social studies extension activity. In addition to this, there is a home reading log where parents are to read to the child for ten to twenty minutes. I consider the home reading log to be the most important element of the homework assignment. However, when I check homework, I frequently find that the logs are blank or contain only a few entries. And heartbreakingly, I once found that a student had entered in the column "Who did you read with?" the word "myself."

Communicating with the parents who do not speak English is difficult. We encourage them to read to their children in their native language, but materials are not readily available, and many parents don't understand the merit of this activity. They feel that because the reading is not being done in English, it is not furthering their child's ability to read. Cultural issues also come into play. In Mexico, parents are not encouraged to participate in school activities, and are only summoned to the school when their children are in serious trouble. Many of these parents' own school experiences were not positive, making them reluctant to become involved.

Assessment

The Fullerton School District has devised several different assessments to gauge the progress of our first-grade students. These include a beginning phonics skills test, a phonemic awareness test, a writing sample on a set topic given at the beginning and end of the year, a spelling test of 25 basic sight words, and the running records described earlier.

When I gave these assessments in September, only one child knew all the letter names, no children knew all the vowel sounds, and none of the children were able to read or write more than a few words. Their phonemic awareness levels—the ability to blend and segment words and recognize rhymes and beginning and ending sounds—were low. On the running records, 17 were unable to read the easiest passage, and only three could read at the readiness level.

On the December running records, three of my 19 children were still nonreaders. Eight students were at the pre-primer level. Six students were at the primer level—right where they should be halfway through first grade. Two students read at first grade level. (One student had moved.)

At the end of the year, I still had 19 students, but one had moved and another had come about a month before the testing. I gave my running records one last time. Twelve students read at or above grade level. Four students were just below grade level—well on their way to becoming fluent readers! Two students were at the pre-primer level. The new student, who had only been in my class for one month, was my only nonreader.

Looking Forward to Next Year

If you had seen my children at the beginning and end of the year, you would have no doubt that Four-Blocks—with some intensive Building Blocks™ activities early in the year—works! Using what I have learned, I anticipate even more success this year. My goal for this coming year is basically the same as last year's—to have them all reading as well as they possibly can by the end of first grade.

My personal goal is to do a better job with Guided Reading. I have read *Guided Reading The Four-Blocks™ Way* cover to cover—twice! I've gotten a beach ball and can't wait to use it! I'm also looking forward to trying the Prove it! and What's For Reading Today? activities. I am looking for more materials to use during Guided Reading. I am going to ask around (and do some poking around, too!) in my school district to find sets of old reading series books. I want to encourage my principal to buy class sets of books on science and social studies themes. I also want to try getting class sets of books with my book club bonus points and explore writing a grant to purchase books. While I am basically very happy to be using Scholastic's *Literacy Place* as my basal, it doesn't have a lot of nonfiction or some of the other genres I know I need to use more of during Guided Reading.

I am basically happy with my Writing Block with two exceptions. I hope to start editing and publishing a little earlier and to help the children learn to use more descriptive language in their writing. I am planning minilessons for editing, publishing, and descriptive language.

One of the major sources of help for me has been the Four-Blocks mailring at *Teachers.Net*. I have gotten so many wonderful ideas there and on the Four-Blocks chatboard. However, it's also nice to talk with teachers "in person" about problems, successes, and experiences using this model. I am still the "Lone Four-Blocks Ranger" at my school, so I don't have the opportunity to share there. However, there seems to be the beginnings of a Four-Blocks discussion group that meets "for real" (as opposed to via computer) here in Southern California! I want to thank Marti Plumtree for getting this going! We have met twice, and I am very hopeful that this will become a valuable resource for all of us.

If I think back to where I was two years ago in my comfort level of implementing Four-Blocks instruction, I know I've made lots of progress! I'm sure I can make headway this year on improving my skills and developing techniques that will work, not only for the ELL students in my class, but for all the students in my care.

The Internet, Four-Blocks™, and English Language Learners •

By Lisa Repaskey (with Dottie Hall)

I first met Lisa virtually on the Web as she wrote about her first grade class in California where many of her students were English Language Learners (ELL). Pat and I would lurk on the mailring and sometimes talk about Lisa's wonderful responses to other teachers who had similar children and similar problems. I was fortunate to really meet Lisa in the summer of 1999 at a Four-Blocks™ seminar in Sacramento, where some teachers from northern California had just had a Teachers.Net gathering and stayed for the seminar. Lisa later attended the first Four-Blocks Leadership Conference and has since moved to North Carolina. This is Lisa's story:

As a teacher, I eagerly await the summer months, not just because it means some time off, but also because I have time to catch up on my professional reading. Two summers ago, I had just purchased a new computer. I enjoyed surfing the Web and discovered a whole new world of teaching resources on the Internet. That summer, I had just reread *Classrooms That Work* to prepare for a literacy workshop that I would be giving to teachers in my district the following fall. This time, I read it with "new" eyes and discovered that I had lots of questions. As I surfed the Web one night, I ended up at Wake Forest University's Web site looking for my brother-in-law's work E-mail. Realizing that Pat Cunningham taught there, I searched the Wake Forest University Web site looking for her E-mail address. That is when I stumbled upon her Four-Blocks™ Web site. As I read through it, I was totally amazed! Here was a literacy model that contained every aspect of a balanced literacy program that I had always used in my primary classrooms, in a framework that I could easily use. It was laid out so I could make sure that I taught all four aspects of balanced literacy every day. I had always had students who loved books. Little did I know that in a year's time, I was going to have readers who devoured books!

My Teaching History

Over the past 10 years, I had been teaching grades kindergarten through second grade in a very large urban district in Northern California. My district has gone through its share of controversies and problems over the years. Problems that plagued the district ranged from consistently low standardized test scores, fiscal mismanagement, typical inner-city problems like drive-by shootings, gang problems, teen pregnancies, families "on the edge" of homelessness, and drug abuse to classrooms filled with students from diverse ethnic and linguistic backgrounds. Despite all of the problems that presented numerous challenges to my teaching over the years, there was always a sense of freedom in the way that I taught. I was allowed academic freedom to teach my students in the way that I knew was best. It was always implied that if my students left my classroom in the spring doing well on the standardized test, then I was doing well as a teacher. As long as students left the room as readers, my district never seemed to mandate that teachers all use the same reading curriculum. I felt fortunate not to have someone breathing down my neck and questioning my methods as a teacher.

In 12 years, I had already seen too many programs come and go. I watched my district purchase entire, highly-expensive curriculums, only to throw them away within a year or two. And with the academic freedom that I had, I could try anything—and I had over the years! But I still held onto my beliefs about balanced literacy. I knew that my students must have a "balanced diet" of reading, writing, and phonics to become strong readers. When I found the Four-Blocks Web site, I knew I had found my teaching framework. Little did I know how far the Four-Blocks journey would take me, both figuratively as well as literally!

How I Learned About the Four-Blocks™ with the Help of the Internet

It was near the end of August, 1998 when my journey began. Pat's Web site led me to explore the other links on the pages. Those links led me to Cheryl Sigmon's columns and to the mailrings at *Teachers.Net*. I printed out every single one of Cheryl's columns. I placed them into a notebook that I have read over and over again for the past two years, gaining new insights every time I read them. Being so new to the Internet, I wasn't so sure about the mailrings. But the thought of lots of daily E-mails was definitely enticing! I subscribed and began to meet teachers from all over the country. At first, I was jealous as I read about how entire schools, and even states, were doing Four-Blocks. Even those teachers who had at least another person at their school site to share with were lucky, I thought. I couldn't find anyone in my district who had even heard about Four-Blocks, let alone was actually using the framework. So, I depended upon the teachers on the Four-Blocks mailring to be my "support group" as I implemented Four-Blocks in my classroom, and in the years ahead. As everyone talked and shared what was happening in their classrooms and how implementation was going, I began to get to know teachers around the nation who were all going through the same things I was. It's very interesting how close I felt to these teachers, none of whom I had ever met before. I would go online every night after work to check the E-mails that I had received that day from the mailring. There were several screen names that I would recognize, and I read their postings first.

The First *Teachers.Net* Gathering in Northern California

Over the next year, there were several postings about teachers meeting each other off-line, and how much fun they had together. At some point, there was the suggestion that those of us living in Northern California might meet. That sounded interesting, and a bit scary! I had heard horror stories about people meeting others "in person" that they had met on-line. But, I was eager to meet the other teachers that I had been e-mailing for the past year. There is a strange sort of intimacy on the mailring. Maybe it's because the mailring is so anonymous that a person feels open to sharing personal thoughts. Anyway, I was looking forward to meeting these teachers. About 20 of us met for lunch at a restaurant in Sacramento. It was a two-hour drive for me, but well worth it. Several of us decided that we wanted to have special T-shirts made, and we wore them when we met each other. When I walked up to meet them, I felt an instant connection! We ate and talked for several hours about our common links—Four-Blocks and teaching, as well as about our personal lives. Even after the gathering was over, I continued to talk and e-mail several of the teachers from the gathering. A year later, four of us have become very good friends and continue to spend time with each other in a variety of situations. One way that we've maintained our friendship together, despite the distances we live from each other, is the chatroom on *Teachers.Net*. We log on a couple of times a week and talk with each other about how Four-Blocks is going, and just about life in general.

ELL and The Four-Blocks™

Being a person who typically plunges right into things, Four-Blocks was no different for me. School started just after Labor Day, and by then, I had rushed out to purchase *Month-by-Month Phonics for First Grade*. By the first day of school, I was ready to begin implementing all four of the blocks immediately. Because I was one of very few teachers at my school who had the Cross-Cultural Language Acquisition Development (CLAD) certificate, all of the English Language Learners in first grade would be placed into my classroom. The CLAD certificate means that I have taken some extra training, as well as a multiple choice and essay exam, and

• •

have the expertise to work with students from second language backgrounds. In years past, my classroom looked like a miniature United Nations! This first year of Four-Blocks, my 20 first-graders would speak Spanish, Cambodian, and Vietnamese, as well as English. In fact, only one of them was a native English speaker!

As I read through everything that I could get my hands on about Four-Blocks, I realized that I wasn't finding information about how to do Four-Blocks with English Language Learners. At least, not with as many as I had in my classroom! Could I do it with so many students for whom English was not their first language? I hoped so. I decided to keep an assessment notebook on them that would be ongoing throughout the year. Not having read much concerning English Language Learners in the Four-Blocks classroom, I felt I was entering uncharted territory. I was trying something new and exciting and wanted to be able to document every single detail just in case I had to prove to my administrator that my students were getting what they needed. This was the first program that I was actually excited to use in my classroom. I knew that it would work with my students. Perhaps the notebook was going to be proof of just how far my students actually did "travel" in their literacy journeys.

Fortunately, I had been on a district team that developed an authentic literacy assessment package that every elementary teacher used to assess their students. This literacy assessment, called the "Curriculum Embedded Assessment," consisted of running records, concepts about print, letter identification, high-frequency word lists, and a writing prompt done three times a year for kindergarten through third grade. These assessments were the perfect answer for what kind of assessment to put in this notebook.

First Grade

My 20 first-graders entered the classroom on a September morning, all dressed up in their new blue-and-white school uniforms. Some were obviously very happy to be back in school after a long summer break. As I began to assess them, it was obvious that about a third were in school for the very first time, as kindergarten is not mandatory in California. These students who had not been to kindergarten also did not speak English. The other two-thirds of the class had gone to kindergarten in the room right next door. But because of their very limited English skills, most entered my first-grade classroom recognizing only about half their letters in English, and they knew even fewer letter sounds! Out of the 20 students that entered my classroom that day, there were two that were considered to be good readers by their kindergarten teachers. As I assessed these two, I discovered that they were fantastic "word callers," but had little comprehension of the texts they were able to read.

Because of their English Language Learners status, I began the year fully immersing the students in shared reading of songs, nursery rhymes, chants, finger plays, and poems, as well as stories with repetitive text. This was my Guided Reading Block. Our time together on the rug began with chanting our alphabet. Then, we read and re-read our favorite stories. Favorites soon included *The Farmer and the Skunk*, *The Big Red Apple*, and *Chicka Chicka Boom Boom*. From the first day of school in September, and all the way through Thanksgiving, this is how our mornings began, engaged in the enjoyment of songs and stories.

The Working with Words Block turned out to be one of our most enjoyable and engaging work periods of the day. Luckily, we were at the far end of the building because the Working with Words Block was also our loudest and most joyful time of the day. We chanted our new words with lots of enthusiasm. This block was perfect for learning new vocabulary that is so important to English Language Learners. Our enthusiasm and engagement sometimes got the best of us, and we would have an audience watching us cheer and chant our words. Our most favorite "audience" was the custodian. He was over six feet tall, but when he heard us, he would rush into our classroom and stand on one of our tables to chant and cheer the words with us. By standing on the table, his size would put him right at the ceiling! As the year went on, we created some of our own Word Wall cheers that I shared with the *Teachers.Net* mailring. The two that we created were "Raise the Roof" and "Tigger Bounce." To do "Raise the Roof," you put your hands in the air with the palms up towards to ceiling. Then, you raise your arms for each letter. You also have to "get into the groove" when you do it. To do the "Tigger Bounce," you do "what Tiggers do best"—bounce! You bounce and spell the word. This last one was created for our classroom mascot—Tigger.

There are lots of Word Wall cheers teachers have come up with to vary the daily Word Wall practice. These can be found at *www.FourBlocks.nethop.com* under the section Word Wall cheers. You will find pages of these cheers listed under these headings:

- Cheers that can be done in the seat
- Cheers which are done standing up
- Cheers that can be done in the seat or standing up
- Cheers which are sung
- Add a Cheer to the List

Clapping, snapping, and cheering words has always been a part of the Word Wall activities in Four-Blocks classrooms. The Ketchup Clap, Disco, Box It, and Rocking Horse have been added by teachers who want to get their children actively involved and moving as they chant their Word Wall words into memory!

Writing was the block I was least comfortable with. Part of the assessment binder I kept for the district's literacy assessment was to give a writing prompt three times a year. I administered the prompt and hoped that they would do well because they had been so used to choosing their topics in the Writing Block. Each assessment showed growth. At the beginning of first grade, my students couldn't even write a word. They just drew pictures. At the end of first grade, they all could write a sentence or more in English! A summer school teacher commented about the writing of one of my first-grade girls. She wrote that this child was very expressive and had a distinct voice, something she had not seen in such a young child. This girl went on in second grade growing as a writer in another class. She spent much of her free time writing in her many notebooks.

Besides Writer's Workshop, my students corresponded with three different classes around the nation, one by E-mail and the other two through U. S. Mail. One set of penpals lived just outside of Sacramento, California, and they were the class of a close friend of mine, Katherine. Our two classes corresponded over the course of two years. Katharine and I both commented frequently about the growth we saw in the writing of children in each other's classes. My class went from non-writers to writers in first grade, and they all improved in second grade. Progress was very slow at times, but they were constantly growing. I saw it in their daily writing and in the assessment notebook that I kept!

By January, all 20 students were able to engage in reading for about 15-20 minutes every day for Self-Selected Reading. Instead of book boxes that contained a wide variety of reading materials, I spent lots of time in reading conferences helping children pick "just right" books for their book bags. These were gallon-sized resealable plastic bags with the children's names written on them. Each child had anywhere from 5-10 books in this bag that remained in his or her desk. Most of these books were books chosen at their own ("just right") reading level, with one or two that were easier or harder reads. I didn't want students to "browse" during this time; I wanted them to be totally engaged in their reading. I felt like I could keep better track of what they were reading if they chose books this way. During this time, I would hold reading conferences.

The Internet, Four-Blocks™, and
English Language Learners •

Wanting to Loop with My Students

In January, I did running records as a part of the district's assessment. As I reflected on their progress, I realized that I wanted to see what a second year of Four-Blocks could do for all my students and especially my English Language Learners. I had heard that Clemmons Elementary, the pilot school, "looped" their Four-Blocks classrooms in first and second grade, but from what I could tell, they did not have the language diversity that I had in my classroom. I knew that looping created stability, and my inner-city students craved stability. For many of them, school was the only place where life was consistent. I had read that looping was positive for English Language Learners. They would not have to get to know a new teacher. We could just move on with the learning process from day one. We could easily gain a full month of instruction from not having to go through the "beginning of the year" stuff. So, I approached my principal with the thought of taking my class on into second grade. She liked the idea, and let me "run with it." No other teacher had looped before at this school, or even at other schools where she had been a principal. But, she was supportive of me and willing to let my try it.

In April, my first-graders had to take the SAT9 test. The State of California was not making school districts give their first-graders the test, but my district decided that the first-graders should take it. So, I prepared my first-graders to take the test. It wasn't until right before the test that I found out that my ELL first-graders did not have to take the test, but they could if they had their parents' permission. I approached my class with this information, thinking that would be the end of it. But it wasn't. About half of my ELL children wanted to take the test! (I had told them that they would do well on the test, and it was their job to not be tricked by the test publisher.) While I was testing, the half who didn't take the test spent time with another teacher doing various activities, mainly watching videos. I had the students take their "book bags" of just-right reading material with them to the other room, but figured that reading just wouldn't compete with the chance to watch videos. A few days into testing, the teacher who had been with those not taking the test came up to me to tell me about what she had seen with my students. She was absolutely amazed! As they were watching these videos, every once in a while she would see them sneak peeks at their books and read! She had never seen students choose to read when they could have been watching a video!

Before the test began, I had heard from the mailring that the reading comprehension part of the SAT9 was excruciatingly difficult for first-graders. Too much reading in a very short time! It totally floored me when all 10 who chose to take the test ended up finishing the Reading Comprehension with time to spare! These students weren't just bubbling in answers, but really reading! I realized that they had the capabilities of reading for about 20 minutes because they had done it every day during Self-Selected Reading. Then, I got the test results back! In reading comprehension, all 10 children who took the test scored above the 50th percentile, with five scoring above the 75th percentile! At my inner-city school, almost no one scores at that level!

As the year ended, there was some controversy about me being allowed to "loop" with my class to second grade. I wouldn't be allowed to take the entire 20 students on to second grade, but I could take 8 of my students. I had to decide which of the 20 first-graders would continue on with me into second grade. This was a very difficult decision, but I finally decided to choose my lowest readers. These eight students had struggled the most with learning English and with learning how to read. Their reading levels ranged from Levels 4-16 (Reading Recovery levels). Those students who went to the other second-grade classrooms were reading on or above grade level, with a few reading as high as fifth grade level. The eight who stayed with me were also "followers." They had not had a chance to shine. But now they would because they knew my routines and expectations. I was expecting them to be the leaders in the classroom, showing the others the "ropes." And shine they did!

Second Grade

Before my second-graders entered my classroom, I had expected that the eight that I was looping with would be among the lowest students in the classroom. Never did I imagine that those eight would actually be my most proficient readers. The second year together was amazing! From that first day of second grade, I knew right where these eight "loopers" were academically. I didn't have to spend the first month assessing them to figure out where I needed to begin my instruction. I could begin right away!

As the year progressed, I assessed all of my students, but was especially interested in the progress of those eight ELL students who had looped with me. At the start of the year, these eight read at levels ranging from beginning first grade to beginning second grade level. By the end of the year, six of the eight were reading above the third grade level.

One of my ELL girls stood out to me. She had been one of my first-graders that I was most concerned about. She came from Mexico in April of her kindergarten year. When she walked into my room last year, she barely spoke any English and knew very few letters and sounds. By the end of first grade, she read at an early first-grade level, which was sort of an amazing feat in itself! But she was not through, by any means! By mid-year in second grade, she went from a first-grade level to a early third-grade level. And by the end of second grade, she had topped out on my district's running record levels — that is at the sixth-grade level!

In early Spring, one of my ELL boys came into class with a couple of picture books in Spanish. His parents were teaching him to read in his native language at home. This sparked a huge interest in my classroom with the other seven students. Very soon, each of them began making attempts to read in Spanish, using what they had learned about reading in English, as well as their own knowledge of the Spanish language. It was amazing to watch them go through this process, and on their own!

Teacher Interest in Four-Blocks™

Since I had moved up to second grade, I had a new "team" to work with, as well as the "old" team of first-grade teachers. Each of the first-grade teachers began to realize that they really could implement Four-Blocks in their classrooms. One went "whole hog" and implemented all four blocks like I had. The other two were a bit more reserved, and tried a couple of blocks. By the end of the year, all of the first-grade teachers were convinced. They witnessed their own students making amazing growth in reading. All of their students seemed to be better readers and writers than the year before. That sold them! The two who had not done all the blocks wanted me to help them fully implement Four-Blocks in their classrooms the next year. At this point, the second-grade teachers were ready to try. As part of instructional materials that were ordered for the next year, I ordered them all Word Walls, *The Teacher's Guide to the Four-Blocks™*, and *Month-by-Month Phonics for Second Grade*.

Looking Forward to Next Year

In past years, I had been around for my students to come and visit, and share their accomplishments as they grew at school. This time, it will be different. I am not going to be there in the fall. My journey as a teacher has taken me to the other end of the country, far from these precious students who allowed me to be with them as they took amazing risks on their literacy journeys. It began at a computer in Northern California two summers ago. Two years later, this journey has taken me across the country, miraculously where Four-Blocks began twelve years ago…in Winston-Salem, North Carolina.

I will be teaching first grade in a year-round school—not much of a vacation from a late-June ending in California to an early-July beginning in North Carolina! I have 21 students and no ELL students this year! I do have one Spanish-speaking student, but she is bilingual, understanding both Spanish and English. My school is not a Four-Blocks school, but the (new) principal hopes to lead it in that direction with my assistance. Since it is a year-round school, I have already begun my Four-Blocks instruction. My students enjoy interviewing each other, and I like finding out about my new students. I really saw my class come together when I introduced them to partner reading during the Guided Reading Block. They not only became partners during Guided Reading time, but during playtime as well. One little boy who has been a challenge from the first day of school followed his partner's rules better than mine! I know I will have other challenges; that's teaching! Where will my journey take me next? It's anybody's guess.

Four-Blocks™ In Spanish •

by Kay Fulton, Guadalupe Lucero, and Norma Nuñez
(with Pat Cunningham)

For the past several years, at every workshop I did, someone would come up to me at the break and ask, "Can you do Four-Blocks™ in Spanish? What would you have to change? What would you do in the Working with Words Block?" I always answered that I was sure that Four-Blocks would be an appropriate organizing framework for teaching children to read in Spanish (or in any language). The most basic principle underlying Four-Blocks is that children come with their own personalities and that any one approach to teaching reading is not going to be successful with all children. "The Four-Blocks are really four different approaches to reading," I would remind them. When you have four "roads" which you take children down every day, more children are going to arrive at the goal of fluent reading and writing than if there are only one or two roads that you can take to get them there. "I don't know anything about teaching reading in Spanish," I would explain, "but I do know that what language you speak doesn't change the fact that children all have their own personalities and learning preferences, and that no single approach is going to teach all children of any language background to read." I would then encourage them to be brave and try the Four-Blocks™ framework with their children and write me and let me know how it worked, what materials they used, what changes were needed, and other details.

A few years ago, I was invited to Albuquerque, New Mexico. Several schools in Albuquerque were piloting Four-Blocks, and some classes were doing the Four-Blocks™ framework in Spanish. I jumped at the chance, and three airplanes later, I arrived in a lovely southwestern state I had never visited before. I observed and met with teachers in several schools, including East San Jose Elementary, where Lupe, Norma, and Kay were teaching. Four-Blocks is used at East San Jose in both the English and Spanish classes, but I wanted to see it happening in Spanish. I had a wonderful day at East San Jose and left begging them to capture the instruction on video. (They did, and I treasure my copy of East San Jose teachers doing Four-Blocks and Building Blocks™ in Spanish.)

Currently, Kay is not based at San Jose, but has been given the awesome job of heading up the Four-Blocks™ framework in Albuquerque as many

more schools choose to implement the framework. Lupe is a special read-
ing teacher at East San Jose, and Norma teaches second grade. Here is their
story of what you would see if you were as lucky as I was and could fly to
Albuquerque and see Four-Blocks in Spanish. Kay wrote the story, but she
insists that it is really Lupe's and Norma's story, and she wrote it as they told
it to her.

East San Jose Elementary is located on South Broadway Street in the heart of
the Albuquerque Enterprise Community, also known as the "Pocket of Poverty." It
is a School-Wide Title I kindergarten through fifth grade school where 100% of the
students receive free or reduced lunch. Spanish is the predominant home language, with over 92% of our students categorized as Hispanic, and 74% of our
student population considered LEP (Limited English Proficiency). The school is
one of nine elementary schools and two middle schools which feed into Albuquerque High School. Albuquerque High has one of the highest cohort drop-out
rates in the district, with a rate of 40.9%. Each year 40% of the incoming freshman
class reads below the 25th percentile. Most people believe the correlation between the two rates is not coincidental.

East San Jose is in the third year of implementing the Four-Blocks™ Literacy
Model. What sets the school apart from the others across the country is the dual
language focus of the instruction. The program emphasis is supported by research
that demonstrates that native language instruction strengthens second language
literacy development through the transfer of necessary skills. This research was
conducted by Wayne Thomas and Virginia Collier and is summarized in "Language Minority Student Achievement and Program Effectiveness."

In 1998, East San Jose began implementation of the Four-Blocks™ framework
through Title I district and financial support. Carolyn Robinson and I (Kay) were
the Title I Resource Teachers. We received intense training in Four-Blocks, so that
we could serve as trainers for the staff. We worked with all the staff, including
Lupe and Norma, who were dual language teachers when we began.

Prior to implementation of the Four-Blocks, East San Jose had adapted a model
of dual language instruction in the classrooms. Dual language kindergartens are
90/10 classes in which 90% of instruction is delivered in Spanish and 10% of
instruction is delivered in English. In first grade, two classes follow the 90/10 model,
and one class follows a 50/50 model. Second grade has three 80/20 classes, and

third grade has two 70/30 classes. This model of dual language instruction progresses into a 50/50 bilingual program as the grade levels increase.

Implementing the Four-Blocks™

The primary staff began implementation of the Four-Blocks that first year with enthusiasm. The Writing and the Self-Selected Reading Blocks were easiest to implement because they sustained instruction in either language. The students wrote in their own language during the Writing Block. Teachers needed to make adjustments in their minilessons to model the Spanish grammar rules for children. An example is the punctuation at the beginning and at the end of a question or adding an exclamation mark.

¡Me gusta mucho! ¿Como te llamas?

Finding enough Spanish books to keep the kids in books during the daily Self-Selected Reading Block was a challenge. We spent thousand of dollars purchasing books to support Self-Selected Reading. Children are encouraged to read in whichever language they like during Self-Selected Reading, and we tried to order matching text in both languages whenever possible. Although more companies are publishing children's texts in Spanish, they are still difficult to find and more expensive. Some publishing companies have large Spanish collections, including Scholastic, Hampton Brown, Crossroads, and The Wright Group.

The Guided Reading and the Working with Words Blocks, however, were frustrating to the dual language teachers. Which language should they be done in? We eventually decided that these blocks needed to be presented in Spanish. Then, we had to go out to find the materials and make up the lessons!

For the Guided Reading Block, we used the adopted Houghton Mifflin Reading Series, *Invitations to Literacy*, which included a companion series of Spanish texts. For the easier reading days, we purchased additional *Watch Me Read* books, also available in Spanish. As we worked our way through this block, we realized we needed multiple copies of informational books to support the integration of science and social studies with Guided Reading. These books, readily available in English, are less available in Spanish. Good Spanish resource publications to support Guided Reading include Crossroads publications, such as *Storytellers* and *Explores*.

Guided Reading in Spanish looks much like Guided Reading in English. We followed the Four-Blocks™ framework for developing comprehension skills. We built prior knowledge, taught vocabulary, and used KWL charts, story maps, graphic organizers, webs, and data charts for comprehension skills.

We added posters to Guided Reading in Spanish to help children learn cognates. Cognates are words that are spelled the same and mean the same in both English and Spanish (radio, radio). As we came across cognates in our reading, we wrote and illustrated them, and displayed them on cognate posters. These posters were helpful in developing meaning and reading vocabulary in Spanish and English.

Working with Words was the hardest block to implement. The first issue was the Word Wall. What words should be included on the Spanish Word Wall? The first-grade teachers decided that the Word Wall words should be mainly high-frequency from the Guided Reading text, as well as some words children used in their writing. Second-grade teachers decided the Word Wall words should come more from students' writing, and some difficult first-grade words should be put on the second-grade Word Wall again if children had not mastered them. Using these criteria, Lupe and Norma created Word Wall lists appropriate for first- and second-grade classrooms.

Palabras De Mayor Frecuencia en Primer Grado
(High-Frequency Words for First Grade)

A amo, ayuda, aquí, amigo, allí, algo, así

B bonito, bien, bueno, busca

C con, como, cuando, casa, cada, cual

Ch chiquito

D dice, donde, dijo, después, día, de, del, dos

E es, ese, en, están, el, ella, eso, era, estoy, este

F fui, fueron, favorito

G gusta, grande

H hay, había, hoy, hacer, hola

I ir, íbamos

J jugar, juntos

L la, los, las, le, libro, leer, luego

LL llego, llamo, llevar

M me, mi, mío, mamá, muy, mucho, miro, más

N nada, no, niño, nos, noche

O otro, oye

P papá, pasa, para, por, pequeño, pero, pone, perro, puedo, porque

Q que, quitan, quien, quiero

R rápido, rato, risa

S sale, se, su, ser, si, son, sabe, suave

T todo, tener, tu, tengo, también, tuyo, te, tan

U uso, uno, ustedes

V voy, ver, viene, vamos, vez

Y yo, y, ya

Z zoológico

Palabras De Mayor Frecuencia Del Grado Segundo
(High-Frequency Words For Second Grade)

A	alguien, aquí, alli, ahora, algunos, ayer, afuera, agarrar, ayuda, atención, abajo, añadir	M	mucho, mover, muy, más
		N	nada, nunca, nuestro, nomás, necesitamos
B	bien, bueno, bastante, bonito	O	otros, olvidar, oye
C	cuando, conmigo, crecer, cuidar, callar, caer, casi, cual, colorear	P	porque, puedo, pequeño, poquito, prestar
Ch	chaparro, chiquito	Q	que, quiero, quedar, quería, querer, quitar
D	después, donde, dicen, desde, dijo, decir, debajo	R	recoger, rápido
E	ellos, entonces, está, encontré, estaba, estoy, empezamos	S	siempre, suave, seguimos, sabe, siguiente
F	fui, fácil, favorito	T	tiene, también, todavía, tuyo, tener, todos, trae
G	grande, gente		
H	hay, hacía, había, hasta, haciendo, has, hizo	U	ustedes, único, último, usar
		V	veo, veces, vamos, viene, vez, voy, ves
I	íbamos, igual, interés		
J	jugar, juntos, juegos	Y	yo, ya, y
L	luego, limpio, leer	Z	zapato, zoologico, zumbar

Once the words were chosen, the teachers followed the usual Word Wall procedures. They added words gradually, and the children practiced five words each day, chanting and writing the words.

Late in the second semester, second-grade teachers add an English Word Wall, separate from the Spanish Word Wall. After the English Word Wall goes up in second grade, the five new words introduced are done in English. Thus, begins the transition into the English language. In third grade, we do both an English Word Wall and a Spanish Word Wall. Both Word Walls are begun early in the year and displayed separately in the classroom environment.

Just as in English Four-Blocks classrooms, we do a second activity following the Word Wall practice each day to focus on letter/sound patterns. Guess The Covered Word activities work the same in Spanish as they do in English, and the children love to do them. Rounding Up the Rhymes works the same in Spanish, except that it is more difficult to locate the rhyming books on which to base the lessons.

The Houghton Mifflin Spanish series has big books that support rhyming strategies, and we use these for Rounding Up the Rhymes. Two Spanish authors, Alma Ada and Francisca Isabel Campoy, publish many rhyming and poetry books. A favorite of the primary teachers is *Dulce Es La Sal*. The *Rimas Y Risas* series is also popular. We also use a series of musical tapes called *Lyric Infantil*.

The structure of syllables is the foundation of the Spanish language. Before beginning Making Words lessons (in which children manipulate individual letters), we do an activity similar to Making Words in which students manipulate syllable cards. The students are introduced to one vowel at a time. They manipulate their syllable cards to form words as the teacher models. Once they have made words with the syllables, they read some simple sentences containing these words. Here is an example:

On Monday the vowel "a" would be introduced along with the syllable cards: ma, da, la, sa ,ca, and va. Students combine the syllable cards to form words. Masa, dama, lama, sala, vaca, casa, saca, cada, and mala. The teacher has the sentences, "Mamá va a la casa," "La dama saca la vaca," "Mamá lasa la lama," and "Mamá lava la cama" written on sentence strips. The children read all four sentences using the words made from the syllables.

In first grade, we introduce a new vowel every week and continue these activities for five weeks. The vowels from the previous weeks are constantly being reviewed and included in the daily lessons. (In second grade, we use syllables to make words for the first week or two of school.)

Once the Making Words with syllable cards lessons are complete, the children make words with individual letter cards. Of course, there are no "premade" lessons available in Spanish as there are in English! So, after grumbling for awhile about this, we got busy and made lessons. Just as in English, we tried to connect the secret word to our district curriculum, and we integrated science, math, social studies, and seasonal vocabulary. Here is an example:

families

Lotteries: a a i i f m l s

Palabras: a, mi, la, Al, si, mix, meal, Sal, las, más, mala, fame, lama, Lisa, sala, mesa, mist, isle, flame, false

Superior: la, ma, Al, sa

Transferencia: papa, coma, nodal, balsa

The Working with Words Block was the biggest challenge for us in delivering the Four-Blocks in Spanish, but we have worked together, solved the problems, and created lessons which we are now sharing with others who are teaching Four-Blocks in Spanish.

Building Blocks™

We have all kinds of kindergarten classes at East San Jose! We have one full day English-only kindergarten and one half-day, English-only kindergarten. We also have 90/10 kindergartens—two full-day and one half-day. We did training in Building Blocks™ early in the year using the *Building Blocks* video and *Month-by-Month Reading and Writing for Kindergarten*. The kindergarten teachers in the 90/10 classrooms do four 45-minute sessions in English each week, and the rest of their instruction in Spanish. The kindergarten teachers decided to do Building Blocks™ activities in both Spanish and English, and used the four English segments each week for Building Blocks™ activities in English. They varied which activities they did in English and Spanish.

The "Getting to Know You" names activity was usually done in Spanish, and it was very easy to adapt the procedures to Spanish. In the East San Jose parent community, the names became a family affair. Many family members or extended family members joined the students in celebrating and cheering the spelling of their names.

Just as in Four-Blocks, finding materials in Spanish was a problem for the kindergarten teachers. When the school adopted the Houghton Mifflin series *Invitaciones* for the kindergarten classes, the teachers were much happier. The series included big books, posters, tapes, and multiple copies of literature to support the Spanish learner. The series also contains a Spanish resource book, *Mi Libro Rimas y Canciones*, which has rhymes and tongue twisters in Spanish. The teachers were delighted when they discovered the book, *Tortillitas Para Mama*. This book is filled with Spanish chants and rhymes and became an integral part of the Spanish Building Blocks curriculum.

There are not as many rhyming words in Spanish so the teachers found the rhyming activities a challenge. A favorite of the teachers and students was *Chocolate*.

Chocolate
Uno dos tres cho
Uno dos tres co
Uno dos tres la
Uno dos tres te
Chocolate
Chocolate
bate, bate, el chocolate.

The kindergarten teachers have grown in the implementation of the Building Blocks™ framework in Spanish. In fact, these teachers have progressed to giving district trainings for other kindergarten teachers. They have been particularly helpful to dual language teachers who are trying to include the Building Blocks™ principles while maintaining the Spanish language. They recently presented at the Cosecha, a regional conference for bilingual education in Albuquerque.

Looking Forward to Next Year

School has begun again, and the school community of East San Jose Elementary in Albuquerque, New Mexico continues to be a model dual language Four-Blocks/Building Blocks™ school. They graciously host visitors from far and near who want to observe in the classrooms. Norma is not only an exemplary second-grade bilingual teacher, she also welcomes visitor upon visitor to observe her implementation of Four-Blocks strategies in Spanish. Lupe supports the dual language classes as the lead Title I teacher. She conducts on site-training for the staff and supports dual language Four-Blocks implementation in classrooms.

I have taken on a new responsibility—district trainer and coordinator for Four-Blocks. We now have many schools in Albuquerque in various stages of implementation. Some of these are implementing in English and others in Spanish. I also support other schools and districts as much as my schedule allows. The last two years have been two of the busiest and most exciting (and some days, most exasperating!) years of my life. Four-Blocks—in any language—is appealing to teachers and children, and we in Albuquerque are doing our best to promote it in as many classrooms as possible!

Four-Blocks™ in Spanish and English•••••••••••••••••••••

by Anne Oulahan (with Pat Cunningham)

Anne's census forms was one of the first to arrive by "snail mail" rather than E-mail. I scanned it as I was opening my mail and was amazed to read, "I do Four-Blocks™ in both Spanish and English. I have two Word Walls. Guided Reading and Writing are done in two languages. For Self-Selected Reading, the students choose the language they want to read in. It is hard, but it can be done!"

"Wow," I thought, "How can it be done?" I learned a little more from reading the rest of the information Anne had included on the census. But, I wanted to know all the nitty, gritty details. So, I wrote Anne a letter—a real letter, put it in an envelope, stamped it, and mailed it off to Milwaukee. Anne responded quickly with a nice note telling me she was too busy finishing the school year to write and tell me everything I wanted to know. She did, however, promise, to write me a long letter "when things settle down."

Just when I had given up hope (knowing how seldom things settle down!), my mailman brought me Anne's letter explaining how she does it all. She was right. It can be done! Here is how Anne Oulahan does Four-Blocks™ in both English and Spanish.

I teach at La Escuela Fratney, a city-wide school in the Milwaukee Public School system. We have a blend of African-American, Hispanic, and Caucasian children from all over the city, and 75% of our children qualify for the free/reduced price lunch program. Our school's focus is a dual language, bilingual program. Our goal is to have all our children be bilingual. Our English-dominant children learn Spanish, and our Spanish-dominant students learn English. There are no entrance requirements, other than an English-dominant child has to have some background in Spanish if he or she comes to us after the first grade. The percentage of the day taught in Spanish varies from grade to grade. By the time the children are in third grade, their day should ideally be 50/50.

In first and second grades, children receive their language arts instruction in their first language and the rest of their instruction—science, social studies, math, etc.—in Spanish. So, for children whose first language is English, they spend a larger portion of their day getting instruction in Spanish. We decided to do this

True Stories from Four-Blocks™ Classrooms

because we found that when we divided the instruction more equally between Spanish and English, our English dominant students were not becoming bilingual as quickly as our Spanish dominant students. Some of that is because of the environment. That is to say, our Spanish-speaking children have much more English support by way of TV, radio, community, etc., than our English-dominant students have in Spanish. Most of our Spanish-speaking parents recognize the necessity of learning English, while many of our English-speaking parents value learning Spanish, but don't feel the same urgency for their children to learn the second language.

The focus for kindergarten and first grade is oral language development in the second language as the students learn to read and write in the first language. We transition to formal reading and writing instruction in the second language toward the end of the second grade, or when the child has reached a good, solid third-grade reading level in their first language. My Spanish-speaking children get 45 minutes daily of oral English instruction from an ESL teacher. When my Spanish-speakers go to their ESL class, I give the English-speaking children Spanish lessons which consist of games, songs, poems, riddles, etc., to build their Spanish oral language. I also introduce orally some of the new Spanish content area words and concepts we will use in upcoming math, science, and social studies lessons.

I have taught first and second grades, and have sometimes looped with my first-graders to second grade. This year, I taught first grade and had 18 first-graders. I had a teaching assistant for two hours who did some follow-up lessons with the children in one language while I taught lessons in the other language. Here is how I did Four-Blocks in Spanish and English.

Guided Reading

During the Guided Reading Block, my assistant and I alternated working with the children who spoke Spanish or English. On some days, I worked with the English readers, and my assistant worked with the Spanish readers. Other days, she worked with the Spanish readers while I worked with the English readers. We used all kinds of materials—big books, books from reading series, tradebooks, and whatever else we could find. It was easier to find materials for the English readers than for the Spanish readers.

Some days, we worked with the children in small groups. Grouping was flexible, that is, groups changed constantly depending on the needs and interests of the children.

Working with Words

I had two Word Walls right next to each other, because it was the only space big enough. The one with the blue alphabet was the English Word Wall; the green alphabet signified the Spanish Word Wall. The Spanish words were taken from a Spanish high-frequency list and the students' reading books. When we did the Working with Words Block, my assistant took one language group, and I took the other. I always did the primary lesson, and the teaching assistant did the follow-up activities. So, while I might be introducing the words of the week to the Spanish group, she may be doing Rounding Up the Rhymes with the English group.

The groups usually listened to each other when the Word Wall words were being practiced, probably because of the noise created by the spelling, clapping, and "dancing" of the letters. That didn't worry me because students had a chance to learn the words in two languages, and it didn't seem to cause any language confusion for the children.

On some days we would be doing the same activity in the two languages. When we did Guess the Covered Word, the children would want to know if I used the same words in both English and Spanish. (I didn't.)

We did weekly spelling tests—at the children's request! At the beginning, the children did it in their primary language, but as the year went on, many began asking if they could learn the words in the other language, and began studying them, also. So, both lists of words went home on a weekly basis for those who wanted to challenge themselves. I held them responsible for the words in the primary language, and encouraged them to do the second language words if it was appropriate for them.

Writing

During the Writing Block, the minilesson was given to the language group. But then the children were together for writing, and they chose the language to write in. At the beginning, they generally chose to write in their dominant language, but as the year went on, many words in the second language began to appear in their journals.

Self-Selected Reading

The Self-Selected Reading Block was done at the end of the day, right before the bell rang. The children got ready to go home 30 minutes before the bell rang.

All notes and homework were distributed, book bags were packed, jackets were collected and at their desks, etc.—all of this was done beforehand. Then, from 3:00-3:30, everyone had "drop everything and read" (DEAR) time. During this time, I conferenced with children, took a quick running record on some days, and encouraged students in their reading efforts in whatever way was appropriate for that particular child.

I had both Spanish and English books available, and the children were allowed to choose books in either language. All the buckets and bins were coded for English and Spanish—English books in blue bins and Spanish books in green ones.

This is where I saw the most interaction with children choosing books in both languages. Some challenged themselves to read more difficult books, but some would challenge themselves to read in the second language. It was great!!

Assessment

In our district, we give informal reading inventories to all our children at the end of the year to determine instructional levels. We use the Basic Reading Inventory for the English readers, and the Cuentamundos Reading Inventory that comes with the MacMillan/McGraw-Hill series for the Spanish readers. This year, which was my third year fully implementing the Four-Blocks in my classroom, I was pleased to see that all but two of my first-graders read at second-grade level or above. One child with ADHD was reading at the end of first-grade level. One child with a learning disability was reading at a beginning first-grade level. She was, however, absent more than 50 days this year!

In past years, I have looped with my children from first to second grade and have noticed excellent results, especially in second grade, when I can keep them for two years. Last year, more than half my class of second-graders transitioned to formal reading in the second language by Christmas time. This included both native Spanish and English speakers. It was the first time so many children were ready so early.

I am bilingual, but teaching in Spanish has always been more challenging for me, because Spanish is my second language. In English, I might be able to explain something three different ways to help a child understand it. But in Spanish, I probably can do it one way, two at most. The Spanish readers seemed to really benefit from the consistency Four-Blocks offers and from the amount of time the children actually spend READING! Most of the children have very few or no Spanish books at home, and between Guided Reading and Self-Selected Reading, they read a lot every day at school.

Looking Forward to Next Year

Next year, every kindergarten and first-grade classroom will have two teachers teaming together to teach 30 children. This system with two teachers, rather than a teacher and assistant, should be more effective. I felt like I had to plan and teach all the initial lessons in both languages. I also had to touch base with the children the assistant had worked with to make sure they were progressing as we would like, as I was ultimately responsible for their progress. With two teachers, these responsibilities can be shared.

I won't get to see how the teaming actually works, however, because I will be on sabbatical. I am taking some classes in the area of learning disabilities and bilingual education, and am hoping to do some work on developing Four-Blocks resources in Spanish. Having to make everything up as you go along is the hardest part of teaching Four-Blocks in Spanish—particularly when there are now so many resources for English readers. I hope in a year to have some Making Words lessons, Writing minilessons, and Guided Reading lessons I can use and share with others.

Four-Blocks™ Works
in My Multiage Classroom ••••••••••••••••••••••••••••••••

by Linda Holland (with Pat Cunningham)

Whether by choice (in which case they are called multiage) or by chance (commonly called split or combination classes), many teachers have two or more grade levels of children in the same classroom. Teachers who are doing Four-Blocks™ with their multiage classes usually find that Writing and Self-Selected Reading work quite well. This makes sense because Writing and Self-Selected Reading are the two blocks which are most naturally multilevel. Working with Words and Guided Reading, the two hardest blocks to make multilevel, pose real problems for many teachers of multiage children. "Which words should I put on the Word Wall?" and "How can I make Guided Reading multilevel if I have two levels of a reading series to teach and test on?" are commonly-asked questions.

When the census forms started to flood in, we paid particular attention to the responses of the multiage teachers, hoping they knew some of the answers to these often-asked questions. Sure enough, these clever teachers have found ways to make Four-Blocks work in multiage classrooms. Here is Linda's story of how Four-Blocks works in her multiage classroom:

I teach at Adams School in Tulsa, Oklahoma. I have a multiage class composed of, at the beginning of the school year, five-, six-, seven-, and eight-year-olds. Tradition would call it first and second grade. I have approximately 20 students per year and have students with all ability ranges—gifted, average, and special needs. The ethnic composition of my class is about 30% Native American, 25% African-American, 8% Latino-American, and 37% Caucasian. Approximately 90% of my children are on free/reduced price lunch.

When you join the MAC room (my name for our program—<u>m</u>ulti<u>a</u>ge <u>c</u>lass), you stay until you enter third grade or move. I strongly feel that because we will be working together for two years, then we must form a community of learners where each of us will share in teaching and facilitating. I feel that I can best assess a student's understanding of a concept when I witness that student "teaching" that concept to a peer. We become a school family that works together, learns together, plays together, gets frustrated with each other, but above all else, cares about each other, and therefore, wants everyone to succeed.

Four-Blocks™ Works
in My Multiage Classroom •

I have been teaching multiage for seven years, and have used the Four-Blocks™ framework for four years. I like teaching multiage, and liked it before Four-Blocks, but I am convinced that Four-Blocks enables my students (and me) to be more successful in the multiage setting.

Self-Selected Reading

The easiest block to implement in a multiage class is the Self-Selected Reading Block. This was the first block I tried, the year before I began the entire Four-Blocks program. I have always enjoyed reading aloud to my students and "blessing" all kinds of books as "one of my favorites." I also firmly believe that to become a reader you must be read to. I've heard it stated that you need to hear about 3,000 books read aloud. My children come at least 2,500 behind, so I must endeavor to do my best to bring them closer to the goal.

My students sit in "pods," each pod contains a basket of books placed in the pod, and each basket has approximately 20-30 books. At the beginning of the school year, the books range from wordless picture books to chapter books. (Some of the books are accelerated reader books. My school uses the accelerated reader program, and the older students are encouraged to take the test upon completion of an accelerated reader book.) This block was easy to implement because the "olders" model how we read and the "youngers" imitate. We begin the school year with the children reading for seven minutes, and build to 20 minutes by the middle of the year.

I have found that conferencing with each student at least once a week is a great way to encourage and assess their reading progress. Early in the year, my "youngers" may meet with me a couple of times a week. Sometimes, I meet with a couple of them together, and we work on reading fluency. I firmly believe that emergent readers need to practice reading to someone. My older students thoroughly enjoy this time to read. Most of these children beginning their second year with me are reading on or above level, and are on their way to becoming lifelong readers.

I have discovered that if I rotate the books in our baskets approximately every two weeks, my children have plenty of reading material. I encourage them to reread their favorite books, and to read books written by their favorite authors. I incorporate books from all genres in my reading baskets. In addition to books, I include magazines, pamphlets, menus, *Scholastic News*, and old basal readers. My children enjoy a great variety.

The biggest problem I've encountered is with my "youngers," who want to read books that may be way above their level. It takes a lot of patience on my part, and frequent conferencing with some children to get them accustomed to choosing books on their level. My "olders" choose some books on their level and some easier books. I am convinced that fluency comes from repeated readings, and thus, I have no problem encouraging them to enjoy an easy book along with their own level books.

Working with Words

The second block I began was the Working with Words Block. We usually do Making Words lessons two or three days a week. We also do at least one rhyme family lesson and one Guess the Covered Word lesson.

My Word Wall is probably the most important area of our room. I add five words per week from the list of high-frequency words for first- and second-graders. I choose some from each grade level each week. By doing it this way over a two-year period you would have every high-frequency word on the Word Wall. I choose words from these lists that correlate with the theme or big book I'm using. A few words will appear both years, but these are usually words my students are having difficulty with in their journal writing. On Monday, I introduce our five new words, we spell them and say them several times, and I make certain my students understand what each word means (i.e. two, to).

I have discovered that when we write the words, this is a great opportunity to teach correct letter formation. Toward the end of the year, when we are practicing cursive, we all write the words in print and cursive. This allows me to teach my second-graders the beginning of cursive writing (a requirement in my building), but in actuality, if they were with me the previous year, they received the lesson as a "younger" and as an "older."

On Tuesday through Friday, we do Word Wall activities and games. My class loves the "Mind Reader Game" (as we call it), and they love playing "WORDO" with the Word Wall Words. My school has a spelling homework policy, so I use the Word Wall words as my basic spelling words.

My Word Wall is very simple to construct. I use 14" x 24" pieces of white construction paper, laminated with a large uppercase letter and matching lowercase letter at the top. I then write our Word Wall words on the paper using four different colors of permanent markers. (The permanent markers work better and are brighter than the transparency markers.) I place a smiley face sticker on the rhyme family words. I am lucky in that I have cabinet doors that the Word Wall cards fit on perfectly. I configure the shape of the word, and they are easily seen from anywhere in the room. The Word Wall allows me to meet the needs of first- and second-graders with the same lesson, and often gives review of needed material, as well as an early introduction of some material, which keeps my gifted children eager to learn.

The bonus of a good Word Wall is that your students are so familiar with the basic sight words that their reading ability and fluency increase significantly, giving them the intrinsic feeling of success.

Guided Reading

The third block that I implemented was the Guided Reading Block. This block has become my favorite block. I can teach all the skills demanded by my state objectives, and do it without workbooks or busy work, and my students think that learning is fun. I have a special area for Guided Reading, composed of a rocking chair, a big bookrack, and a large piece of carpet. My Guided Reading selection is often related to the theme that I am currently using, which allows me follow-up with many hands-on activities.

The hardest part of Guided Reading is deciding upon the material to use. My school has a basal reader, but my principal allows a lot of freedom and encourages the use of literature. I start the year using big books. (I don't know what we did before big books came along: they are super in teaching the concept of print flow, tracking, picture detail, etc.) I have leveled all of my big books, and I choose books on both grade levels during the course of the week.

We begin on Monday with a book or selection that is on second-grade level, and we work with it for three days. On Thursday and Friday, we work with a book or selection on first-grade level. Some weeks I reverse this, depending upon the readability of the selection. Many books on first-grade level have extremely high interest and are very easy to teach multilevel lessons from. By the end of the year, we are usually reading chapter books during Guided Reading time.

I choose from a wide variety of books. A few titles I especially like for the beginning of the year are *Gunnywolf* and *Mouse Paint*. I also use *Lazy Lion* or *The Mitten* when working with folktales.

My students (boys and girls alike!) love a series of books about a little girl named Junie B. Jones. They are on an early second-grade level with extremely high interest. When we read a chapter book, we use the ERT (Everybody Read To . . .) format, and then discuss what we have read.

I also use the *Little Celebration* series, which are great informational books on first- and second-grade level. My students love to use sticky notes and read two or three pages, writing down a fact or two they have learned or words they do not know. We then gather as a group and discuss the facts we have learned or go over the words we do not know.

My class loves to "picture walk" a book. By the end of the year, they will "picture walk" any book they are reading on their own, before they begin to read. I use picture walking as a way to prepare them for the reading, and to increase their vocabulary. My students lack a lot of experiences and are always weak in vocabulary. Many times we spend 10-15 minutes in engaged conversation about what is shown and taking place in the illustrations. I also draw their attention to the printed form of these new vocabulary words. I make certain that my students understand what the word means and can identify it in the book.

When we do Shared Reading, I have a rule that the first reading is my turn to read—they will have many opportunities to read with me later. This gives my "youngers" the opportunity to hear the story and not feel as though they "couldn't read it." We always close the Guided Reading lesson with a discussion: what happened in the story? Who were the characters? What was the setting? What was the plot? We also do many story maps and webs.

We do a lot of rereading, often using choral reading, echo reading, or partner reading. In addition to rereading the current selection, we always do a quick re-reading of the Monday selection again on Thursday and Friday, which are usually our days for reading easier selections. The following Monday we reread the Thurs-day selection. I discovered several years ago that when we reread the selection many times, students retained the vocabulary (both meaning and sight words) much better. Their comprehension and fluency also increased dramatically through rereading.

Writing

The last block I implemented was the Writing Block. I was really afraid of this block, but it is the one where I saw the greatest gains in my students' performance.

Four-Blocks™ Works
in My Multiage Classroom •

I had always felt inadequate in teaching writing. Before Four-Blocks, my students would always write just a few words or maybe a few sentences, but now they write a lot. They are totally unafraid of putting their thoughts on paper.

I always begin my Writing Block with teacher-modeled writing. I sit at the overhead, think aloud, write, rewrite, brainstorm, and demonstrate the writing process for my students. Many of my students see someone writing for the first time in their lives. The modeling of how to write a piece is not done at one sitting. I often write the first draft one day, demonstrating how I stretch a word out to spell it, and how I use the Word Wall and other print in the room. The next day, I work some more on the piece, and have the children help me add, change, and edit. I only wish someone had taught me to write using this method!

The Writing Block is completely multilevel. You could be at first- or fifth-grade level and still work side by side. At the beginning of the year, I have students at all levels, from drawing pictures with no words to writing, and from picture drawing with a couple of sentences to complete pages of writing. By the end of the year, everyone writes pages!

We have folders that students keep their writing in—on the left side is finished work, on the right side is what we are currently working on. When they have completed four or five pieces of writing, the students may select one to publish. The students then conference with me and we edit the work. They may choose a variety of methods to publish, from rewriting in manuscript to using the computer. Each student has a variety of choices in putting their books together. They love to publish!

Evidence of Success

My students are tested each year on a district-mandated test. The second-graders take the Gates-McGinite Reading Test in the fall and spring. They also are tested on the ITBS. My first-graders also take the Gates-McGinite test in the spring. My second-graders showed an overall class average of 3.6 in March of the second-grade year, which is astonishing when you remember that my class is a total-inclusion class with many children with special needs! My first-graders scored at a 2.3 overall, and this included children with special needs and an ESL student. These scores are consistent, year after year. I have never had a single student, including special needs students, who did not show at least six months growth from fall to spring since I began to use the Four-Blocks™ model.

Looking Forward to Next Year

Four-Blocks is developmentally appropriate for any classroom. The teacher must know the levels his or her students are on and design the curriculum to fit the student. Textbook publishers so often make the student fit their profile. A good teacher knows that a student cannot learn unless the curriculum is designed to meet the needs of that student. A multiage class has a wider diversity than a single grade class, but the individual students in all classrooms must have their needs met to enable them to experience success. Four-Blocks is a framework which allows me to design the curriculum to allow ALL my students to experience success.

As I am doing my final edit on this story, I am just beginning a new school year. After only four days of school, we are back into our Four-Blocks routines. The beauty of a multiage class is that half of the class knows your routine and can begin work immediately. I'm very excited about having a reading teacher who will be in my class for one hour each morning. We are planning to work together during Guided Reading. I'm lengthening the Writing and Self-Selected Reading Blocks a little because my students want and need more time for both of these.

When my "olders" (second-graders I had last year as first-graders) entered on the first day of school, they brought me stories they had written over the summer. They saved them and wanted to edit and publish them! The "olders" also were very eager to begin the "Interviews" again. They love the daily interview and writing about each person. I love the interviews because they allow us to get to know each other, build community, teach phonemic awareness, and model correct sentence structure—all while having fun. I am one excited teacher, anticipating another great Four-Blocks year!

My First Year to Do Four-Blocks™
and a Combination 1-2 Class ●

by Andrea Smith (with Pat Cunningham)

Linda Holland chose to teach a multiage group of children. Andrea Smith was asked to teach a combination first and second grade class to make the class size numbers work. Fortunately, Andrea had taught both first and second grades and felt comfortable having both grade levels of children in her classroom. What she hadn't done before this year was to use Four-Blocks™ as her organizing framework. Andrea tells a wonderful story of how Four-Blocks worked in her combination class. The biggest surprise to her was how well the Guided Reading Block worked. Here is Andrea's story:

I have taught for fourteen years, and for ten of those years, I taught first or second grade. As the 1999-2000 school year began, I was teaching at Indian Springs Elementary in Columbus, Ohio. Our school is part of an urban district, but our school's community would appear statistically as a more suburban school with only 20% qualifying for free lunch. Our school has a minority population of around 25%.

Our district has adopted the Four-Blocks™ Literacy Model, and I was excited about trying this approach. I had done some parts of the model before, but this year I was going for full implementation. I was a bit apprehensive, however, because I was asked to teach a combination first-second grade class. This class was established mainly because of the numbers, rather than with the benefits of a multiage setting in mind. However, I have worked in true multiage settings, so I developed a community and curriculum around the multiage belief system.

The first-graders selected for the class were typical first-graders with a wide range of abilities. Many of my first-graders entered already reading and had control of many writing words. Seven out of the 12 first-graders entered the class reading at a Level 10 or higher. I had three first-graders reading between Levels 4 and 6, and two first-graders reading between Levels 1 and 2. (We use the DRA-Developmental Reading Assessment at the beginning of the year to determine reading levels.)

A majority of my second-graders had been considered for retention and were considered "below average" or at risk, especially in reading. Only two of my second-graders read at a level 18, the reading level anticipated at the beginning of

True Stories from Four-Blocks™ Classrooms

second grade. The remaining second-graders read well below grade level, with two at Level 6, two at Level 4 and three at Level 2.

So, I had a wide range of reading levels and literacy experiences in both my first- and second-graders. I had been reading all summer about how the Four-Blocks was multilevel, and I "crossed my fingers" that it was going to be multilevel enough.

Working with Words

One of the biggest questions I had was which words to put on the Word Wall. At the beginning of the year, I used the first-grade Word Wall list from *Month-by-Month Phonics for First Grade* as an assessment tool and found out which words the kids already knew how to read and spell. There were only a few of these (is, the, a, I), but at least there were a few! I added these words to the Word Wall first. I didn't know whether to use the second grade or first grade lists, but decided to follow the suggestions of a few *Teachers.Net* and *Readinglady.com* mailring members to select three words from each grade level's list. I selected these words by looking at the students' writing and thinking about patterns needed for reading.

I began by holding my second graders responsible for all six words and my first-graders for the three first grade words. I encouraged my first-graders to try to learn all six words, however, and most of them were eager to show me they could.

For the second part of the Working with Words Block, I chose activities from both *Month-by-Month Phonics for First Grade* and *Month-by-Month Phonics for Second Grade*. I had given everyone Marie Clay's Hearing Sounds In Words Test (from *The Observation Survey*). This sentence dictation task told me a great deal about what they knew about letters and sounds and how they applied this to writing. This information helped me choose and adapt Working with Words activities from both books.

My children responded very well to the Working with Words Block. They liked the Word Wall activities, Guess the Covered Word, Making Words, Rounding Up the Rhymes, and generating rhymes from a weekly word family chunk. I think the children saw the direct benefits of these activities because they saw how the experiences helped them gain and strengthen important reading strategies. It was actually much easier to stretch the activities to meet the needs of both grade levels than I had thought it would be.

Guided Reading

This was the hardest block for me. We have limited reading material for early readers, and I felt so rushed to accomplish a lesson, practice, discussion, and closure in 40 minutes. Guided Reading was also a challenge at first because I was used to teaching small groups based upon abilities while the other children rotated through literacy centers. (Being a Columbus, Ohio resident, it is hard not to have been influenced by the Early Literacy Learning Initiative/Literacy Collaborative at The Ohio State University.) The approach to Guided Reading as described by the Four-Blocks™ Model was so different to me, so I really researched what to do over the summer.

I read all the Four-Blocks material, including *The Teacher's Guide to the Four-Blocks™* and Cheryl Sigmon's Four-Blocks columns at *www.teachers.net*. I also read *Mosaic of Thought* and (later in the year) *Strategies That Work*. I focused my Guided Reading lessons on the comprehension strategies suggested in these books and the quarterly benchmark guides my district designed in alignment with our state proficiency test.

I presented comprehension minilessons to the whole class, and then the children applied what we talked about with selected reading materials. On some days, the children read different texts close to their instructional levels. On other days, we all worked with the same text and supported one another's reading. I utilized paired reading and literature circles often, and tried to mix in enough shared reading with guided support as needed. I included my struggling readers in at least three quick support groups each week to monitor how they were doing. I assigned different reading partners or teams throughout the week so I met with all of my other children at least once or twice a week.

Our district just adopted the Harcourt Brace series. I used only the first-grade books because most of my second-graders could not handle the second-grade text levels. It was recommended that my first-graders not read the second-grade level books. I also provided appropriate texts by using multiple-copy book sets from our resource room. The book sets were used for book clubs and research teams during the Guided Reading Block to support a science or social studies theme ongoing in our class.

We spent a great deal of time working with nonfiction materials this year, and the children loved it! Different thinking strategies for non-fiction were taught and expanded upon throughout the year. The children learned to identify important ideas, supporting details, and the author's purpose for writing the book. During a plant unit called "Out In The Garden," I used the term "Research Teams," and each team was responsible for reading a text and later identifying the important ideas, details, and author's purpose. I collected different book sets at varying levels and big books about plants. I also found several plant books and made audiotapes so my less able readers could use these kits at our listening center. I knew they could understand the concepts when provided the strongest of text support. Children were given the choice of working alone, with a partner, or as a team to read about plants. Mixed ability groups had the opportunity to work with me, and we read a big book together. After reading a selection, the children recorded a summary of the book and any interesting supporting details in their Research Journals. They could add information about something new they had learned or something they found to be unusual about plants. To close each Guided Reading Block, the group met and discussed what was learned and any pertinent information or new questions were added to our class KWL chart. The class KWL chart and the Research Journals were later used by the children to write their own books or magazines about plants.

My support groups contained two to three of my struggling readers, regardless of grade level, and two to three other children. It was important for my struggling readers to have models in their group to demonstrate the ways a reader deals with text challenges, and to model thinking strategies when discussing the books. By rotating different children into the small groups, I could observe my capable readers working with different kinds of text and offer them the one-on-one time that makes Guided Reading groups so appealing. I met briefly with my struggling readers three to four times a week, and with my other kids one to two times a week during Guided Reading. The composition of the groups changed all of the time, but the purpose remained the same.

Despite my concerns about the lack of leveled groups in Guided Reading instruction, the children all did very well during the Guided Reading Block, especially my struggling readers. (I really did not think doing Guided Reading the Four-Blocks way would work, but am I glad that I was wrong!) I think relinquishing the control of learning from me to the children made all the difference in the world. All children, regardless of their instructional levels, deserve the opportunity to read and discuss books for their meaning and personal connections. All children can do this. They just need the opportunities to focus on meaning and comprehension. Having these opportunities with a wide range of peers is critical, too. I now realize why the research shows that low-achieving children often miss out on higher level comprehension lessons, and spend too much instructional time on decoding skills and too little time on the quest to make text make sense. Instructional text levels do not define how well a child can think about text!

Writing

Writing Workshop is a favorite time of our day. The kids were comforted by the routine of minilesson, independent writing time, and then our sharing circle. My minilessons were guided by several important thoughts, and this kept my writing instruction and interactions focused and effective. First, I thought about the range of abilities and what my kids needed to learn as blooming writers. After presenting the initial procedural lessons regarding how Writing Workshop would flow, I presented many minilessons on how to simply get my ideas from my head to the paper. My kids needed help with taking risks to use invented spellings with confidence, and they really needed help in coming up with ideas for their writing. I did lots of modeling and brainstorming about how you get ideas.

After the children understood the procedures and how you get ideas, then the lessons could focus on organization, style, mechanics and conventions, editing, real-world connections for writing, poetry, and expository/non-fiction writing. The critical foundation of Writing Workshop was finding out what my children needed, presenting many opportunities for them to see writing modeled, and then using my conference times to observe my children and their individual strengths and challenges. From the children's perspective, I tried to make sure they understood why we met for minilessons, how their independence and ideas were the energy of Writing Workshop, and how the cooperation and community of helping one another during Writing Workshop or the sharing circle was both fun and helpful.

Everyone has their own style for organizing materials and keeping samples of students' writing over the course of the year. A few simple things have kept me together, because once the year starts, I want a low-maintenance way of keeping track of materials, paperwork and documentation for writing portfolios.

My kids sit at tables with a communal basket of supplies, so the pencils and crayons are always handy. I have a writing bookshelf that holds a variety of paper, index cards, art supplies for publication/illustrations, and book cover materials that the children get as needed. On the same shelf is a crate holding everyone's writing folder. It is someone's job to pass out the folders from our community area at the end of each minilesson, as the children leave to begin writing. I like keeping the folders in a crate so I can lug the whole crate to a table after school, or take the crate home when I want to look at pieces for assessment and progress. I keep my clipboard for student observations in the same crate.

On the same shelf, I keep a crate with hanging legal folders that are labeled for storing each child's writing portfolio. I have a copy of our district's writing rubric taped to the folder to make assessment easier for me, and I have it available to show parents at conferences. I also have a paper that shows examples of children's writing as they pass through the developmental stages, so parents have a handle on where their own child is on a continuous scale, rather than a grade. At the end of each month, children select the pieces they want to store in their portfolio. I have the option of adding pieces, too. If a child wants to keep working on a piece, but wants the current sample in the portfolio, we just make a copy of it and add it. We take part of one writing period each month to pick a piece and add it to our portfolio. It takes some modeling and assistance at first, so you don't end up with an out-of-sequence portfolio, but it is worth the time. It allows the children to see their progress.

Not one of these ideas is original or fancy. Most teachers will probably have all of these materials at school. I was always encouraged to try to set up classroom writing materials in a way that worked best for me and my kids.

Self-Selected Reading

I started Self-Selected Reading on the very first day of school, and used the first five days to explain the procedures and expectations. I modeled selecting books from the baskets, and reviewed picture walks as a previewing strategy. I modeled how to put books away carefully, how to find books of interest, and what to do if a book was too difficult to read independently. The children were very excited to be given an opportunity to read without interruptions, and they seemed to be very engaged from the start. I really emphasized how Self-Selected Reading gave them a chance to practice their reading strategies and skills, while allowing them to discover new authors, genres, and topics of interest. Practice was the way to become a better reader.

After a week of observing my students, I realized that my transitional and fluent readers were making the most of their Self-Selected Reading time and spent the entire block reading. On the other hand, my emergent and early readers were struggling with the limited number of books they could read in the rotating book tubs. Once they read and reread the books within their independent levels, they quickly tired of looking at more difficult books and only telling a story through the pictures. What first appeared to be engaged reading was really page flipping while those developing readers waited for the end of Self-Selected Reading and the call to meet in our sharing circle. The book tubs held some books at their independent levels, but apparently not enough titles. With the range of readers in the split grade class, I would need bathtub-size tubs to hold enough books for this diverse group! I was frustrated by the number of kids losing interest in Self-Selected Reading because I wanted my kids to enjoy and benefit from this block.

I decided to take a problem-solving approach with the children, so I met with the emergent and early-level children, and we brainstormed a way to solve the problem. After exploring our classroom library together, we decided that during this block, they would choose books from book baskets I had organized by Reading Recovery Levels in our classroom library. In addition, they could select a book basket according to a topic of interest. For example, one student was reading at a Reading Recovery Level 10. He would read from the basket holding Level 8, 9, and 10 books. He would also select the "Snakes" book basket because he was very interested in snakes—one of his neighbors had several boa constrictors! Once the children realized they could spend Self-Selected Reading time with books they could read independently, and then challenge themselves with more difficult books of interest, they became more motivated readers during this block.

As children demonstrated independence, I allowed children to read in places other than at their work tables. They loved being able to stretch out on the rugs around the room, share big pillows as seats or headrests, sit on chairs with cushions, or choose the most coveted place—our classroom couch. They would pick at least three books from their book tubs and select a place to read. I monitored who could handle this much freedom and who needed to remain at the work tables until they developed enough focus and self-direction to read in the alternative places. I know many teachers require their children to read at their seats, but I thought about my own preference for reading on the couch at home rather than at the kitchen table. As the children accepted the responsibilities of Self-Selected Reading, allowing them to read around the room seemed like a natural progression.

That is how my Self-Selected Reading block evolved during the first nine weeks of school. By honoring the idea that children wanted books they could read independently, while still having the opportunity to pick more or less challenging books, SSR time was more productive. The children were truly involved with reading, allowing me to begin my individual conferences.

Assessment

I use a variety of assessment tools to monitor reading development. At the beginning and end of the year we establish instructional text levels using the Developmental Reading Assessment. (I administer this assessment two additional times to my struggling readers to make sure their reading levels are increasing and their comprehension is improving.)

In addition, I give our district's quarterly benchmark tests. Our district worked with the Evans-Newton Corporation and aligned our curriculum to match our state proficiency test. To "monitor the delivery of curriculum" and "assess student achievement," Target Teach tests are given at the end of each quarter. Each grade has target reading benchmarks, and all students take an end-of-the-quarter test to see if they mastered these reading benchmarks. The tests are a combination of multiple choice and short answer responses.

In the children's reading portfolios, I add running records and my notes from Self-Selected Reading conferences. These notes record a child's responses to books, but I periodically add questions regarding a benchmark (Tell me the problem and solution in the story. Do you think the character made a good choice?).

For writing, we have a district portfolio with a rubric that we use to assess samples throughout the year. Each month I ask the children to pull a favorite writing piece, and I select one, too. I use the district's writing portfolio rubric to score each piece, and then put the samples in the children's writing portfolios. To see how children are growing in their word knowledge, I give the Hearing Sounds In Word Test sentence dictation test and Richard Gentry's Developmental Spelling Test four times throughout the year.

How My Children Progressed

Four-Blocks has been extremely successful with this group of children, and I believe assessments and results support this statement. My first graders all did exceptionally well. On the end-of-year Developmental Reading Assessment, 11 out of 12 first-graders read and comprehended a Level 24 book successfully. (We did not assess beyond this level, but I know many of them could have read well beyond level 24.) This included one girl who was reading between Level 1 and 2 in September. She now exceeds grade level expectations, reads *Junie B. Jones* books, and can lead a literature circle like a pro. My other first-grader who began the year at a Level 2 progressed to a Level 16.

My second graders, all but two of whom were reading below level in September, also did exceptionally well. The text levels improved for all of my second-graders, even those identified as learning disabled. More importantly, their comprehension strategies improved, and the students were able to monitor their own comprehension while reading. When they listened to read-alouds or had assistance with more difficult text, they were still able to discuss the books in terms of literary elements and higher level thinking strategies, such as evaluating the solution used by the story character to solve a problem. I found that graphic organizers greatly enhanced their understanding of nonfiction text and visually showed them ways to organize their thoughts. These organizers had a positive carryover to their writing as well.

Second Grade Students: 1999-2000 School Year

*denotes student identified with a learning disability with and IEP

Student	Entering DRA Level	Exiting DRA Level
A	18	34+
B	18	34+
C	6	34+
D	2	28
E*	2	12
F*	2	10
G	4	12
H*	4	14
I	6	24

I have taught for 14 years (10 of these in first or second grade) so I know how enthusiastic young children get when they are first learning to read. However, this class, half of whom were struggling second-graders, has astounded me. The students all love to read and write and look forward to it each day. Parents tell me that their children love to read at home this year, whereas last year, it was a struggle to get them to read each night for their homework requirement.

I got my first inkling about how strong their enthusiasm for reading was in November when one of my shy little girls, who came to me with few literacy experiences, said to me, "Mrs. Smith, I start thinking about you and our books the minute I wake up in the morning." Now if that doesn't sum it all up for this model, then I don't know what could!

Looking Forward to Next Year

As of now, I will not have a multiage class next year, but things can change! I would love to have a combination first/second grade class again. I think I am more relaxed with the model now and understand how I can incorporate my school district's curriculum, our school's resources, and the Four-Blocks™ Model more effectively. I knew before I started the model how beneficial Self-Selected Reading and Writing were to the literacy development of children. I will work even harder to protect the conferencing times in these blocks, so I can spend more time really talking with children. I was surprised at the huge impact Working with Words had on the children. Traditional phonics programs are usually so uninspiring to the children and teacher; more importantly, I question the benefits of some phonics programs for true literacy. Working with Words allowed my children to gain truly useful strategies for dealing with reading and writing—things they could think about and use independently as they read and write. The biggest shock (still) is how well Guided Reading went, and the excellent progress so many children made. I was very hesitant to change from my small, ability-based Guided Reading groups, but enough people supported the notion, so I took a risk. I will approach the new year with so much more confidence regarding reading. I've spent the summer planning how I will support the development of truly useful thinking and reading strategies for readers, young and old alike.

Come to think of it, I have a renewed sense of confidence in myself as a teacher because the model really promotes the idea that children need to be taking control of their learning, while learning alongside caring adults who know when to gently guide them and when to stand back and observe. I am looking forward to an even better year!

How I Adapted Four-Blocks™ for My Multiage Classroom •

By Karen Seitler (with Pat Cunningham)

Like Linda, Karen Seitler chooses to teach a multiage class. Karen has 20 years of teaching experience and has taught many different grades and special education. Karen is a teacher who has a clearly-defined philosophy of teaching and a clear concept of herself as a teacher. Many teachers at upper grades have difficulty adapting Four-Blocks™ to their older children. Karen has adapted Four-Blocks for both her third- and fourth-graders with great facility. When I read Karen's census response, I found myself thinking, "What a clever lady!" (This opinion had nothing to do with the fact that she too is a Rhode Islander!) No matter where you are from, I think you will agree! Here is Karen's story of how she adapted Four-Blocks for her multiage classroom: ·

I am very privileged to teach a multiage third and fourth grade class at the Captain Isaac Paine Elementary School in Foster, Rhode Island. Foster is a cozy New England community with approximately 4,300 people. Our school has about 420 students in grades K-5. I began teaching in 1980 as a special education teacher. Then, I moved into grade three inclusion, and now I am a multiage teacher. This has been a steady progression towards the classroom that I now have.

Teachers must, of course, assume a variety of roles, but I see myself primarily as a facilitator of my students' growth and learning. My students are encouraged to be self-directed and to take responsibility for their own education. I use the beliefs of the Responsive Classroom® approach, and have found the book, *The Morning Meeting*, to be very helpful. I feel that it has changed how my students and I view the day, and how we communicate with each other. My classroom is run as a community of people who value each other, both teacher and student. I feel that this directly affects how the students feel and how they learn. They respect each other's strengths and weaknesses. My classroom would best be described as a differentiated classroom. I recently read *The Differentiated Classroom* and realized that is a very close description to what I believe a classroom should be. I chose to teach a multiage classroom, and the most valuable book I have seen on multiage is *A Multiage Classroom: Choice and Possibility*.

My classroom is standards-based. Standards provide the direction and goals for our learning. In my opinion, the most valuable part of our standards is the Applied Learning sections. These standards challenge the students to use what they have learned and apply their learning to real-life situations. These expectations have forced me to stretch as a teacher, and begin to look at my instruction with new eyes. When the *Reading and Writing: Primary Literacy Standards for K-3* came out last year, I carefully read through to see if Four-Blocks™ was going to enable my students to succeed in the standards. I feel confidently that all four areas in reading are needed for students to attain the standards.

Technology is a major component in my classroom. Technology provides a wonderful vehicle to allow students to find purpose in their studies, because they have many ways on the Internet to gain an audience for their work and to participate in real time events that are currently taking place somewhere in the world. I have found that students will attempt to read material that is difficult when they are trying to locate information on the Internet and the topic is of high interest to them.

A few years ago, I went to a conference and heard a teacher from Texas describing how she ran her classroom. What caught my attention was that all of the different viewpoints on reading were incorporated into the day. I had always loved to read aloud to my students, but often felt I should be doing something more important. I also loved the silent reading time. This idea gave value to what I had always believed. Upon returning from the conference, I immediately put buckets together with books for each table, and we had silent reading and teacher read-aloud daily.

My reading specialist saw what I was doing, and said, "I think that there is an actual program that puts together all the different approaches. I think they call it Four-Blocks." I went searching and located *Classrooms That Work: They Can All Read and Write* and *The Teacher's Guide to the Four-Blocks™*. I think that the books are most helpful for kindergarten, first, and second grades. I adapted for third grade last year, and have been adapting for my third and fourth grade multiage class this year. Here are some things that work particularly well in my multiage classroom and some of the adaptations I have made.

Self-Selected Reading

We have Self-Selected Reading every day. I try very hard not to miss this time. I initially began with buckets, but have stopped them. They were a great way to get started, but I found them confining to the students and myself. I have some students who are such avid readers that it is a challenge to keep up with them. I have other students who need a lot of low-level, high-interest books. I found that putting them all in the same bucket often caused conflict. I have many books in my classroom. Each student has a folder for silent reading, and they often tuck their book into the pocket of this folder. Every student has access to all of the books on the shelves. The students choose their books when they have time during the day. They are expected to always have a book ready to read for Self-Selected Reading.

I call shorter, easier books "Quick Reads" or "Sit Back and Enjoy Books." I sometimes use them for Teacher Read-Alouds. I also use nonfiction "Quick Reads" to help us learn key information. I discuss how valuable "Quick Reads" are with the class so students never feel badly choosing them. At the beginning of the year, I model "Quick Reads," and often the students applaud or cry at the end of these books. My strugglers often choose two or three "Quick Reads," and this helps to avoid having students wander around looking for books during silent reading.

During my discussions with students, I take notes of student interests and preferences. When I locate a book I think a student might enjoy, I share it with the student and show the student where it will be located for future reading. I regularly provide "book commercials" to introduce books to the class. "Book commercials" are my way of getting kids excited about new books, and to share my excitement and reasons for choosing them. During a "book commercial" I get very excited, and describe the treasures I have found. I often hug each book as I present it. As I discuss the book, I describe what kind of book it is, why it might be interesting, and where it will be located. Some of the books I place on the corner of my desk because I just can't wait to read them. Of course, anyone may read the books on the corner of my desk, as long as they put them back for me. (These books don't stay on the corner of my desk very long.) I have found these techniques very helpful in encouraging kids to read.

When I begin a unit such as Weather, Iditarod, or Australia, I gather a wealth of books on the topic. At the beginning of our units, we immerse ourselves in learning everything we can about the topic. During this time, I do limit the students' reading during silent reading to the topic that we are beginning. This is something that I have never read about, I have just developed it on my own. My students love this. We pretend that we are researchers becoming experts on a subject. Each student is also in search of something that really interests them, so they choose a topic to research more in depth and become the classroom expert on that topic. This immersion in unit-related books usually lasts two to three weeks. Then, we return to selecting any book for Self-Selected Reading.

Teacher Read-Aloud is my favorite time of the day. I use this time to read many different kinds of text for many different reasons. If we are starting a unit, I read books on the topic we are studying. I read more nonfiction books than fiction. My students have always read fiction easily, so I use this time to present them with new content. I discuss how authors use different techniques to present information. This often gives students ideas as to how to present their information in writing and in their projects. I have found *Mosaic of Thought* to be one of the most invaluable books that I have ever read. It, like the other books mentioned, gave value to what I had always believed. During my read-aloud time, I use many of the think-aloud techniques described in this book.

Guided Reading

This is the most difficult block for me, because I am not sure if I am doing it correctly. I have adapted what I have read to what I think is best for third- and fourth-graders. I use mostly sets of actual books, short stories, poetry, and nonfiction. I only use a basal if the story I want to use is complete in the basal, as if it were a book. I have found that using plays really helps to improve my student's oral reading fluency. The best source for plays that I have found is a magazine put out by Scholastic, titled *Storyworks*. I save the magazines and use them again and again. Music is an integrated part of our day. Students will put great effort into learning to read words fluently when they are singing. Music can be found for almost any topic, and students often learn a lot of content about the subject at the same time.

To teach comprehension, I use the strategies described in *Mosaic of Thought* and *Strategies That Work*. We have used all of the formats listed in *The Teacher's Guide to the Four-Blocks™*. My students enjoy the Book Club Groups the best. I have used a lot of ideas from *Literature Circles*. The most valuable technique that I have begun to implement in the last few years is teacher modeling. I think that teacher modeling, or thinking aloud as you read and process in front of the students, has an incredible impact and has drastically changed the level of work that my students produce.

Writing

In Rhode Island, writing is a major focus in third and fourth grades. Students are tested in writing by the state at both levels. I spend a lot of time modeling good writing. I initially did not like to teach writing at all. I have taken many courses on writing, and I'm always looking for a really good book that will shed new light on how to teach children to write interesting stories. I can truly say that now I love to teach writing. For writing, I follow very close to what is in *The Teacher's Guide to the Four-Blocks™*, but I add a lot more to it for third- and fourth-graders. *What A Writer Needs* and *Craft Lessons* are my two most treasured books on teaching writing.

I think the best way to teach writing is to model, model, and model. In addition to having students write on their own topics, I do focused writing in which I connect the writing with our reading or a unit we are working on. Once a month, I give prompts to prepare the students for the state assessment.

I love using poetry in my classroom. I think poetry writing is just as important as writing stories and reports. (*Awakening the Heart* and *Three Voices* are awesome books on poetry in the classroom.) My students will write many more poems than they will other types of writing. Poetry frees them to write a lot, and their writing improves in all areas. I find that the techniques that I am modeling for the students in my lessons often show up first in their poetry, long before they show up in their written stories. If I am teaching similes, for example, I present a poem with many similes, and the students find these similes. Often, they begin to apply the use of similes in their own poems with little frustration. The students take great pride in their poems, and we applaud all their efforts. This success encourages them to write more.

Many of our poems are written about the content area that we are studying. Before we begin to write poetry on the subject, the students learn a lot about the subject. I have used many books on the subject during Read-Aloud, we have researched it on the Internet, and the students have read books, sung songs, read poetry, and created vocabulary lists. This allows the students to write poetry easily because they don't have to search for a topic, and they are eager to write because they feel they are experts on the subject. I model how to write the poem and provide examples before the students begin to write. I weave all of these things into different times of the day and into different lessons. I have learned from reading the students' poetry that I can quickly assess exactly what the students are learning and what they really understand about the subject.

We write poems for gifts, print them on attractive paper, and laminate them. This provides a chance for families to applaud their child's writing achievements and to display them. There are many sites on the Internet where students can share their poetry. When they see their own poems on the Internet, it is very satisfying to them. Some of our poems can be found at the addresses below:

Iditarod Collaboration Project 2000

http://www.indep.k12.mo.us/Elementary/impact/schrik/exchange/bookclub/
    clubhome.html

Poetry 2000 Project

http://www.geocities.com/poempoets/Poets2000/Seitler.html

Working with Words

This block has been tricky because I have two grades this year. I put the third-grade words on the Word Wall, because all of the students need to spell and use those words correctly. I do a Making Words lesson once a week. I use ideas from both the *Month-by-Month Phonics for Third Grade* and the *Month-by-Month Phonics for Upper Grades*.

My students love the activity from the third-grade book, *Spelling Change Banners*. I make a banner, and as students are reading, they add words they find to whatever we are currently working on. They can do this at any time during the day when they find a word in anything they are reading.

If a student can spell all of the words on the third- and fourth-grade Word Wall, then I move them on to the Nifty Thrifty Fifty words. At times I take this group of students and just work with them, because it would be too frustrating for the other students. But, I don't limit this group to fourth-graders. If a third-grader can spell all the words, he/she joins the group. I do groupings that change all of the time, so groups don't bother the students. I have had students who finish all of those lists, and then I move into vocabulary development. (*Words, Words, Words: Teaching Vocabulary in Grades 4-12* has been very helpful.)

Our Schedule

I do most of my teaching by integrating a topic and using the topic to teach from. We do not follow a set schedule every day. We always have Read-Aloud and Self-Selected Reading. At times we do Guided Reading one day, and then do Writing in response to the reading the next day. I have used many techniques from *Nonfiction Matters: Reading, Writing, and Research in Grades 3-8*. The techniques presented for utilizing reading and research, and then enabling students to produce a high-quality written project, have been very helpful at this age level.

How I Adapted Four-Blocks™ for My Multiage Classroom ●

Sometimes we take all day to do all four blocks. When we studied Australia, for example, Monday often looked like this. (I have no specials on Monday, so I use Monday to set the stage for the week.)

- Morning Meeting
- Making Words Lesson (20-30 minutes)
- Self-Selected Reading—books on Australia (30 minutes)
- Read Aloud—books on Australia (20-30 minutes)
- Guided Reading—Short story or informational piece related to Australia, modeling lesson (45 minutes)
- Writing—Students respond in writing to the reading (30 minutes)
- Lunch
- Math (60 minutes)
- Reading/Writing/Research based on current topic (rest of the afternoon) I don't follow the same schedule every day or every week. I structure my schedule around where the students are and where I plan for us to go. Some days, we write a lot. Other days, we read a lot. This is quite a change from my former teaching, but I have found that the quality of the students' work has greatly improved. I decided that students need time to complete high-quality work.

The basis of my day is Four-Blocks, in that I truly believe that all four areas must be covered for a child to learn to love to read. But, I also feel that education must be integrated and not so many different chunks of things that students never understand how to use it altogether. As I plan my schedule, I think across a week—rather than a day. That way, I can give attention to each of the blocks, but have longer blocks for Guided Reading or Writing, and integrate the two through research on some days.

Looking Forward to Next Year

This fall, my third-graders from last year will return as fourth-graders and new third-graders will join us. This will be my third year using Four-Blocks. The first year, I tried many techniques with third-graders only. Last year, I used it with third- and fourth-graders. Multiage was new to me, and I also utilized technology much more than I ever had before. I felt that I was doing many new things, and the progress of my students was much improved. I look forward to improving my

True Stories from Four-Blocks™ Classrooms

teaching in the Self-Selected Reading Block. I am going to work on my techniques for conferencing with students and providing them with appropriate reading materials.

I have been reading *Guided Reading The Four-Blocks™ Way* and *Strategies That Work* this summer. This has helped to clarify some of my concerns about the Guided Reading Block. I am eager to try these techniques. One specific "new year's resolution" I have made is to use more graphic organizers to enable my students to better comprehend informational text.

I spent two weeks in intensive training this summer to learn how to better integrate technology into the classroom. The goal is to use technology to teach in ways that are not currently possible without technology. I used PowerPoint last year to teach and assess students comprehension of their reading. When the students created their own PowerPoint presentations, it was quickly evident to me what they understood and what they didn't. PowerPoint challenges students to clearly state main ideas and specific details. This then gave me the opportunity to implement activities to improve upon their comprehension. I have learned many new ideas to improve on what I did last year, and I am looking forward to a very exciting year!

Rounding Them Up in the Library and Doing Four-Blocks™ •••••••••••••••••••••••••••••••••••

by Jean Reid (with Pat Cunningham)

What do you do when it is halfway through the school year and you have a whole grade level of children who are not reading and writing well, and you just know Four-Blocks™ would help them, but the teachers don't know how to do it and are understandably anxious about totally changing their teaching right in the middle of the year? This is the problem Jean Reid faced, and her solution will astonish you with its boldness, workability, and common sense. Here is Jean's story of how they "rounded them up" in the library and did Four-Blocks:

The 1999-2000 school year was my thirty-second year of teaching. I have taught reading in six different schools. For the last four years, I have been a reading teacher at Cora Kelly Magnet School in Alexandria, Virginia. We are a magnet school for science, math, and computers, so 15% of our population comes to us from all over the city. Our children come from middle- and lower-income families, 75% of them are on free/reduced price lunch. Approximately 60% of our children are African-American, 20% are white, and we have lots of Latino children. We have some multiage classes, and several teachers who will be looping with their children to the next grade.

This year, we had several primary grade teachers who were using Four-Blocks™ in their classrooms. I loved the framework, and went into their classrooms to help and support them. I asked each teacher in which block she thought she would need me most, and that's the one I helped to teach. As the fall went on, I became even more convinced that the Four-Blocks was the kind of balanced reading instruction our children needed.

At the same time, I was worrying about our fourth-graders. Scores on the Stanford achievement tests, given at the end of third grade, had been very low, and we knew they didn't reflect what the students are capable of. Our principal called together a group, including members of our leadership team, and some of our professional development school partners from George Washington University and the National Education Association. We brainstormed ideas for what we could do to give our fourth-graders a boost. The team agreed that the children would really benefit from Four-Blocks instruction, but we didn't know how to go about getting it up and running. I thought about it over the holidays and came up with a plan. Everyone agreed it was worth a try, so we decided to "give it a whirl." This is how it worked.

Rounding Them Up in the Library

Three of the fourth grade classes had interns from George Washington University for the second semester. For two hours each day, two of the fourth-grade classes, along with their teachers and interns, gathered in the library. We divided the children into four heterogeneous teams and rotated them through the four blocks. (The other two fourth-grade classes, along with their teachers, one intern, and another reading teacher, used a similar procedure in two classrooms which open to each other.)

We wanted the teachers to learn all the blocks, so we decided that each teacher would teach one block to all four groups of children for a month, then take on the next block, and the next, and so on. By the end of the year, the teachers would feel confident with all the blocks. We planned together each week and coordinated as much as we could between the blocks. Because we were all right there in the library together, the teachers knew what their children were getting and could make links between the blocks and the rest of the curriculum. Our proximity also eliminated transfer time. We changed groups and blocks in less than a minute!

How We Did the Blocks

We tried to use a wide variety of materials for Guided Reading. We have the Houghton-Mifflin reading series, but had not used it much with these children because it was too hard for them. But, we supported them with partner reading, Everyone Read To…, and other ideas from *The Teacher's Guide to the Four-Blocks™*, and for the first time, our children were able to be successful with the grade-level textbook. We also used a lot of materials that connected to our social studies curriculum and included poetry, magazines, and newspapers. We tried hard to vary the reading selections throughout the week and to have a good balance of fiction and informational text.

I had just finished reading *Mosaic of Thought*, and it has really influenced my thinking on the Self-Selected Reading Block. I began modeling every day when I was reading aloud. (The students think it is so funny when I "think aloud" as I'm reading. They know immediately when I stop "to think" because I take my glasses off.) I also tried to be much more thoughtful in my conversations with the students during our Self-Selected Reading conferences.

Our Writing Block was Writers' Workshop, which we had all been doing for a long time. We model something every day in the minilesson, give the students time and opportunity to write, conference with them, and share. In addition to letting students write on topics of their own choosing, we did some focused writing lessons to prepare students for the type of writing they will need to be able to demonstrate on the state writing assessment given in fifth grade.

In Working with Words, we used many of the activities from *Month-by-Month Phonics for Upper Grades*. We had a Word Wall, and the children enjoyed all the Word Wall activities, especially Wordo. We did two Making Words lessons each week. On several occasions, we used the social studies book to create Guess the Covered Word lessons. What Looks Right? was also a big hit with all the students. I can't remember a single activity we did in the Working with Words Block that they didn't enjoy.

How We Know It Was a Success

Achievement tests are not given at the end of fourth grade, so we don't have comparison scores. We did do a writing prompt similar to that used for the state writing test at the beginning and end of the year, and scored these using the rubric used by the state. Each paper was graded on a 1-3 score for content, written expression, and usage. All children's scores improved from the first test to the end-of-the-year test; many students showed dramatic improvement.

Our major source of data for our strong belief that Four-Blocks is working is our children's reactions. They love coming to the library for their blocks and enjoy moving every thirty minutes. When they can tell that the group next to them is enjoying something, they are eager to get there and do it, too! Amazingly, they stay totally on task, and we have very few discipline problems during these two hours. One day, we had to cancel because half of the students were going on a field trip. When I passed the other group in the hall, they were begging me to have Four-Blocks just for them. I can't really explain the phenomena, but these children love being together with four different teachers. I think they appreciate both the structure and the variety.

Looking Forward to Next Year

Next year, the entire staff is "going for broke." We will all be doing Four-Blocks, learning together. The fourth-grade teachers are going to mentor the fifth-grade teachers. We joked with the fifth-grade teachers about how they were inheriting a group of kids who could teach THEM the framework. We are figuring out how to do this training, grade level by grade level. We have folks all along the continuum of learning about Four-Blocks, so we are going to try a variety of things.

We are providing release time for teachers to come and move with a group through the Four-Blocks. We have a book study group that started with *Classrooms That Work*. We are meeting weekly to discuss strategies, assessment, etc. We do expect for teachers to take some initiative about this and get online and read all of the great stuff on the mailrings. We consider Cheryl's Four-Blocks columns at *www.teachers.net* a must. Our principal is 100% behind us, and says he'll do whatever it takes to make this undertaking successful.

Kindergarten will begin using Building Blocks™. The kindergarten teachers will be provided with the "Building Blocks™" video, *The Teacher's Guide to Building Blocks™*, and *Month-by-Month Reading and Writing for Kindergarten*. They will have an in-service together in August and meet throughout the year.

Our original intent was for the fourth-grade teachers to teach all Four-Blocks independently next year. To my surprise, they are adamant about continuing to work together in some configuration. They feel that the children have flourished from being exposed to different types of teaching styles as they move among the four teachers. Also, they believe their planning is more effective.

So, next year, two pairs of fourth-grade teachers will work together. One teacher will teach the Working with Words and Writing Blocks, while the other teacher does Self-Selected Reading and Guided Reading. Then, the children will switch, and the teachers will teach the same two blocks again. This way we can shorten Working with Words and add to Writing without disrupting the schedule.

The fifth-grade teachers (one of whom is a trained "blocker") will use the same plan. We think this is going to be a great group to watch because all of the children are "blockers" already. I've told the children they'll have to be very supportive of their teachers as they are learning to do the blocks. One student offered to do the teaching until the teacher is ready!

We are in a professional development partnership with George Washington University and the National Education Association. This partnership supports our work, and we will have at least four full-time interns from their graduate program next year. We are thinking about how to use these interns to provide the most support to our teachers as we move to implementation.

We had a block party toward the end of the year, and it was a big success. There are twelve teachers in our school who are "blockers" already. We gathered for refreshments (always a MUST for our faculty), and then met in informal groups by grade levels. Attendance was voluntary, but most classroom teachers came. The "blockers" briefly explained the Four-Blocks, and then the discussions were off and running. The enthusiasm is high, but we know we have a lot of work to do. We have a whole-day, schoolwide workshop with a national consultant scheduled for the end of August and hope to be ready to begin the blocks in all the classrooms at the beginning of the year.

Three Teachers Collaborate and Make Maximum Use of Space, Materials, and Time •••••••••••••••••••••••••••••••••

By Claudia Le Rud (with Pat Cunningham)

After the first 100 responses, reading and coding the Four-Blocks™ census forms became a laborious task. "I'll do one more and take a break," I decided, as I picked up a form from the stack. I coded the information from the short form side, and then turned it over to note (somewhat woefully) that there was lots of information on the long form on the back. I skimmed this quickly and noticed that three first-grade teachers were moving the children to three different rooms. "Oh, no," I thought, "Departmentalized Four-Blocks in first grade! I just hope they aren't dividing the students up by level and giving someone all the struggling readers!" As I read more carefully, my initial chagrin was replaced with delight. "What a neat idea. The teacher moves with the children, and the rooms can be set up perfectly for each block!" I could just visualize the Writing room with computers and publishing center, the Guided Reading room with a big carpeted space for the whole group and some small tables for partners and playschool or book club groups, and the Working with Words room with the overhead and red pens for Word Wall and a pocket chart for making and sorting words. One concern about moving children is the time that is lost in the transitions. But, when I read that the children stay in their original room for the Self-Selected Reading Block, then follow that in their own room with whatever block that room is set up for, and make their first move as they return from recess, that concern also was allayed. I attacked the stack of forms with renewed gusto after reading Claudia's form, saying to myself "What other great ideas might these clever teachers have thought of?" Claudia Le Rud, Tracy Dennison, and Connie Coston teach first grade at Wilamette Primary School in West Linn, Oregon. Here is how they shared their thinking and made maximum use of their space, materials, and time. (Claudia is the storyteller.)

In the spring of 1999, another colleague and I happened upon *Month-by-Month Phonics for First Grade* and really began to "do" the Word Wall. (We'd had Word Walls for a long time, but were not really doing the activities which make the Word Wall truly useful to all the children.) I then became curious about the

Three Teachers Collaborate and Make Maximum Use of Space, Materials, and Time •

entire Four-Blocks™ program as I read some general overview material in the *Month-by-Month* book and ordered *The Teacher's Guide to the Four-Blocks™*. I was intrigued! I began to talk with my colleagues about it, and three of us talked with our administrator about implementing the Four-Blocks in our classrooms the next school year. We decided to do the Working with Words and Writing Blocks the "Four-Blocks way," but because our school had a long-standing tradition of using small, leveled reading groups, we decided to keep our leveled groups. To find time to do this, we decided not to do Self-Selected Reading. We would do Guided Reading the "Four-Blocks way" during the Guided Reading time and our leveled reading groups in place of Self-Selected Reading.

At the same time as we were planning how to implement the Four-Blocks framework, we began investigating the possibility of team teaching in the downstairs area. Our principal told us that we might be able to hire another first-grade teacher in order to reduce our class size, but room space posed a problem. We needed to free up a classroom for the new teacher. The downstairs area, which was actually two and a half rooms, was at that time being used by two teachers. We began to dream about how the three of us could use that total area, thus freeing up a room for a new teacher. We each wanted to teach our separate first grades, yet have them be somewhat of a community as well.

The three rooms are side by side. There are two full-size rooms and one room which is quite a bit smaller. However, all three rooms are equipped as classrooms, with sinks, closets, white boards, etc. They have inside doors connecting one to another and an outside hall door. The smaller size of the third room made staying in it all day for everything very unappealing. That's when we began to dream about moving ourselves and the kids to different rooms for the different blocks. We drew out a floor plan of the three rooms. The largest room seemed best suited for the large rectangular tables and computer space needed for writing. The middle room was best suited for round tables which we wanted to use for our math center time in the afternoons, and it contained the shelving needed to house the tubs for these centers. It also had the best long wall needed for a Word Wall that could easily be seen by all the children. (All our rooms do, however, have the exact same Word Walls.) The smallest room actually had the largest carpeted, whole-group area that would work well for Guided Reading. The remaining space in the smaller room could be used for several small tables that could be used for partner reading, playschool groups, and book club groups. We then began to "pool" the classroom furniture that we each had and realized that by combining it and doing a bit of trading, we could furnish the three rooms nicely.

We jumped in at the beginning of the 1999-2000 year with the Guided Reading, Writing, and Working with Words Blocks. In February, all three of us attended Pat's workshop in Seattle. As we talked about what we heard that day, we decided to abandon our leveled groups and add the Self-Selected Reading Block.

Planning for Integration

After school was out, we packed up our rooms and the janitors moved us to our new space. During the summer, we planned. We had been asked to develop a curriculum map for our district's new social studies adoption. Our job was to look at the new first-grade social studies curriculum and plan how the main ideas and concepts could be interwoven into the other curricular areas of first grade. As we got excited about integrating, we wanted also to include science, so we ended up planning ways to integrate both science and social studies with our Guided Reading.

The PTA had given each grade level some money to use for social studies and science materials. We ordered reading materials at various levels that we could use for social studies, science, and Guided Reading. Because we were using one room for Guided Reading, we only needed to order one class set or one half-class set (for partner reading), or one big book. That saved a lot of money and allowed us to order more! We also went through our current basal series, our previous series, and big books to find selections that fit in with our social studies and science curriculum map for the year. Of course, not all of our Guided Reading could be integrated with social studies and science, but we found that much of it could be!

Mapping and perspective were two important concepts from our social studies curriculum. In addition to our big book social studies text, we used *Me On the Map, Maps,* and *As the Crow Flies* during Guided Reading to teach these social studies concepts. Another concept from our social studies curriculum is "Our Country and Its Heroes." We did shared reading with a big book version of *Young George Washington,* read *Honest Abe,* and used some reproducible selections about other American heroes. We then did book club groups using five different Troll First Start Biographies—*Young Helen Keller, Young Orville and Wilbur Wright, Young Amelia Earhart, Young Jackie Robinson,* and *Young Clara Barton*. We later used the book club format again with our science study of wetlands. The books we used were *Ducks Don't Get Wet, Beaver Stream, Tale of a Tadpole, Dragonflies,* and *It's Best To Leave a Snake Alone.*

In addition to informational books, we found some fiction books which tied into our social studies and science units and included these during Guided Reading. We read *The Very Hungry Caterpillar* and *I Know an Old Lady Who Swallowed a Fly* during our insect unit, and did an author study using some of Jan Brett's more "wintry" books (*The Mitten, The Hat, Annie and the Wild Animals, The Wild Christmas Reindeer,* etc.) during our weather unit.

Because we wanted the children to learn the differences between fiction and nonfiction, we tried to include one of each book whenever possible. During our fall unit, for example, we used both the fiction big book, *Pumpkin, Pumpkin* and the non-fiction big book, *From Peanuts to Peanut Butter.*

We also found many books we could read aloud to our students which would tie into our units. In the fall, we read books about hibernation, apples, pumpkins, and fall holidays. In addition to the biographies we read during Guided Reading, we read some more sophisticated biographies. We read aloud all of Eric Carle's insect stories as we studied insects.

Integrating science and social studies with Guided Reading and Teacher Read-Alouds seemed like a daunting task, but when we got right down to it, we discovered many wonderful books and found that the hard part was not finding the books, but choosing which ones we could take the time to read. Later in the year, when we began Self-Selected Reading, we included in the book tubs many unit-related books which we didn't have time to read aloud. Many children gravitated to these books and chose them to read and share.

Making the Schedule

With the curriculum mapping done, we were ready to schedule our Four-Blocks. Once we were given our recess, lunch, and specials schedule (we have 30 minutes of P.E., music, or library per day), we began to put our day together. We wanted it to flow smoothly and the transitions to be quick.

We all spend the first hour and 40 minutes in our own rooms. We do a morning math/calendar activity (20 minutes) and Self-Selected Reading (40 minutes). We then stay in our own rooms for our next block—the one that is done in that particular room. For example, my room is the Guided Reading room, so I do that block next. Tracy does Writing, and Connie does Working with Words because that is what is housed in their rooms.

After this second block, there is a recess break. When the children come in from recess, they know to automatically go to the next room. My kids and I go to Tracy's room for Writing; Connie and her kids go to my room for Guided Reading; Tracy and her kids go to Connie's room for Working with Words. After that, there is time for one final block before lunch. The kids move quickly and are prepared for what's next when they get there. It is fun for the kids to see their friends go and come, and it is a joy for teachers to briefly touch base if need be to give quick suggestions about any lesson changes or to relate a memorable moment! It is a quick, but welcome break for all!

When we enter a room, everything is set up and ready to go. The books are set out and ready for Guiding Reading, with a clean sheet of paper on the easel and anything else needed for the lesson on the tables. I set that up for my class first thing in the morning since we were the first to do Guided Reading. Each teacher, with help from the kids, is responsible for setting the room up for the next class.

The overhead is ready for the Working with Words Block, with the new Word Wall words on cards ready to talk about. Pencils and red pens are on the tables. Anything needed for a Words activity or an "on-the-back" is there and ready. (Connie sets that up for us, and we each return it to the original condition when we leave.) The writing supplies, folders, and anything else needed for the Writing Block that day are ready in Tracy's room.

The transitions are very smooth. You would think we would lose teaching time, but just the opposite is true. Because the children know the transitions so well, putting away and moving is quick and easy. (It has to be, you have another class on your tail!) It also keeps us teachers from extending the block and therefore not getting everything in that day. The move is a chance to wiggle, and because the children know what is next, they are mentally ready for the next block. We actually think we gain 10 to 15 minutes each day!

In the afternoon, we also run "blocks." One room is for whole-group math, one for math centers, and the third room has centers for other curricular areas including science, social studies, art, and health. Children and teachers rotate through these rooms, just like in the morning. We then have our specials and a short choice time.

Three Teachers Collaborate and Make Maximum Use of Space, Materials, and Time •••••••••••••••••••••••••••••••••••••

Planning and Organizing

Getting this to work smoothly does take a lot of planning! The planning and organization were much more tedious at the beginning of the year when we were really feeling our way. Now, things are easier. We meet for a big planning meeting every Wednesday after school. That is a sacred time for us, and we try very hard not to let anything interfere with it. At that time, we plan each block (day by day) for the next week. Some of our planning time is spent looking beyond the next week, particularly when we are beginning a new unit. We choose our Guided Reading selections, plan before and after reading activities, and decide how the selections will be read.

We choose next week's Word Wall words and plan the week's activities for the Working with Words Block. Some of these activities need be prepared only once for all of us to use. For others, such as Tongue Twisters or Guess the Covered Word sentences in which we use our children's names, we each plan our own. We discuss the writing our children are doing, but we plan our minilessons individually to meet the needs of our own classes. The same is true for Self-Selected Reading. We choose some books that everyone reads—books to be recycled into the Working with Words Block for Rounding Up the Rhymes, and books tied to our science and social studies units. Other books we choose ourselves (although when we find a particularly good read-aloud, we usually end up passing it to each other, knowing that all our children will enjoy it).

We also jointly plan our whole-group math lessons and our centers. We decide on various homework assignments. During our planning meeting, we divide up all the preparation work. At first, we each just took various jobs, making sure they all got done. Now, that has fallen into a pattern as we have found what we each enjoy doing and don't enjoy doing. Some jobs are best done together, and we do that as well.

In addition to our weekly planning meeting, we are always talking and planning—before and after school and during lunch and breaks. It is so nice to be able to talk over how lessons went and how we should modify for the next day (or next 10 minutes!). It is also wonderful to get each others' advice on how we can teach specific students.

True Stories from Four-Blocks™ Classrooms

Involving Parents

We have a good group of parent helpers. Planning a few days ahead lets us prepare the things that they can do to help us. For example, after we choose the Making Words word(s) for the next week, one of the parent helpers gets our individual folders all stuffed and ready (we only need one set because we share them).

We each do our own weekly newsletter, featuring our own children and their work, but some things are included in all our newsletters. Once every month or two, for example, we write a curriculum reflection for parents. Each of us writes about a different curricular area, and parents find out what we are doing in all areas. I think the parents appreciate knowing that all our first-graders are getting basically the same curriculum.

Getting Started

I had to look back at plans to remember how we began implementing the movement with the children at the beginning of the year. I had thought we did it gradually, but as I look back, we really just jumped right in on the second day of school! The children loved the set-up and adapted easily. We moved with our children from room to room, but kept the individual classes together so that each small community could develop. We wanted the students to develop comfort and safety with their own teacher. We did the names activities described in *Month-by-Month Phonics for First Grade*, including the personal interviews and writing about each child. This really helped the children feel like they knew each other, and they developed a sense of "family."

Once each class had "bonded," we began to bring the three classes together as a whole community for some activities. Our first social studies unit focused on our school community. We began that study by developing our own neighborhood community. Each class named themselves (Investigation Corner, Discovery Place, Exploration Lane), and we wrote and learned a community song about our neighborhood.

We read them many books about being and making friends, including *Friends, The Rainbow Fish, The Best Way To Play, The Meanest Thing To Say, Howdi Do,* and *It's Mine!* For Guided Reading, we read *The More We Get Together, Sing, Sing, Sing a Song,* and *The Little Red Hen.*

We opened up all the rooms for their afternoon choice time, and the children moved freely through these rooms during that time. While the children spent most of the day with their own teacher, we occasionally divided the children up into "mixed class" groups for a special activity or project with each teacher taking a different group. The children soon felt at home in their own rooms, and in the other two rooms as well. They had no doubt about which teacher "belonged to them," but they also felt comfortable with the other two teachers.

Looking Forward to Next Year

Our space makes our set-up ideal. However, we have so enjoyed working together this year and feel that the children have benefited so much, that even if we were to move back to regular rooms, we would run our program as much the same way as we could (that is, if we could have rooms that were close to each other). The children would not be able to leave and enter a classroom at the same time like we do now, but with some adjustments, they would learn the routine, and it could be done. It would be entirely worth the extra effort!

We are looking forward to beginning the year with all of the Four-Blocks in place at the beginning of next year. We are a little apprehensive about this since we had leveled groups until February this year, but we are planning to use many of the kindergarten activities from *The Teacher's Guide to Building Blocks™*, as well as the activities in the August/September chapter of *Month-by-Month Phonics for First Grade*. Our children all read and wrote so well at the end of this year when we were learning the framework as we were teaching it, we can't wait to see how they do next year!

A "Techie" Meets First Grade and Four-Blocks™ •••

by Joe Fuhrmann (with Pat Cunningham)

I remember distinctly the phone call from Kankakee asking me to come and work with them to implement the Four-Blocks™ framework. I was way over-committed and was waiting for an appropriate pause so that I could graciously "beg off." At some point in the conversation, I asked if Kankakee had a lot of mobility. Student mobility is a big hindrance to providing good literacy instruction, and I was preoccupied with it at that point in time. "Kankakee has almost one-third turnover every year," the principal explained. "But it is mostly within district, and that is why we need a consistent frame-work in all our schools." I was hooked and soon found myself on two airplanes and one long car trip going to Kankakee.

Kankakee is a small district with high in-district mobility and a large percentage of children on free or reduced price lunch. In the 1998-99 school year, they implemented Four-Blocks and Building Blocks™ in their three primary schools. Joe Fuhrmann was returning to the classroom that year after three years as Technology Coordinator. His story reveals how an experienced teacher, new to first grade, implements the framework and extends himself to helping others implement through face-to-face and across-the-Internet interactions. Here is Joe's story, along with lots of Web sites for you to explore at your leisure.

My Four-Blocks™ story begins in the summer of 1998, as I was looking forward to returning to the classroom. I had spent the past three years as a Technology Coordinator. The work was interesting, and I learned a lot about computers and networks, but I missed having my own classroom. I eagerly awaited the beginning of the school year and the chance to once again teach third-graders. During the summer, I reread all of the stories in our reading series and scanned through some of the wonderful lessons I had developed. It was going to be a great year!

Suddenly in mid-August, 10 days before the start of school, I was asked to meet with my principal. She greeted me with a warm smile, and we chatted a little about our summer and our families. Then, she came to the true reason for our meeting. A first-grade position was available, and she wanted me to take it! After 19 years of teaching, I felt very comfortable going into almost any second-, third-, or fourth-grade classroom. I had some experience with first-graders as the

Technology Coordinator, but it wasn't all positive. I didn't think first grade was where I belonged, but I could tell that it was where my principal wanted me, so I reluctantly agreed. I went home and spent the weekend wondering what I had gotten myself into. I took some consolation in the fact that the other first-grade teachers were terrific teachers, and I could count on them for encouragement, suggestions, and support. I looked forward to seeing them on Monday when we would all be attending a district workshop about something called Four-Blocks.

Over the next two days. I listened intently as Pat Cunningham presented us with a framework for the best practices in reading and writing. Her framework, called Four-Blocks, provided a structure for developing literacy using multiple methods. It provided for the differing levels of the children and their diverse learning styles. She talked of a balance between teacher-centered and student-centered blocks. Four-Blocks seemed so practical and provided a framework for the best practices in reading and writing I believed in. The suggested time limits for each block would make sure that I did not overstress any one way of developing literacy. I was hooked. I went home very excited. Needless to say, I felt much better about the upcoming school year. The other first-grade teachers were also excited, and we spent a great deal of our break times brainstorming ideas for implementing the Four-Blocks.

My First Weeks of First Grade and Four-Blocks™

On the first day of school, 26 excited children entered my room. We only had a half-day of school that day, but I was determined to accomplish two things. First, I started the "Getting to Know You" activities I read about in *Month-by-Month Phonics for the First Grade*. I was the interviewee. We cheered the letters of my name. The class, with my help, read the interview questions from the pocket chart, and I provided the answers. Later on, we used the answers I provided to fill in the blanks of a pocket chart story I had created earlier. The class became really excited when I told them each day we would interview a different person until everybody had a chance to be the interviewee.

Second, I started the Writing Block. For my minilesson, I wrote about how scared I was on this first day of first grade. I wrote it on chart paper with the children sitting on the floor around the easel. The children loved it. It was only three sentences long. After writing, I spent a few minutes drawing. I took out my pencil and traced in my simple drawing of a teacher at the chalkboard. Then, I colored it in.

After a brainstorming session about possible topics, the students went to their seats to write and draw something they wanted to tell me. As I walked the room, I noticed a wide range of abilities. Many children wrote a sentence or two, stretching out words to varying degrees. Some scribbled. Some wrote what I call "shopping list" stories (I like ____. I like ____.) Of course, a few had to be encouraged and coached.

After five minutes, they all were allowed either to finish their writing or draw a picture. To my amazement, most picked up a pencil to sketch in the drawing first. This made an immediate impression on me about the power of modeling. For years, I had tried to get my third- and fourth-graders to sketch drawings in pencil before adding color. My first-graders caught on just by watching me. Shortly before dismissal, the children shared their written and illustrated pieces. I was very pleased with their first attempts at writing.

At noon, the children went home. During lunch, my first-grade colleagues and I discussed the first day and Four-Blocks. The day had gone well for my colleagues, too, but they had many years of experience and lots of lesson plans and materials. They seemed to be planning on trying to combine what they had done in the past with the Four-Blocks™ framework. I, on the other hand, had no experience in first grade and nothing to give up. I believed that Four-Blocks could work, and I was determined to implement it to the best of my understanding.

As I began working with the blocks each day, I began to see the Four-Blocks as four fenced-in yards. In presenting each block each day, there were things I had to do—structures and procedures I needed to follow. These structures and procedures were the fences. At the same time, I still made many professional and personal decisions about what I did within each block— choosing the selections we read, choosing the follow-up activities, writing the Guess the Covered Word sentences, selecting what would be modeled during the writing minilesson, and many others. These choices are the yard I got to roam and play in. The Four-Blocks™ framework allowed me to make decisions about what to do within each block, as long I stayed within the structure (the fence) for each block.

During those first weeks, many exciting things happened. Student interviews were conducted every day, and follow-up stories were created. The stories were then put into a book, which was sent home with each student to share with his or her parents. The student names and responses from the interviews were used to learn many important concepts about sounds, letters, and words. Predictable charts were created for a wide variety of subjects. These charts were later used to make class books, which were placed in the class library. We also created a class ABC book. I was so proud of the students' collaborative work that I posted it to the school's Web site (Link #1 on *www.JoesStory.nethop.com*).

Parents' Night

Having the ability to create things on a computer is a lot of fun, however, it can lead to being asked to do a lot of extra things. One of those extra things was a request from my principal for a PowerPoint presentation about Four-Blocks for Parents' Night in late September. I pulled together the limited resources I had at the time—my notes, the book *Implementing the 4-Blocks™ Literacy Model,* and the *Month-by-Month* books. Of course, being the "techie" that many accuse me of being, I did a search on the Internet. To my amazement, I found Pat Cunningham's and Dottie Hall's Web site (Link #2 on *www.JoesStory.nethop.com*). Creating the PowerPoint presentation started becoming a positive experience.

The presentation went well, even though it ran 15 minutes too long. (I tried my best, but couldn't provide an overview of Four-Blocks in 15-20 minutes.) I thought other people would like to have access to what I had created. The result of that brainstorm was the beginnings of the Four-Blocks Web site which I have managed ever since (Link #3 on *www.JoesStory.nethop.com*).

The Year Continues

Soon, weeks turned into months, and a pattern starting developing in my implementation of Four-Blocks. In Guided Reading, I made sure that for three days a week, we read an on-grade-level selection. On the other two days, we read an easier selection. I also started developing a repertoire of comprehension activities that I modeled, and then, to an ever-increasing degree, allowed children to do in their flexible groups. These activities included story maps, sequence activities, and character maps. Later, I added completing Cloze summaries, which led to the students writing their own summaries during the Writing Block. I began these activities before we read and tried to follow up on these activities at the end of each day's Guided Reading Block. I soon realized how easily time got away from us. It was then that I bought an electronic kitchen timer. I also trained the children to help me remember to set the timer. Not only did I stay within the time constraints, but the children learned some time concepts, too.

The Writing Block was always an exciting time in the class. I am still amazed at how quickly the children started developing fluency. Sharing seemed to foster many wonderfully creative pieces. Of course, much modeling had to be done. Many students got caught in the "shopping list"-type stories. It took many days of modeling how to elaborate before the children tried it themselves. The Writing Block was the class's favorite block. They simply loved to share their stories at the end of each day. But Friday was their favorite day of all. Fridays were DoodleLoops Day. We turned our writing upside-down. We drew first, using the DoodleLoops materials, and then we wrote (Link #4 on *www.JoesStory.nethop.com*).

The words and strategies acquired by the children during the Working with Words Block were being applied to other reading and writing activities. Different chants/cheers were done routinely on different days (many which are listed at Link #5 on *www.JoesStory.nethop.com*). A routine was also developed for On-The-Back and the other Working with Words activities. As it turned out, I liked Making Words and a modified Rounding Up the Rhymes activity, and the children were more excited about Guess the Covered Word and Word Wall.

Christmas arrived along with a new computer at home. Needless to say, I spent a little of my vacation time on the Internet. I don't like doing useless searches, so one day I entered Four-Blocks into my search engine. The search lead me to the Teachers.Net Four-Blocks mailring (Link #6 on *www.JoesStory.nethop.com*). I soon discovered an international community of fellow Four-Blocks teachers. Ever since that day, I have routinely read the 50 or more messages received each day. My students and I have benefited from the many fantastic ideas and solutions that have been garnered from the mailring. I also found many other helpful resources at Teachers.Net. Most noteworthy was Cheryl Sigmon's "Sifting & Sorting Through the 4-Blocks™ Literacy Model" articles (Link #7 on *www.JoesStory.nethop.com*). These practical articles deal with questions and topics that have surfaced on the mailring or at various conferences.

During Christmas break I also started to create some of my Four-Blocks materials on my computer. I redid my Word Wall words using a 200-point size of the Century Gothic font and posted them to the net (Link #8 on *www.JoesStory.nethop.com*). I also made and posted the materials for the Making Words activities listed in *Month-by-Month Phonics for First Grade* (Link #9 on *www.JoesStory.nethop.com*).

January, February, and March were very exciting times in the classroom. The children made gigantic steps in becoming fluent readers and writers. The excitement in the classroom was contagious. The school's Reading Recovery program provided a critical intervention during these months. Many students just needed a few weeks of this intense one-on-one instruction to make big leaps in their reading abilities. Reading Recovery and Four-Blocks are very compatible.

That final day in June was fast approaching. I was busy completing my end of the year Developmental Reading Assessments and selecting student work to place in their portfolios. It was amazing to see their growth in reading and writing. My first-grade colleagues and I agreed that the students we were sending to second grade were the most fluent readers and writers ever produced at our school. I found myself looking forward to the next year. I learned so much, and of course, there were many things I wanted to add or do differently.

Summer, 1999

During the summer I changed hats and moved to the school district's Information Systems department and became a full-time "techie" for approximately two months. One of my many jobs during the Summer of '99 was to create Web sites which would be utilized by the teachers and students of the Kankakee School District. I knew a Web site providing information and support for our district-wide K-3 Four-Blocks initiative would be extremely appropriate. I developed some of its initial content and then set the Web site aside as the school year approached.

In July, Pat Cunningham and Dottie Hall came to Kankakee for two days of workshops. Each grade level spent a day with one of them. Pat presented to the first-grade teachers. She outlined the transition activities we should do to move children from their kindergarten Building Blocks™ experience to the Four-Blocks™ framework in our classrooms (Link #9 on *www.JoesStory.nethop.com*). The presentation helped me plan for the beginning of the next school year.

My Second Year of First Grade and Four-Blocks™

Soon, it was the beginning of the new school year. This year, I had 23 excited children. I made sure to use the transition suggestions provided by Pat and added some of my own. I thought maybe we could move into the Working with Words Block routine in a gradual manner. So, the first week we began the Word Wall with only two words (I, like). The next week we added three new words to the

Word Wall (this, is, my). The third week we added four new words (we, can, see, the). I selected these words because they went with the predictable, patterned blackline mini-books from *25 Emergent Reader Mini-Books*, which I was using for Guided Reading. We used these words in writing our Predictable Charts, and the children immediately got in the habit of using the Word Wall as they did their daily writing. (These lessons can be found at Link #10 on *www.JoesStory.nethop.com*).

Fred the Frog is an important character in our class, and this year he was introduced as part of the names activity on the very first day. Fred is a puppet that often speaks to children. Every year we write about Fred. Last year's class wrote a book about Fred, so I of course read this to the children during the teacher read-aloud part of Self-Selected Reading. Some students chose to write about Fred. Even on the first day of school, it was easy to incorporate a simple theme across some of the Four-Blocks. (The students' "Meet Fred the Frog" can be found at Link #11 on *www.JoesStory.nethop.com*).

By late September, a routine for each of the Four-Blocks was established in the classroom. Having the past year's experience certainly helped. Of course, some tweaking was needed because every group of children is different. In fact, this group of children was different every week for the first two months of school. I had six students move away and six students move in. The new students adapted quickly. The multilevel approach of Four-Blocks and the repetitive nature of some of the activities certainly helped. It also was apparent that the structure that had been developed created a great deal of student confidence. In turn, the students' confidence resulted in their ability to provide an unusual amount of help and encouragement in assisting the new students to adjust to our classroom.

Again this year, the Writing Block became the class's favorite block. The children seemed to energize each other as they came to respect and enjoy the creativity, humor, and experiences of their classmates. One example of this is the Writing Block activity we did for the 100th day of school (Link #12 on *www.JoesStory.nethop.com*). After posting this activity on the Four-Blocks mailring, we received nearly 80 comments from Alaska to Colombia (South America). It was exciting to read the messages and mark the sender's location on a map each day.

Just before the break, the school district presented me with an unexpected Christmas present. They sent me, along with two principals and another teacher, to the Four-Blocks Leadership Conference in North Carolina over the Martin Luther King, Jr. weekend. It was a great conference. The assumption was that the attendees were already aware of and practiced in the basics of Four-Blocks and involved in helping others implement Four-Blocks. The presentations were designed to move the participants to the next level in the understanding and practice of Four-Blocks. There were lots of topics to pick and choose from. The ones that helped me most were Pat Cunningham's discussion of coaching by the teacher and students to help children decode unknown words, Jim Cunningham's thought-provoking presentation on the Writing Block, and Dottie Hall's talk about creating focus groups in our schools and districts to support the implementation of Four-Blocks. I also learned more about kindergarten and Building Blocks™ from Elaine Williams's presentations. (Notes from this conference have been posted to the Web, see Link #13 on *www.JoesStory.nethop.com*).

Another outgrowth of the Leadership Conference was the beginning of conducting focus groups in our school district. These discussion groups on a pre-specified topic were led by Keri Romaneghi, the other teacher to attend the Leadership Conference, and myself. We would bring information to a group of 5–10 teachers to launch a discussion. The result was an awesome collaborative session of brainstorming, troubleshooting, and encouraging. In order to stay on task for an hour and fifteen minutes, we made an agreement with the group to deal with issues other than the topic at hand during the final 15 minutes of our gathering. We held two focus group meetings, one on conferencing and one on coaching, during early spring. We intend to continue these focus groups next year and have selected three topics (comprehension activities to use during Guided Reading, grade-level, appropriate mini-lessons for the Writing Block, and preparing for the state writing assessment) to get us started.

Late April found me headed for Indianapolis and my first International Reading Association national meeting. Teachers and administrators from 11 school districts presented their experiences implementing the Four-Blocks at a preconvention session. I felt honored that our Elementary Curriculum Director asked me to be part of the Kankakee team. For many of the attendees, this was a bit of a reunion. We were old acquaintances through the Four-Blocks mailring, even if we had not seen each other face-to-face before. Our presentation seemed to be well-received by those in attendance (Link #14 on *www.JoesStory.nethop.com*).

After five exciting days at the IRA convention, I came home and made the following observations, which I shared on the mailring:

> I guess the biggest thing I took back with me is the confidence I gained after attending many sessions on teaching emergent and early fluent readers. They all promoted the practices you and I are doing through the implementation of 4-Blocks. It also was a lot of fun talking to people that have not heard of 4-Blocks. One person at my table during the luncheon today said, "I can tell it must work, you get really excited just talking about it!" From what I heard, many of you also have been spreading the word. Many people said something like; "I just was talking to somebody in the last meeting about that (Four-Blocks)!" I think it is great to be part of something so positive! Kids are learning to read and write all over the world because of 4 Blocks. That's exciting, and you and I are part of its success.

I returned home to once again do end-of-the-year assessments. This year, 80% of my class scored at or above grade level, and 33% of the class scored a full year or more above grade level. Even the children below grade level showed consistent improvement throughout the school year. Fortunately, our school district is participating in the Illinois Bridges program during the summer, and the program is using the Four-Blocks™ Model. It was wonderful to know that my children who had come so far, but were still below grade level, would get another six weeks of beneficial instruction.

Looking Forward to Next Year

Summer found me working as a Professional Development Provider (PDP) for the consortia of schools in my area that were involved in the Illinois Bridges program. As a PDP, I was able to hear Pat Cunningham speak for a third time in four months. To my surprise, I found myself still taking notes and gathering more ideas about improving my own Four-Blocks classroom. In giving my presentations and workshops this summer, I hope what I have learned and my excitement towards the Four-Blocks will encourage others to implement it in their classrooms (Link #15 on *www.JoesStory.nethop.com*).

I also have some goals for improving my Four-Blocks instruction in my own classroom next year. These include: developing a sequence of writing minilessons for use in my classroom and other first grades, improving my skills at conferencing with children during the Writing and Self-Selected Reading Blocks, and making a focused effort during the second half of the school year to train all children in the steps of Coaching to Decode Unknown Words. I also plan to explore the possible uses of computers during Four-Blocks (see Link #16) for a discussion of "The Use of Computers in the Four-Blocks Classroom."

Two years after attending a required workshop to learn about "something called Four-Blocks," I am still learning and still exploring the vast yards bordered by those fences.

Building Blocks™:
The Wonderful World of Kindergarten • • • • • • • • • • • • • • • • • • •

by Elaine Williams (with Dottie Hall)

Elaine met Pat many years ago when she took a graduate course in reading which Pat taught at Wake Forest University. This started Elaine's journey toward Building Blocks™, as she used the activities she heard about in that course to teach her kindergarten children about reading and writing. I met Elaine in 1988 when she came to teach at Clemmons Elementary, and we have worked together ever since! I will let Elaine tell you her story and the story of how Building Blocks™ was born.

In 1980, I began my career as a kindergarten teacher. My school was in the country, where cows grazed in the fields next door and huge oak trees covered the front lawn. Prior to coming to public school, I had taught in federally-funded preschool programs and was thrilled to have my own kindergarten class. Students bused from two downtown public housing projects, as well as from the nearby community, afforded me a classroom rich in cultural diversity. On the other hand, the school was labeled "at risk" due to the large number of students receiving free or reduced lunch. It was clearly going to be a challenge, but I was ready to change the world, one child at a time.

Every day I arrived at school early and stayed late preparing lesson plans, activities, and centers, as well as studying the North Carolina Standard Course of Study and the goals of the local school district. Those goals were focused on preparing children for the demands of first grade. The reading program consisted of learning the alphabet, beginning and ending sounds, some high-frequency words, and rebus reading. Students who mastered these basic skills were allowed to move into the preprimers and participate in the take-home reading program. I still shudder at remembering the scope and sequence of that particular reading curriculum.

The first unit focused on teaching the letters "F," "D," "M," and "G." I planned numerous activities to teach the letter "F" in addition to the lessons from the skills charts, workbooks, and worksheets. I added the letter people to my instruction, and the class made funny feet and went on a walk looking for things that had the "F" sound. I integrated autumn themes into reading; I took the class to the fair, where we found the fudge maker and subsequently were able to sample some delicious fudge. Thinking I had planned fun, educational activities, I frequently congratulated myself for going above and beyond the basal lesson plans.

However, when I assessed their learning, I discovered that while many of my students had easily mastered the letter "F," over thirty percent of my class, it seemed, had never been introduced to "Mr. F" at all! I also suspected that my top students knew all about the letter "F" before they arrived.

I was now forced to face the reality of the wide range of abilities in my kindergarten. My class was made up not only of redbirds and bluebirds, but also of buzzards, and I was beginning to lose sleep at night worrying about those buzzards!

I was also horrified to witness the way in which many of my students looked at books during our USSR (Uninterrupted Sustained Silent Reading) time. They were reading to themselves, but they held the books up as if showing the pictures to others. I realized that they were mimicking the way I read to the class. It was obvious that they had not been read to at home, and they were unfamiliar with the concept of translating words on a page to spoken words. I began poring over all available resources in an effort to find a better way to teach letters and sounds to kindergarten students.

What I Learned from Pat

I signed up for a reading course at Wake Forest University taught by someone named Patricia Cunningham. Although unfamiliar with her work, I was eager for any opportunities to learn, and it didn't hurt that I was an avid Wake Forest fan. At the first class meeting, she talked about ways to teach young children to read without first having to teach readiness. She showed us a tape of her teaching a "Structured Language Experience" lesson to a group of "unready" kindergarteners, and my life was changed forever. I could see the pitfalls in my previous methods of teaching letters and sounds. My students needed to see that words are made up of letters, and that people read from left to right. They needed to know an essential language concept—what you say can be written and what is written can be read. Dr. Cunningham advocated letting young children dictate and "read" their texts, and *then* focusing on sentences, words, letters, and sounds. A great deal of my students' inability to comprehend basic reading concepts was a result of the lack of literacy experiences in their environment.

I thought of my goddaughter, Eleanor, who understood when she was only a year old the links between talking, writing, and reading. During dinner at a Greek restaurant with her mother and me, Eleanor became bored with her toys. Her mother gave her a check deposit slip and a pen. Eleanor scribbled as most babies do, but then she picked up the slip and proceeded to "read" it: "de do ba ba ta." I was amazed! Eleanor already knew a lot more than so many of my students because she had lived for ten months in a world filled with words and books, raised by parents who were English majors and journalists. In contrast to the children I taught, reading and writing were a part of Eleanor's daily experience. I realized that this was what was necessary for my students. They needed to be saturated with words and books, and they needed to be exposed to the kind of print-rich environment they may not have ever known.

Back in my classroom, I modeled the structured language experience approach step-by-step. My students began READING! They could now read some or all of the charts, and even my "buzzards" were dictating and reading their own sentences with pride. They no longer had to be segregated into ability-based groups, but could be taught as a whole because the instruction was multilevel. Regardless of their level, each child could learn something from the reading and writing provided in the structured language-experience method. The self-esteem of my children skyrocketed. A miracle had taken place, and I felt that my students had been transported out of darkness into the light.

I learned a key phrase from Pat Cunningham: "1,000 hours of literacy experiences." That is the prior experience which children who easily learn to read enter kindergarten with. Most of my students had not had 100 hours of being read to and engaged in literacy encounters, much less 1,000!

I soon became a Cunningham groupie. I took more courses at Wake Forest, read her books, subscribed to *The Reading Teacher*, used her ideas, and practiced her methods daily in my classroom. As my years of teaching kindergarten went on, I began to receive praise from parents and recognition from other educators. What pleased me the most was that my students were finally excited about the world of reading. Reading was no longer the privilege of an exclusive kindergarten club for the chosen few, but an enjoyable experience which could be shared by all the students.

Working with Dottie

By 1988, I needed a change in my educational environment, and decided to apply for transfer to another school. Although I applied to five schools with strong leaders and good reputations, I was especially interested in Clemmons

Elementary because of the principal, Daisy Chambers, and the large size of the school, which I hoped would increase the chances of there being an opening. After several interviews, Daisy asked me to join the Clemmons team of intelligent, hardworking, and dedicated professionals. I found myself in awe of the professionalism and constantly found myself saying, "transferred to Clemmons…now in heaven!" I looked forward to meeting with the curriculum coordinator because I wanted her to know that I planned to integrate Pat Cunningham's methods into my curriculum. When I broached the subject, she just smiled and replied, "Of course you can do it! After all, Pat Cunningham is my friend and mentor!" My curriculum coordinator was Dr. Dottie Hall, the other half of the famous Cunningham and Hall duo. I had landed in a gold mine, and my life was about to change forever again.

During the next year, Dottie and a group of teachers began exploring alternative approaches to teaching reading. Under the leadership of Dottie Hall and Margaret Defee, the Four-Blocks™ Model was born just "down the road" from my classroom. As a kindergarten teacher, I began to examine our literacy program for ways in which it would support the Four-Blocks™ Model. I was already doing a lot of shared reading with big books, as well as a weekly predictable chart (structured language experience chart). Most of the writing, however, was done in the Writing to Read lab along with other parts of the IBM program.

It was time for a change, and with the Dottie's help, I began a writing program in kindergarten that incorporated three components: the writing center, journal writing, and coached writing. I became aware that I needed to do additional writing *for* my students, as well as writing *with* them. The first writing I added to the day was a morning message. Each morning, I wrote a message on chart paper while my students watched. I wrote about school and other events in our lives, and my students would read back sentences to me that I had read to them. I taught them about capitalization, punctuation, and other conventions of print. My class was asked to search the message for the longest and shortest words, rhyming words, and opposite words. I asked a few students each day to use pointers to track the print while reading the message aloud.

The most exciting part of the morning message was when children would circle the words on the chart they could read. Because they chose their own words, it was a non-threatening experience for my students. It soon became necessary to expand the variety of words in the morning message, because most of my students could read all of the text! They began to recognize the words we had used in the morning message when we read big books during shared reading. The combination of the morning message, predictable charts, and shared reading was much more successful than the "letter of the week" approach I had previously used.

The next addition to the kindergarten literacy program involved making the changes to the writing program. We stopped going to the Writing to Read Lab and began doing writing in the classroom. Writing center activities had always been a part of our curriculum, but now I examined very carefully the kinds of activities that would promote an interest in writing. I stopped focusing only on handwriting skills at the writing center and promoted children's writing. I filled the center with cards, stationery, envelopes, sticky notes, and all sizes and colors of paper and markers. The class loved communicating with each other, as well as with parents and teachers. I created monthly picture dictionary boards that centered on specific themes, as well as on the seasons and holidays. The class would copy some words and illustrations to make little books with great pride. I added other writing tasks that integrated the curriculum, but I always left plenty of time for children to write whatever they desired.

Journal writing was introduced right after the Christmas break. As I began the journal process, I wanted my students to know why and how people write, so I designed a lesson plan that actually demonstrated all of the stages of writing. Years earlier I had learned from Pat Cunningham that many students do not know the purpose for reading or writing, and it is important to discuss it. I also wanted a climate that promoted a respect for each child's writing, so I knew I had to dignify every stage of the writing process. I modeled drawing, scribbling, random letters, copying, letter-sound associations, invented spelling, words, phrases, and sentences. Promoting an atmosphere of freedom to take risks, I believed that the students should pick their own writing topics each day. I felt strongly that they could write best about what interested them, instead of using writing prompts. I also started using unlined paper so that no one would be frustrated by handwriting.

Dottie was instrumental in helping me to understand that there was no need to edit kindergarten writing, and that it was fine to publish their writing with their own phonetic spelling. She explained that my children would take risks as authors if they did not have to worry about correct spelling, and that many kindergartners would not be able to read their own stories if they were edited. Dottie continually advised me to be a cheerleader for what children can do—not an editor for what they can not do!!

Now, years later, this philosophy continues to drive my instruction. I was amazed at the writing progress of my class. Every stage of writing was taking place in my classroom, and the children moved up to the next stage when they were ready. It was easy to see the influence of the daily morning message instruction on the students' writing. Students often wrote their own morning message for a journal entry. They usually spelled high-frequency words correctly in their journals—particularly those words I used again and again in writing our morning messages. I was pleased with the writing progress, but at times, I felt like my students could do more.

I discussed my concerns with Pat Cunningham, and she helped me add "a little something" which made a big difference. What I had been doing was putting everyone's journals on the tables and having them write as soon as they entered the room. After they wrote, I would have a few share their writing each day. Pat suggested that I gather the children for big group first and model writing "something I wanted to tell them."

So, I added an eight-minute, big group minilesson in which I modeled how to think of something to write and then wrote it. The students were always eager to read what I was telling them. They also loved helping me sound out my words, and we talked about capitalization and punctuation. Before dismissing the class to begin their writing, I would check in with them and ask what would they be writing about today. Everyone left big group on a mission to write, and it helped to eliminate students sitting at their tables doing very little at writing time. After adding this step to my daily journal writing, I saw huge progress, especially in content areas. Students seemed more focused in staying on a topic rather than just writing lots of random thoughts. It was amazing to me that such a simple eight-minute (or less) activity could be so powerful.

Last year, one of the student teachers at Clemmons took over for a teacher on maternity leave after Christmas. One afternoon, she examined some of my students' journals and asked for some advice on how to motivate and promote journal writing. I explained my own experiences and how Pat had rescued me. After a week of doing this with her students, she came rushing into my room and exclaimed, "Wow, that modeling and asking them what they plan to write really works!"

In the spring, I added the final component to my writing program. During center time, I worked with each student individually for about ten minutes each week. This small amount of time was designed for me to see exactly what each student knew about words, letters, and sounds. I would "coach" their attempts at writing about topics they chose. After coaching for several weeks, many students knew exactly how to sound out words. Others were ready to create simple stories with a beginning, middle, and an ending. I found other students were ready to learn something about describing words, details, and opening and closing sentences. These short, individual coaching sessions really helped me move all the children along in writing from wherever they were as far as they could go.

After a student wrote a simple five-sentence story, I would publish it in book form. The students would illustrate the pages, and I would help them with the dedication and "about the author" pages. I began celebrating the year of literacy in kindergarten each May by having a "Young Authors Tea." The students selected a published book to read aloud to the parents, followed by an old-fashioned tea party.

Each year, I still get a little emotional as I watch each child read with pride. I think about where the year started on this journey of literacy and where the journey has ended. Every year there is a wide range of reading and writing levels in my class and it confirms that Building Blocks™ is a multilevel program. I shudder to think about all the time I wasted teaching isolated sounds and sight words, and I still seek forgiveness for the error of my ways. The students' genuine writing samples have given me a mirror to see exactly what they know about phonics and what skills I need to teach during shared reading, predictable charts, morning message, or environmental print lessons.

Spreading the Word

It wasn't long before Clemmons School was on the map as a Four-Blocks and Building Blocks™ Model School, and people were coming from all over the United States to observe instruction. Dottie coordinated visitation days and conducted seminars and workshops with Pat all over the country. The Southeastern United States became a primary focus for training, and during the 1996 school year, Cheryl Sigmon asked me to work with some kindergarten teachers in South Carolina.

I vividly remember my first consulting experience. Leaving at 4:30a.m., I gazed at a beautiful crescent moon and wondered what in the world I was doing! In

South Carolina, I worked with teachers and children in several schools where most of the children lived in poverty and had few literacy experiences when they entered kindergarten. As I worked with the teachers and children, I knew what I was doing. Literacy is not an exclusive club for the chosen few in America— literacy is for everyone. The wonderful teachers and children of South Carolina touched me deeply and are in my heart forever. I noticed over and over again while consulting that I was learning so much from other teachers, and it was exciting to validate the strengths of Building Blocks™. I soon traded my old, "not-too-reliable" car for a new one and traveled all over South Carolina, spreading the "Gospel of Cunningham and Hall" and avoiding "catfish stew."

In 1998, I began consulting with Educational Resources Group, and I continued to marvel that large groups of educators filled hotel rooms to learn about Building Blocks™. After all, I am just a kindergarten teacher. I have learned that being a kindergarten teacher brings authenticity to my training, and twenty plus years in the classroom is valued and appreciated. Last year, Dottie asked me to co-author *The Teacher's Guide to Building Blocks™*. It was an honor and a privilege to write with Dottie and share Building Blocks™ with educators. I have come a long way since the days of Mr. Funny Feet and the letter-of-the-week routine. Now my classroom is filled with reading and writing activities that have meaning. I still get upset when I see kindergarten students doing mindless rote activities that involve copying on lined paper and other skill-and-drill worksheets. It is my hope that kindergarten students will be successful and find great joy in reading and writing. Where will Building Blocks™ take me in the twenty-first century? It's time to buy a new car and see where the journey takes me!

Four-Blocks™ and FROG

by Dottie Hall and Pat Cunningham

When Four-Blocks™ began at Clemmons Elementary School in 1989, 25-30% of the students were labeled "at risk." Some schools, both in Winston-Salem and around the country, are almost a mirror image of these statistics. The first school to really look at what was happening at Clemmons and adapt Four-Blocks to change its instructional program was an "at risk" school across town, Easton Elementary. Near the end of the pilot year, Connie Prevatte, the curriculum coordinator at Easton, heard about what was happening in Margaret's classroom and came to visit. Connie was looking for a way—any way—to get the students at Easton reading and writing and to get their annual test scores out of the "cellar."

She observed Margaret teaching the Four-Blocks and thought this framework would benefit the students at Easton. All summer, Connie worked to design a new instructional program for Easton based on the Four-Blocks™ framework. She made some adaptations because of the population Easton served and the Title I and other support available there. She reconfigured the Title I program, which had been a pullout program serving the lowest-achieving children, into a program which would give reading support to all first- and second-graders. She named this extra support FROG (Facilitating Reading for Optimum Growth).

Several years later, Connie left Easton, and Margaret Defee, the Four-Blocks pilot teacher, went to Easton to become the curriculum coordinator. While at Easton, Margaret fine-tuned both the Four-Blocks™ Literacy Model and FROG. Many of the original teachers have left Easton for one reason or another, but they remember what it was like before Four-Blocks and FROG, and how it changed after. This is the story of how one "at risk" school implemented Four-Blocks and FROG, and how these changes benefited the entire school community.

Easton Elementary, a small school situated southeast of the center of Winston-Salem, was once a school in trouble. Many of Easton's students came from homes with limited book experiences and difficult home situations. Prior to Four-Blocks™ and FROG, the students scored low on state mandated achievement tests and had poor attendance records. The parents were not a part of the school and often viewed the school with hostility. Poverty was common, and approximately 80% of the children qualified for free or reduced price meals. The majority of the students were working below grade level. Behavior problems consumed valuable teaching time. The teachers were working hard, but their instruction seemed fruitless.

Teachers taught reading with a basal and had three or four reading groups in each classroom. No matter how many groups the teacher had, it seemed as though some students did not fit in any of these groups. The children knew who was "smart" and who was not. The children in the lowest groups were difficult to motivate and teach. The biggest problem was not teaching the group, but what the other children did while waiting for their group's turn to read. The children had a hard time doing anything independently. Worksheets and workbook pages were hurried through—if the children could do them at all. Centers were "played" in; discipline was a problem!

Easton, like many other schools with large numbers of poor children, had a pullout Title I program. They had several Title I teachers, but still could not provide reading remediation for all the children who needed it. Worse yet, the children receiving the pullout instruction were not making much progress—often not meeting the minimum goals set by the Title I program.

Teachers at Easton were committed to making changes because of their frustration over the lack of student success. When Connie Prevatte described to teachers what she had seen in Margaret's classroom and how she thought Four-Blocks and FROG could better meet the needs of all their students, teachers did not hesitate to give the new programs a try. Reading groups were abolished and pullout programs were eliminated. The new schedule for first- and second-grade classes included daily instruction in reading using a grade-level basal (Guided Reading Block), reading on the student's own level from individual copies of trade books and emergent readers (Self-Selected Reading Block), writing (Writing Block), and daily Word Wall practice (Working with Words Block). It also included 45 minutes of FROG. The new schedule and instructional changes began on the very first day of school in the fall of 1990. Staff development began the week before school started and continued all year long as the teachers were supported in change.

FROG

FROG was designed to provide the small-group instruction needed to assure the success of all students. The roles of existing personnel in the school were redefined to provide the necessary number of teachers to implement the program. Title I and other special teachers converged upon each classroom for 45 minutes each day. The students in each class were divided into small heterogeneous groups that included one strong reader, two or three average readers, and one struggling reader.

FROG groups received daily intensive instruction with one of the FROG teachers or the classroom teacher. This instruction included those components of the Four-Blocks that the teachers felt could be better carried out in small groups. Each FROG session included four ten-minute components.

One part of the FROG lesson included WEB (Wildly Exciting Books) time. The children brought a book to their FROG group that they had read previously during their classroom Self-Selected Reading time. Each child read aloud a little from the book he or she had brought. Often the FROG teacher set a focus for discussion, asking each child to think about characters, setting, plot, theme, mood, and other elements of literature. When children brought informational books, they discussed the most interesting things they had learned from these books. The first- and second-graders at Easton were still engaging in Self-Selected Reading in their class-rooms, choosing and reading their books and having their weekly conference with their teacher. FROG assured that each child got to share a little from a self-selected book every day. The children were very motivated by getting to share each day at the beginning of FROG. It was delightful to watch them gathering with their FROG teachers as they came to pick them up in their classrooms—every child with a book in hand, prepared to read and share a little from that book.

After the sharing of self-selected books, each FROG group participated in the shared reading of a big book. One book was used in a variety of ways for a whole week. Children learned to "picture walk" through the book and to make predic-tions. Teachers taught print concepts, sequencing skills, and any other skills ap-propriate for a particular big book. Children read and reread each book, using a variety of shared, echo, and choral reading formats. By the end of the week, most of the time, all the children in the group could fluently read the big book. This provided the children at Easton with a successful experience with reading every day. As the year went on, the number of big books (and little book versions, when available) they could read grew, as did their confidence in their own reading abilities.

In the classroom, teachers used the adopted basal reading series and trade books for the Guided Reading part of the Four-Blocks™ Model. As much as possible, FROG teachers selected big books through which they could teach the same skills that were included in the basal series' scope and sequence.

The third element of FROG was a Working with Words activity designed to help children learn to decode and spell. Classroom teachers did the Word Wall part of Working with Words with their whole class. Making Words, Guess The Covered Word, Rounding Up the Rhymes, and other decoding activities were done during the FROG lesson. The FROG teachers often selected the secret word for a Making Words lesson from the big book they were reading, or from a selection everyone was reading in the Guided Reading Block in the classroom. Because they only had 10-15 minutes for this component, they often made words one day and then did the sort and transfer step the following day.

First- and second-grade teachers at Easton worked extremely hard to have wonderful writing. The old Writing-to-Read lab was transformed into a writing lab, and each class went there daily for their Writing Block. The teacher did the minilesson, and children wrote on paper or at the computers (alternating who wrote where so that all children learned to write on paper and at the computer). An assistant was assigned to the computer lab to help children deal with computer and printer problems, so that the classroom teacher could concentrate her time conferencing with children about their writing. The writing lab had a Word Wall to support children's spelling of high-frequency words and a publishing center with all the materials needed to make books. Children and teachers looked forward to their daily trip to the writing lab, and wonderful writing was produced.

In addition to the daily self-selected writing done with the classroom teacher, each FROG session ended with a brief writing response to reading. Early in the year, children wrote one sentence responding to the big book. They often agreed on a sentence starter (My favorite part was. . .; The pig looked. . .; The mom wanted. . .; etc.). All children's sentences began the same, but they wrote their own ending. FROG teachers gave assistance as the children wrote. Because there was only one struggling reader in each group, that child could get individual coaching while writing during FROG each day.

As the year went on, children made more choices about what they would write. On some days, they wrote about the book they had shared during the WEB component of FROG, and on other days, they responded to the big book. The writing component of FROG was always writing in response to reading and looked like a learning log.

A Sample Day with Four-Blocks™ and FROG

9:00-9:30 Writing Block
Classroom teacher does a minilesson, modeling writing and teaching needed writing skills. Children write. While children write, teacher has writing conferences with individual children. Block ends with Author's Chair, with children sharing a piece they have written since their last day in Author's Chair.

9:30-9:45 Word Wall Practice
Classroom teacher leads all the children in practicing Word Wall words, including on-the-back activities to extend Word Wall patterns to other words.

9:45-10:30 FROG
FROG teachers come and pick up their FROG groups and take them to their FROG group space. Classroom teacher keeps her FROG group and does FROG in the classroom. Each heterogeneous FROG group does four activities:

- **Web (5-10 minutes)** Children read and talk about the book they read yesterday during classroom Self-Selected Reading.
- **Shared Reading (10-15 minutes)** Children and teacher read a big book which they reread every day that week. Comprehension and print-tracking skills are taught. Children develop confidence as they are almost always able to fluently read the book by the end of the week.
- **Working with Words (10-15 minutes)** Children participate in a Making Words, Guess the Covered Word, Rounding Up the Rhymes, or other activity to teach decoding and spelling patterns.
- **Writing (5-10 minutes)** Children write a sentence or two in response to reading. Teacher coaches children, giving a little extra attention to the struggling readers.

10:45-11:15 Guided Reading
Classroom teacher teaches Guided Reading to the whole class using a variety of materials, before- and after-activities and a variety of formats. Comprehension skills and strategies are taught and practiced.

1:00-1:30 Self-Selected Reading
Classroom teacher reads aloud to the class. Children read in their self-selected books and conference with the teacher.

FROG teachers' schedule:
    9:00-9:45 Mrs. Moss's first-grade class
    9:45-10:30 Mrs. Patrick's second-grade class
    10:30-11:15 Miss. Howie's first-grade class
    11:15-12:00 Ms. Revel's second-grade class

As teachers and children began to experience success with Four-Blocks and FROG, many other things changed at Easton. Attendance and discipline improved as children were engaged in meaningful teacher-directed activities in which they could find success. Parents saw their children succeeding and began to feel more positively toward the school. Easton initiated some "Family Fun" nights and parents began to come to school activities with their children.

The children seemed to enjoy the small group setting of FROG and working together as a community of learners during the Four-Blocks portion of the day. No child was labeled "better" or "worse" than any other child. All the children now thought they could read! Little by little, their test scores showed improvement—adding to everyone's feeling of success and reducing anxiety. (For more details and some data from the first year's of FROG and Four-Blocks at Easton, read "Eliminating Ability Grouping and Reducing Failure in the Primary Grades" in *No Quick Fix*.)

At Easton, FROG was often referred to as the "double dose" or "second dose" of reading that the children received each day. Reflecting on the Four-Blocks and FROG, it appears to be a perfect marriage, each supporting the other one hundred percent of the time. Many teachers who work in schools with similar demographics have visited Easton. The question most asked by visitors was which part was most important to the success of the children. The answer was, "We are still not willing to consider one without the other." The Four-Blocks approach is an effective delivery system of the instruction in reading and writing,. and the FROG model as an early intervention works beautifully in tandem with it.

Easton is still doing the Four-Blocks and FROG, but some teachers wonder why they have FROG. According to the "old timers," the new teachers do not know what it was like at Easton before FROG and Four-Blocks so they often do not realize how much the children need these programs. We often take for granted wonderful things, even in schools!

Four-Blocks™ and Reading Recovery:
A True Tale from the Hills of Kentucky ·

By Janet Stahl and Charlene Johnson (with Dottie Hall)

Over and over again, Reading Recovery-trained teachers come up to us to tell us how consistent Four-Blocks™ teaching is with the teaching in a Reading Recovery lesson. The teachers at Clemmons, the pilot school, noticed the same thing when we added Reading Recovery, as an intervention, to the Four-Blocks instruction children were receiving in first-grade classrooms. Both programs are research-based, and both programs strive to teach all children.

Some teachers are natural storytellers. We found two as we read these true stories—Janet Stahl and Charlene Johnson. For me, their story began in Arizona where I did a three-day workshop in June of 1999. One day was spent on Building Blocks™ for kindergarten teachers, one day on the Four-Blocks for teachers in grades 1-3, and the final day was for intermediate teachers on the Four-Blocks in the Upper Grades, which we now call Big Blocks™. In the audience sat two Reading-Recovery trained teachers, Janet and Charlene. At that time, I did not know the story behind their trip to Arizona, nor the coming adventures of these two schoolteachers. Here is their tale:

Once upon a time, in Pendleton County in the hills of Kentucky, lived two beautiful princesses named Janet and Charlene. (Okay, so they were really two reasonably attractive schoolteachers with dreams of royalty, but what's the difference?) Anyway, one day, the teachers sought out the school principal and asked to travel abroad in search of wisdom. (Well, really, he asked us, and if we had known what we were getting into, we would have turned tail and ran; however....) So the two adventurous teachers set off in search of knowledge, which in this case came in the form of Reading Recovery training. And after their training year, the two teachers had obtained much knowledge, deeper insight concerning literacy, and two nervous breakdowns. However, with this imparted wisdom, the teachers began to look around their school and then their district, seeing reading in a whole new light. Or rather, lack-there-of, for you see, there was a dark cloud hanging over the district that came in the form of illiteracy.

The Problem

Upon closer observation, the two teachers began to discover many startling things. Our county has two elementary schools with a total enrollment of 1,425. Many factors contribute to the difficulty our students face in learning to read. Analysis of data shows the following problems existed in our schools:

- One school had 42% of its students on free or reduced lunch, while the other had 53%;
- There were a total of 162 migrant children;
- There were 257 single-family households;
- There were 113 families on welfare;
- Of adults 25 and older, 20% have a ninth grade education or less;
- 43% of adults do not have a high school diploma;
- 42% of the working-age population read below a ninth grade level.

Students affected or influenced by one or more of these factors are at risk for failure. Test scores on the Comprehensive Test of Basic Skills (CTBS), a norm-referenced test administered in Kentucky, indicated that many children were failing. In 1998, the district's lowest achieving grade one students had a grade equivalent of 0.2.

In addition, informal diagnostic measures were used to obtain necessary information. All exiting kindergarten students in both schools were given an evaluation consisting of subtests in letter identification, concepts about print, number of known words, ability to hear the sounds in words, and text reading level. These informal assessments verified that a substantial number of our primary students were heading down a path towards becoming struggling readers. The data showed that students had difficulty with letter identification, phonemic awareness, writing words, and reading text. In addition, concepts about print scores indicated not only a level of weakness, but also verified the lack of consistency in reading instructional methods used throughout the district. The demographic data portrayed a school system comprised of students who have many family-based risk factors that may further hinder their literacy development; the testing data showed a trend of low-reading levels in our school. Combined, our research indicated a definite need for a balanced, district-wide instructional reading approach to stop this cycle of failure.

The Solution

While the two teachers were struggling with depression over this gloomy information, contacts in Reading Recovery led them to the name Pat Cunningham. After hearing her name pop up over and over, and because they were both curious by nature, the two teachers attended a one-day Cunningham workshop in Cincinnati. They received a copy of *Phonics They Use*, and immediately made a Word Wall, thinking it was the greatest thing since sliced bread and sticky notes. The teachers used the Word Wall and Making Words activities with Title I groups and began to read more about the Four-Blocks™ Framework.

The following year, the two Reading Recovery teachers encouraged and assisted two classroom teachers in using Four-Blocks in their classrooms. Word Walls spread like wildfire as other teachers heard the "snapping and clapping" and began to ask, "What's going on?" By the end of the 1999 school year, 8 out of 20 teachers came on board the Four-Blocks boat.

Amid all this enthusiasm, the two Reading Recovery teachers heard of a grant that their state was offering to aid in the implementation of a research-based literacy model. Being the dedicated (insane), hardworking (certifiable) teachers that they were, they began writing immediately. Months and many bottles of Advil later, the grant was completed. Much to their surprise, out of 160 applications statewide, they were among the 24 districts to receive the Early Reading Incentive Grant in 1999.

After much research and consideration, it was decided that to fully meet the needs of our district, a classroom model and an early intervention model were needed. The models chosen for the grant were Four-Blocks and Reading Recovery.

Daily instruction in all four blocks of the Four-Blocks™ framework provides numerous and varied opportunities for all children to learn to read and write. Teaching all four blocks acknowledges that children learn in different ways and provides substantial instruction to support the learning personality of each child.

In addition to funding for implementing Four-Blocks, the grant also funded the training of four more Reading Recovery teachers, two for each elementary school. Documented by 20 years of research and evaluation, Reading Recovery provides intervention at a critical time—before the cycle of failure begins. First-grade children who score in the lowest 20% of their class, based on individual measures of assessment and teacher judgment, are eligible to participate. In our case, Reading

Recovery was selected to provide a safety net for students who were struggling, despite the intervention of a classroom teacher utilizing strategies of a balanced reading program.

Reading Recovery and Four-Blocks are perfect complements to each other. Reading Recovery in and of itself uses a balanced reading approach. Daily 30-minute lessons consist of a variety of reading and writing experiences that are designed to help children develop effective strategies for literacy acquisition. Instruction continues until students can read at or above the class average and have developed a self-extending system that uses a variety of strategies to read text and to independently write a message. The Reading Recovery lesson follows a routine framework of activities that is distinctly familiar to the Four-Blocks. Each Reading Recovery lesson has the following parts:

1. Rereading of familiar books for fluency
2. Rereading of yesterday's book while the teacher observes and records the child's reading behaviors
3. Word work
4. Writing
5. Rearranging a sentence from a cut-up sentence strip
6. Introduction of a new book
7. Reading of the new book

In comparison, the reading and rereading of familiar books at the child's in-structional level resembles that of the Self-Selected Reading Block; the word work in Reading Recovery is very similar to the Working with Words Block in the Four-Blocks™ framework. Children write daily in Four-Blocks classrooms on self-se-lected topics and conference with their teacher. In the daily Reading Recovery lesson, students write in response to what they are reading, getting help from the teacher when needed. Guided Reading in the Four-Blocks classroom and the Reading Recovery lesson has the teacher guiding the students through the reading of a new story or book. Reading Recovery mirrors what is being done in a Four-Blocks classroom; both programs are compatible and complement each other in a way that benefits all participants.

In addition, the two teachers, who frequently visited Four-Blocks Web sites, felt they had Pat Cunningham's personal blessing when they found this quote on her Wake Forest Web site:

> Across the years, many of the schools that have implemented the Four-Blocks™ framework have also implemented Reading Recovery programs. In those schools, the classroom teachers attest to the accelerated progress made by the Reading Recovery children. Reading Recovery teacher leaders who have programs in Four-Blocks schools and in schools not using Four-Blocks repeatedly tell us that they exit children more quickly when Reading Recovery tutoring is combined with a Four-Blocks classroom program.

So, the two adventurous teachers once again traveled to far-away lands in pursuit of wisdom. On this voyage, the two met Dottie Hall, who was giving a three-day seminar in Arizona. Being ever-so knowledge-filled and excited, the two "block-heads" came back to Kentucky ready to take on the world, or at least Pendleton County.

However, as summers sometimes go, this one was not to be without surprises. In addition to the Four-Blocks, the grant also provided funds for a literacy coordinator. The literacy coordinator position was designed to significantly raise the level of literacy attainment in low-achieving primary students by providing a means to fully implement the Four-Blocks. With the use of the Literacy Coordinator available to both schools, ongoing professional development was possible in both schools. Charlene, our very own princess, became the literacy coordinator. And, as fate would have it, through inevitable changes in personnel, Janet became assistant principal of one of the elementary schools in the district. While both teachers missed their former positions, their tiny-little-closet-of-a-room, and most of all, each other, they had discovered the opportunity of a lifetime—instead of politely suggesting good ideas, they now had the autonomy to MANDATE THEM! (Just kidding...well, sort of!)

The rest, as they say, is history. Utilization of the Four-Blocks indeed provided the structured, comprehensive balanced program that our district was lacking. We now have two elementary schools implementing the Four-Blocks in all grades. And truly, the time spent "selling" the Four-Blocks to the staff was somewhat in vain; the framework sells itself. Once upon a time, our students were struggling to read, and our teachers were struggling to teach those readers whose literacy development was slow. However, within two years, and only one of those being at full implementation, our test scores rose significantly. In 1998, our grade 1 national percentile score was 55.0 in reading and 55.8 in language. Our 2000 scores rose to 67.6 in reading and 64.3 in language.

Looking Forward To Next Year (or "They Lived Happily Ever After")

We are currently in our second year of our district-wide Four-Blocks and Reading Recovery implementation and are still going strong. In addition, instead of becoming princesses, Janet and Charlene have become Four-Blocks ambassadors, spreading the gospel of balanced reading throughout their land. Surrounding counties call continually wanting more information and training in Four-Blocks. We keep busy showing off our students and our teachers and sharing information. And, like all good stories, we intend to live very happily ever after in the knowledge that while we still may not be royalty, we have gone a long way towards making the world, or at least our part of it, a better and more literate place.

Four-Blocks™ and Title One •

by Jennifer Bish (with Dottie Hall)

Several years ago, I presented a seminar in Cincinnati, Ohio. It was about the time Pat Cunningham and I were beginning to write the Month-by-Month Phonics *books. The topic of the seminar was "Teaching Phonics in a Balanced Reading Program." I began the day with an overview of a balanced literacy program, and I talked about the Four-Blocks™ because I believe that phonics in only one part of a balanced reading program. Children need to learn how to use phonics as they read and write. Jean McLear, the language arts coordinator for Darke County Educational Service Center, was among those in attendance. She called me later and asked me to speak on the same topic to the teachers in Darke and Preble County just before the beginning of the next school year. The following August, I returned to talk about the Four-Blocks™ framework and to help at a school that was trying to implement Four-Blocks. Jennifer Bish was a Title I teacher at that school. She and I talked at length about how a Title I teacher could best support teachers and children in the Four-Blocks™ Model. Here is Jennifer's story of how she found different ways to support different teachers and students, depending on the needs and desires of the classroom teachers.*

I had been a second-grade teacher at South Elementary in Greenville, Ohio for several years. In the fall of 1997, I became the Title I teacher at this school. Bonnie Bollie was our principal, and she was always searching for ways to help her staff become better reading and writing teachers. She had read *Classrooms That Work* and had our staff use that book as the basis for monthly discussion groups during the 1997-98 school year.

The next fall, using the book *Phonics They Use* as our model, the teachers began implementing the Working With Words Block. Later that year, we also purchased the *Month-By-Month Phonics* books and *The Teachers Guide to the Four-Blocks™*. Using *The Teacher's Guide to the Four-Blocks™* as their guide, several teachers began to implement the rest of the Four-Blocks™ framework. Over the next two years our building and our district continued to implement Four-Blocks. We had several in-services with Dottie Hall, and we sent three teachers to the Four-Blocks Leadership Conference in January, 2000.

As the Title I teacher, my job was to help teach those children who qualified for Title I to read, and once we began Four-Blocks, to help teachers with implementation. I wanted to work with each class in the way that would be most helpful to the children and provide them with the most consistent instructional program. I went into some classrooms to work with my children, and I went in at the time the teacher felt she needed the most help. Invariably, the blocks in which teachers needed my "extra pair of hands" were the Guided Reading and Writing Blocks.

Title I Help During the Guided Reading Block

One of our second-grade classes had 12 children who qualified for Title I. This class also included several special-education inclusion students and received some assistance from a special-education Title I teacher. We gave the Developmental Reading Assessment (DRA) to the entire class at the beginning of the year. The test scores indicated that many children were reading below grade level, and that several students entered second grade reading at preprimer level—a year behind their peers.

The classroom teacher, the special education teacher, and I brainstormed various ways to help these students. The classroom teacher felt that she needed our help most during the Guided Reading segment of the Four-Blocks™ framework. So, at Guided Reading time, the special education teacher and I went to the classroom to do Guided Reading instruction. At the beginning of the year, the special education teacher and I each worked with six children who qualified for Title I, while the teacher did Guided Reading with the other 12 children. We all taught the same strategies during the before and after reading segments of Guided Reading, but the special education teacher and I chose easier texts for our children to read.

We modeled strategies for figuring out words—reading on to the end, looking at the rhyming patterns of the word, saying all the letters in the unknown word, etc. Some days we read as a small group. Other days, the children read with partners where one child read and the other child pointed to the words, and then the partners switched roles. As the partners read, we would move around and listen to them read, coaching and encouraging.

One day each week was designated as an "easy reading" day, and the class read poetry. The classroom teacher had the students read poems in a variety of ways that worked well with the whole class, made all the students feel capable, and helped with building fluency. The students did a lot of echo and choral reading, as well as readers' theater. The teacher included poems with lots of rhymes and did follow-up activities, such as Rounding Up the Rhymes during the Working with Words Block, an activity the whole class enjoyed.

On poetry day, the classroom teacher worked with the entire class. The special education teacher and I pulled individual children and coached them and did running records to assess their progress. We knew how our students were doing at all times, and we could give individual help whenever we saw someone with a need.

As the students' reading improved, they were phased out of the small groups and joined the classroom teacher during the Guided Reading Block. By December, all students were reading grade-level materials with the classroom teacher. At that point, the special education teacher and I used our time to provide one-on-one assistance to students when we or the classroom teacher saw the need for this.

We administered the DRA to the class again in May, 2000. All students had made at least a year's growth in reading, and some had grown much more. It amazed us that by doing Self-Selected Reading, Writing, and Working with Words with the whole class and getting some individual and small-group Guided Reading early in the year, all the struggling readers were making progress and catching up with their classmates!

Title I Help During the Writing Block

In another second-grade class, I helped during the Writing Block. That is where the classroom teacher felt she needed the most help with her struggling students. This class had also been given the DRA in September. Eight of the students began the year reading at Levels 4-6. Every day, the classroom teacher and I modeled writing during the minilesson. As the children wrote, we did individual writing conferences with the children. Having two teachers in the room during the Writing Block allowed struggling readers and writers to get daily help. At the end of the year, when this class was tested again with the DRA, the struggling students tested at Levels 20-28. The extra coaching and help during the Writing Block paid off for the struggling readers in that class!

I also pushed in and worked with a first-grade teacher during the Writing Block. The two of us modeled, modeled, and modeled. The students went from a lot of driting in September to writing three- and four-sentence stories, with many writing two to three pages by the end of the year. The first-graders really liked having another person in the room to conference with, and many of our "struggling writers" got daily coaching conferences. The teacher and I agreed that some emergent writers not only need time to write daily, but regular individual coaching if they are to make rapid progress in writing.

Becoming Word Coaches

At the Four-Blocks Leadership Conference, I heard Pat Cunningham explain the coaching strategies in more detail as she had in the soon-to-be-published book, *Guided Reading the Four-Blocks™ Way*. She explained how teachers could "coach" a child or a small group to use certain strategies when they did not know a word. I immediately returned to school and began using these coaching strategies with my students.

On some days, during the Guided Reading Block, we called together a heterogeneous group of four or five students to read with us, while the others were reading with partners. We explained to the children that they were going to learn how to be "word coaches" and could then coach each other on how to figure out hard words. We set some ground rules. Everyone would read a page to themselves first, and then one child would read the page aloud. When the reader was reading and came to a hard word, the word coach would coach them through the steps of figuring out that word. Everyone except the reader and the word coach was to pretend to be invisible, but to pay attention to the coaching because soon, they would all qualify as word coaches. In the first lessons, the teacher would be the word coach. As the children learned how to coach, they became the coaches, and the child reading a page aloud got to pick his/her word coach. We taught the children four steps, and once they understood these, displayed them on a poster as reminders. The students quickly picked up on these techniques, and we began letting each reader pick another child to be the word coach. The students soon found out that after saying all of the letters of an unknown word, they could often read the word correctly.

I worked with the older struggling readers in a pullout setting. My fourth-grade Title I students were fascinated by this strategy for figuring out words, and used it all the time. They particularly liked the fact that they could be "the coach." They also loved the "Brand Name Phonics" lessons we did from *Month-by-Month Phonics for the Upper Grades*.

We were so impressed with the success the children experienced with these coaching strategies that we wrote a grant and trained tutors to use them. These coaching strategies were also used in our summer school program, and the summer school teachers vowed they would use them during the coming school year.

Looking Forward to Next Year

I retired in June, 2000. (Dottie's note: Jennifer doesn't look like she could possibly be old enough to do that!) (Pat's note: Dottie retired, too, and neither does she!) I continue to help teachers implement the Four-Blocks in their classrooms, working with a number of schools and school systems in Ohio and surrounding states. With so many schools receiving Ohio Reads money and wanting to implement the Four-Blocks, I am going to be busy this year. However, I will be able to continue to do the "teaching" I enjoy because I will be going into classrooms to demonstrate the various blocks. I enjoy helping teachers and students reach their potential with the Four-Blocks™ framework—a framework that makes so much sense and matches my teaching style.

Implementing the Four-Blocks™ in a Large School District

by Tom Roe (with Pat Cunningham)

Tom was one of the very first district-level administrators to become excited about Four-Blocks™. I first met him at the South Carolina statewide Four-Blocks training in Columbia in August of 1996. Men always stand out in my audiences because there are so few of them. Many of the men I do get are administrators, and they sometimes get a "glazed" look when I get carried away with the "nitty-gritty" details of instruction which teachers want and need, but which aren't terribly germane to an administrator's world. Tom, however, sat up front, appeared captivated, took notes furiously, and asked questions at every break. I remember thinking as I left this large group of South Carolina educators that the county that had Tom on their team was going to get some real administrative support. Little did I (or Tom) suspect the extent to which he would become involved with Four-Blocks, and the difference that support would make in Greenville's Four-Blocks implementation. In the months and years to come, Tom communicated with me regularly (first by telephone, and then we both got addicted to E-mail), and he turned up at most of the conferences I did in South Carolina or North Carolina. I took on the role of cheerleader and encouraged him to "just do it" at every step along the way. Here is Tom's story. Most teachers and principals can only dream of this kind of "hands-on" support from the district office!

The School District of Greenville County is a large school district in northwestern South Carolina. Presently, there are 51 elementary schools with approximately 27,831 elementary students and approximately 1,325 elementary teachers. I have worked in Greenville County for 25 years—20 years as a classroom teacher and five years as a language arts coordinator. My first encounter with Four-Blocks was as a classroom teacher. It confirmed my philosophy in the teaching of reading, and instruction in general. In 1996, I became the Elementary Language Arts Coordinator for the District. Before I took this position, the District had already begun offering courses entitled "Literacy for the Classroom Teacher." These were critical teaching needs courses, and they dealt with a variety of early literacy issues regarding reading/language arts instruction. The Four-Blocks™ Model was one of several that was explored during the course. *Classrooms That Work* became the major text the second year of the course offering, and a few teachers started exploring and implementing the blocks.

1996-97

During my first year as the Elementary Language Arts Coordinator, organized district-wide training was offered, based on teacher and administrator interest. I contacted Pat and arranged to have Dottie Hall come and do some Four-Blocks training with first-grade teachers. The plan was to start with first grade and "grandfather" the training to second and third grades. In the midst of this organizational period, the Teacher Forum in Greenville (an organization made up of the Teachers of the Year) spoke with the Superintendent and requested that we provide extensive Four-Blocks training throughout the District. The Superintendent contacted me and was pleasantly surprised to find that the training plans were already in motion.

For the first training cycle, I invited schools to send a team of four, that included the principal, the reading specialist, and two first-grade teachers. I wanted principals there because I believe administrators must understand what teachers are trying to do in order to lend their support. I wanted two teachers at the same grade level because change is hard, even when you want to change. It's safer, and teachers are more apt to follow through with implementation when there is a friend to plan, celebrate, and commiserate with along the way. I had told Dottie to expect 100-200 people, but things got a little out of hand, and Dottie arrived to find an audience of almost 500! Extra teachers just dropped by to "visit."

People are always happier when they have food, so our 8:30-3:00 days included both breakfast and lunch. Each school was given multiple copies of *Classrooms That Work*, *Phonics They Use*, and *Making Words*. I received a grant from Alliance for Quality Education, a local organization that supports the education efforts in the District, and thus was able to provide teachers with all the books, Making Words cards, and organizational materials. Dottie was a real trooper, and agreed that it was amazing to see so many people giving up two days of their summer to come. All but one school had a team present! Dottie did an overview of Four-Blocks at the first-grade level, and we followed this up with a three-hour graduate course in the fall for the original team members. This first effort reached 150 classrooms. A make 'n take session, or "PATtern Party", was provided to help organize the teachers—all 150 who participated. These PATtern Parties were conducted during the summer before their implementation efforts.

During the year, all 54 Reading Specialists were in-serviced on various aspects of the blocks at their monthly meetings. I also visited many schools, observing and providing support and encouragement. My role changed from instructor to cheer-leader, with pom-poms and all the regalia. This was also the year of the state reading adoption, and the district adopted three new reading series. Because of the site-based management status in the district, schools could decide which of the three they wanted to use. All teachers at all grade levels were finding it hard to adjust their teaching to the new series, which contained more authentic literature, a more strategic approach to instruction, and more difficult selections for students to read. The focus changed by having the children read every day and abandon the predictable four-day cycle (day 1: get ready to read the story; day 2: read the story; day 3: workbook pages; day 4: worksheets) that was prescribed by the pre-vious reading program used in the district. Four-Blocks teachers had to learn the new integrated language arts/reading materials as they were trying to implement Four-Blocks.

Simultaneously with our district initiative, two of our schools were participat-ing in the yearlong Four-Blocks training provided by the South Carolina Depart-ment of Education. At the conclusion of the training, these two schools were "crowned" state demonstration sites. At the end of the year, we tested all first-graders in Four-Blocks classrooms with the Basic Reading Inventory. Reading Spe-cialists had been trained in its use and oversaw the testing. The results were phenomenal.

Fall Results		**Spring Results**	
Above Grade Level	11%	Above Grade Level	34%
On Grade Level	59%	On Grade Level	54%
Below Grade Level	30%	Below Grade Level	11%

(This represents the 113 students in the initial study of the Four-Blocks™ Model in Greenville County.)

When the principals saw the results of this testing, they demanded training for their second-grade teachers. By then, Four-Blocks was spreading all over the country, and neither Pat nor Dottie could come and do the training. I saw Pat at IRA, and she assured me I could do it on my own. (She seemed very confident about this!)

1997-98

During the summer of 1997, a local church opened its doors for the second-grade overview. I did a two-day orientation on the blocks followed by a one-day PATtern Party. The graduate course, "Teaching in the 4-Blocks Classroom," followed in the fall. One hundred seventy-five teachers gathered weekly for the course, which began in August and concluded around the first of December.

At the request of some first-grade teachers, monthly support group sessions were begun for those who had already been trained. At the onset, the sessions were poorly attended, with only 20-30 teachers turning out for the first three sessions. I didn't know whether teachers forgot, had too many after-school related obligations, didn't want to come, or hadn't received the information concerning them. I started each session with "helpful" tips or reminders on one or two blocks. Time for teachers to share came next. Finally, I asked the teachers for input on issues to explore for the next session. Eventually, the word got out that the sessions were practical and helpful. By the end of the year, we were averaging 100 participants at each monthly meeting.

Towards the end of the second-grade course, principals started calling to request a Four-Blocks course for their new, reduced-size classroom teachers. Of course, they wanted it as soon as possible! (I even got calls at home on the weekend.) In late November, the course was offered to this group of teachers who had been hired explicitly to fulfill this new initiative. This group was comprised mainly of Title I teachers, and the focus was first grade.

In January, I co-taught an integrated curriculum course for fourth- and fifth-grade teachers. I started infusing the Four-Blocks into the course. Some of these participants started working, in a small way, with the blocks.

Starting in April, I began working with 25 third-grade teachers. (Later I found out that several came out of pure curiosity.) The intent of this early training was to establish observation sites. The end of a school year is a tough time for teachers to attend workshops, but they persevered and were real troupers! The group was composed mostly of seasoned teachers, many of whom had master's degrees—many of which were in reading. Several comments at the end included:

"I've learned more about reading in this one course than I did in both my master's and undergraduate programs."

"This stuff really works!"

"I can't wait until next year when I can put it all together!"

"The Four-Blocks really makes sense for children and for me! I came as an unbeliever, but I'm leaving a believer."

On the last day of our class, they surprised me with a party!

1998-99

Approximately 120 third-grade teachers gathered in our adopted home, the same local church, for the summer kick-off. This crowd of participants included some first- and second-grade teachers. The pattern had been set; this kickoff included an overview and a PATtern Party. (This was the second summer at the church. The ministers at the church found the training fascinating, and they made frequent visits to observe the festivities.) These teachers participated in the fall graduate course, "Teaching in the Four-Blocks Classroom." Monthly support group sessions for previously-trained teachers were held throughout the school year.

Also that summer, the superintendent of schools in Greenville began the process of developing an education plan with community leaders, state board members, college/university professors, business leaders, professionals, parents, principals, teachers, and district office staff. This group became known fondly as the Steering Committee for the Education Plan. Five major goals were established with delineated gateway standards. One of the gateway standards stated that all students would be reading on grade level by the end of third grade. Action teams were formed to develop action plans to carry out each goal and explicitly meet the gateway standard. I was asked to serve on the action team for the "reading on grade level by the end of third grade" standard. This team was composed of district office staff, a college professor, a pediatrician, two elementary principals, the Head Start director, parents, and teachers.

After we were given our charge from the steering committee, our committee's work began. My job was to present the research and trends in reading to the committee. I used the Snow report, *Preventing Reading Difficulties in Young Children*, *Starting Out Right* (the parenting version of the Snow report), and the Learning First Alliance's *Every Child a Reader*. The action team began building. The principals in the group wanted to establish Four-Blocks™ as the literacy framework for all children at the primary level. I also discussed the issue that reading instruction did not end at third grade. For the past four years in the District, the elementary scores had been showing gains, but the middle school scores continue to plummet.

Our plan also addressed a need for one-on-one or small group intervention for grades 1-8. The district had just purchased Houghton Mifflin's *Soar to Success* for grades 3-6 and *Early Success* for grades 1 and 2. In addition, we considered assessments—both traditional and authentic. The authentic assessment portion of the plan will first take the form of an assessment tool kit for classroom teachers in the area of language arts, which will initially include benchmark books, retelling protocols, writing prompts, and an informal reading inventory.

As school started in the fall, I was called to the superintendent's office to discuss "reading" with the executive staff. During this meeting, I was directly asked if the Four-Blocks was the direction that the district should take! Of course, I said, "Yes!" My immediate supervisor, the executive director of curriculum and instruction, and I were charged with the construction of a plan to implement Four-Blocks district-wide. This plan had to be completed in one week.

A week later, after lots of long nights, the first draft was presented to the superintendent, and then to the Management Officers Organization. This first draft went back for two additional revisions. After the third presentation, the plan was ready to be presented to the elementary principals for their consideration and approval. In October, I presented the plan to all the elementary principals. First, I shared the research based on the Snow and Learning First Alliance reports. Both of these reports supported the need for balanced reading instruction. Then, I moved to our action plan, which included implementing the Four-Blocks district-wide over a three-year period. Because of the site-based status of our schools, we were seeking one third of the schools who would like to implement the model school-wide.

As anyone who has worked in schools knows, it is very hard to get a group of 54 people—principals or anyone—to agree on anything. Instead of rejecting this first initiative, they objected that the implementation was too slow! They wanted everyone trained at once! WOW! I was sent back to the drawing board one more time.

The final draft of the plan focused the first year of training on grades 1-3 and the second year on grades 4-5. The plan included a "train-the-trainer" model to train Reading Specialists to conduct the after-school sessions, a course for principals in Four-Blocks, monthly support groups, additional "refresher" sessions for teachers in the area of language arts, and contract stipulations requiring Four-Blocks training for both teachers and administrators. Recognition of exemplary classrooms, classroom assessments, and other language-arts related issues were also included in the plan. The revised plan was presented to the principals two weeks later and was unanimously accepted. This was the first time in the district's history that all 54 principals were in agreement! The superintendent was elated, and everyone, myself included, was amazed.

After this presentation, I was asked to present "the plan" to the Board. The Board gave its one hundred percent backing and support. They applauded our efforts! One member did ask if this meant there would be no direct instruction in reading. Being aware of the broader meaning of "direct instruction," I assured her that there would be even more structure, modeling, and direct instruction in our Four-Blocks classrooms.

In November, I began the training of the reading specialists, who were to become the Four-Blocks trainers. The training and support sessions for trainers continued through April and at the request of the trainers, I wrote a training manual for their use. The manual grew from one 2½-inch notebook into three bulging 2½-inch notebooks. I felt as if I had given birth!

February marked the beginning of our work with teachers. This training was not long enough— twelve 2-hour sessions—but it was the best we could do. Teachers received *The Teachers Guide to the Four-Blocks™* and the *Month-by-Month Phonics* book for their grade level. In-service points were awarded for participation in the training. A level-one certificate was awarded on the last day of training. Most teachers, but not all, were happy with the training.

In spite of all the "voluntary training" we had done and the remarkable consensus we had achieved before implementing Four-Blocks district-wide, not everyone was happy. Change is hard. Time seems to be the biggest enemy. Sometimes "new initiatives" are viewed as an add-on, and to change this mind set and release "favorite" activities, workbooks and/or worksheets, is hard. I view school as a big hard-sided Samsonite® suitcase; there is just so much space (time), and you can't stuff anymore into it. The time restraints or sides of the suitcase don't have any "give" in them. Sometimes rearranging and releasing favorite "things" has to occur in the best interest of the children. Change takes commitment and fortitude, and it is not easy.

An invitation was extended to me by a few schools to answer questions concerning the training, Four-Blocks, and reading instruction in general. I accepted, thinking to myself all the time that this might be a twentieth-century version of the Spanish Inquisition, but the teachers asked crucial, thought-provoking questions concerning various aspects of the plan. At the conclusion of each session, they felt better about the initiative and implementation of the model. Some schools had difficulty giving up their ability groups, even though their test scores showed that the children in the bottom quartile had not shown growth in reading or math. I know we haven't convinced everyone...yet.

The first principals' class, "Administrating and Supervising the Four-Blocks Classroom" started in January. I taught the class every Tuesday night. The "bonding" that occurred during this course was amazing. The participants fondly refer to themselves as the "Blockheads!" (The group still meets once a month for a class reunion! The "Teacher" is invited and attends each reunion.)

During the spring of this year, a few fourth- and fifth-grade "pioneers" came to an early round of intermediate training. The "whole" picture was tackled, including new curriculum issues (newly adopted state standards in two content areas), departmentalized vs. self-contained classrooms, and integration! A by-product of this training was the return by a few to self-contained intermediate classrooms because the teachers felt that full integration would be easier to achieve.

Looking Forward to Next Year

There is more to come! The summer principals' course, "Administrating and Supervising the Four-Blocks Classroom," has just concluded. Thirty-five principals plus District Office Administration attended the course. The range of personalities really gelled, and like the first group, they also have a bond. The Four-Blocks graduation ceremony was held with great pomp and circumstance on the last day of the class.

I have also held three days of "planning" sessions for teachers in grades 1-3. Each day was devoted to Four-Blocks planning for each of the three reading programs used in the District. About 230 teachers attended the three-day event. It's fascinating to watch the various levels of understanding and commitment. Some have deep "block" knowledge and understanding, and some are dipping their toes into the shallow end of the pond, but everyone is willing to at least get their feet wet! Their commitment was evident in their attendance during the summer.

We also held some PATtern Parties. One hundred sixty teachers attended one of the four parties. We discussed organizational strategies for the beginning of the school year. Some of our more reluctant teachers softened, because they realized that I was going to support their efforts with a listening ear, a monthly Four-Blocks newsletter, and monthly Four-Blocks pep rallies. (I originally called them support group sessions, but that label didn't sit too well, so we are now having pep rallies. Labeling matters!)

The big push next year will be fourth- and fifth-grade training. The "pioneers" will already be toiling in the Four-Blocks fields. Several products (an integrated curriculum guide, a yearlong syllabus, and various authentic assessments) will be a part of the end result of this effort. There are lots of concerns about how Four-Blocks can (and should) look different in intermediate grades. The seeds are being planted, and watering will occur along the way.

Bringing Four-Blocks™
to Walnut Grove Elementary •

by Jean Swenson (with Dottie Hall)

When a classroom changes, it is usually the result of a teacher. When an entire school wants change and accomplishes it, there is usually someone who has guided that change and helped teachers with that change. Schools and school systems do not change without leadership. Jean Swenson, the "Title I Resource Specialist," is one of those "leaders" who brought about change at her school. Walnut Grove is a large elementary school with 670 students—68% of those students are eligible for free or reduced lunch; 63% of the students are minorities. Last year, two full-time teachers and another part-time teacher served 70 first- and second-grade Title I students.

I first met Jean when she visited Clemmons Elementary several years ago. She sent Dr. Ivory Johnson, Director of Special Projects for Ferguson-Florissant School System, to visit us next. Dr. Johnson was responsible for my going to this St. Louis area school system to do some Four-Blocks™ training. Most chapters in this book are about "teacher" change; this chapter is about how a "special teacher" (and a special person!) changed a school. This is Jean's story:

Sometimes change happens very quickly, and other times change comes over a period of time in a variety of almost imperceptible little events. For us at Walnut Grove, our change process really began in the early 1990's. It all began with Reading Recovery. I was one of those in the first training class in our district in 1990-91. As we began to implement the Reading Recovery model, we started talking with teachers about running records, prompting for strategies, and teaching from strengths. There were a few key people in first and second grade who wanted to learn all they could about the philosophy and methodology of Reading Recovery. Over the next few years, teachers began sharing, talking, and learning from one another. We began to expand our classroom libraries and make better use of "little books"—those easily accessible texts for early readers. We tried to apply what we knew from Reading Recovery to the classroom. We were looking for a balanced reading program—one that could meet a variety of needs because of the diversity in our classrooms—yet was not tied into one specific methodology (i.e. phonics, whole language, basal).

Our Search for a Solution

In 1995, three things occurred that helped define our search. In browsing through professional books, I came across *No Quick Fix* and *Classrooms That Work*. Knowing the professional reputations of the authors, Dick Allington and Pat Cunningham, I was sure I would enjoy these books, and I was not disappointed! I read these two books over the summer and concluded that they were describing the kind of literacy instruction we were looking for and what we were trying to do in our classrooms. So, I immediately passed these books on to everyone I knew! I shared them with our wonderfully supportive principal, Jeff Vordtriede. I gave them to the first-grade teachers and the sixth-grade teachers. I made copies of certain chapters and left them in the teachers' lounge for all to see. Everyone who read these books was impressed with the descriptions of what really works in classrooms! These books outlined a multilevel, multimethod framework for classroom instruction that really seemed to make sense.

As the school year started, I attended a Reading Recovery meeting and had a conversation with a teacher from the Parkway School District. She described a program that their first-grade teachers were using, which she referred to as the "Winston-Salem Project." I realized that this was the program I had just been reading about. I was thrilled to discover that classrooms were using it in our local St. Louis area.

The third event occurred when a first-grade teacher, Rochelle Bain, transferred to our building and brought with her a book called *Making Words*. Well, it didn't take long for us to put all of this together, as everything seemed to be pointing in the same direction. We had finally found our balanced program to meet the variety of needs and levels in a classroom. Soon we were using Word Walls and making words in all four of our first-grade classrooms.

Now, I will say that our first attempts at Word Walls were less than perfect. We were probably doing what Pat and Dottie call "having a Word Wall"—not really "doing a Word Wall." Our Word Walls were large and colorful, and they had lots of important words on them. Our mistake was that we were not really using them to support writing with high frequency words; we were using them for basal vocabulary words, content area words, and seasonal or thematic words. Every important word went on the Word Wall. They were enormous!

We had better luck with our Making Words lessons. Several of our first- and second-grade teachers tried this concept and really saw the benefits. As the reading teacher, I went into classrooms and demonstrated these lessons. We introduced it to our entire staff at a workshop the next year and got some converts in some of our upper-grade classrooms. We purchased the *Making Words* and *Making Big Words* books for every classroom teacher. We also purchased the first book out on the Four-Blocks, *Implementing the 4-Blocks™ Literacy Model*, and had a little more support and guidance to implement the program.

During the 1997-98 school year, we continued to try various aspects of Four-Blocks. In spring of 1998, I was planning a trip with my family to Charlotte, NC, and it occurred to me to try to visit some schools in Winston-Salem. After a few calls to directory assistance, I was on the phone with Dottie Hall, and a few days later, I was at Clemmons School visiting the most wonderful first-grade classrooms. Seeing these classrooms and the teachers was truly amazing! I came back with glowing reports to teachers and administrators that Four-Blocks classrooms were places where children were actively involved and truly becoming readers and writers. And, I knew we could do the same thing!

Implementing the Four-Blocks in First Grade

In the late spring of 1998, our district was moving in the direction of implementing the Four-Blocks™ framework in four low-achieving schools. Since we at Walnut Grove already had a significant start in this direction and a great deal of interest among our first-grade teachers, we literally begged to be included in the training for the program. With the blessing of our principal, I went to the office of JoAnn Jasin, Area Director for Elementary Education, and pleaded our case to be able to share in the staff development for the Four-Blocks training. Again, things fell into place, and our first-grade teachers participated in summer workshops which began our official implementation of the program.

In June, teachers from Parkway School System came to our district and helped teachers get started on materials for Word Walls and Making Words. In August, Dottie Hall came to our district for the first time to give teachers an overview of the Four-Blocks™ Literacy Model. When school started, we had some significant staffing changes, as Rochelle had transferred to one of the four low-performing, now Extended School Year schools, where she would also be using the Four-Blocks™ framework. Leslie, another first-grade teacher, left due to health reasons. Losing both of these classroom teachers caused us to realign our program, but we found that we still had an extremely strong, enthusiastic group of teachers for our first full year of implementing the program. Luckily, Janet and Kelly were still with us to provide professionalism, continuity, and experience to our group of fairly new teachers. They participated in ongoing staff development during the year, some in our building and some within the district. They visited other classrooms; they shared ideas; they asked questions; they tried new things. It was a great start for us!

Implementing Four-Blocks™ at Other Grade Levels

In the spring of 1999, we had the opportunity to apply for a Comprehensive School Reform Grant. The focus of our grant was the Four-Blocks™ Literacy Model. Our goal was to continue implementation of the Four-Blocks in second grade and then in third grade. We also intended to implement as much as possible in the intermediate grades—specifically the Words Block and the Self-Selected Reading Block. We were thrilled when we learned that we had been approved for our grant. The grant provided funds for a number of things; most importantly we could fund continued staff development. Dottie came to our school in the fall of 1999; Pat and Dottie both came in the spring of 2000. These were significant visits for our teachers. Having them visit our classrooms, engage in dialogue with our teachers, and answer questions really added to the credibility of the program. Teachers felt validated for their efforts. (Pat and Dottie talk about "blessing books" when we read aloud to children. Well, Pat and Dottie "blessed" our classrooms and our teachers when they came to visit Walnut Grove.)

In the spring, I arranged for our third-grade teachers, who had been a bit reluctant to embrace Four-Blocks, to visit the third-grade classrooms at Bermuda Elementary. Remember Rochelle who had transferred to Bermuda, an ESY school? Well, she had worked with her colleagues in third grade to develop a wonderful model of implementation for that grade level. (And the Four-Blocks does look different in third grade than it does in first grade!) Those four teachers came back so excited with what they had seen. Where before they were mumbling about this program "that Jean wants us to do," now they were asking, "Will you let us do this next year?" I knew they were sold! Again, in my role as a facilitator and support person, I knew I just needed to get teachers the right information, resources, and training. In this case, a site visit to another classroom was the key element.

The grant also provided funds for materials for classroom libraries. We were able to purchase a wide variety of books for all of our classrooms, K-6. We continued to talk about the importance of reading aloud to children, and the importance of children selecting books to read at their independent level. We trained teachers to take running records and monitor progress. Teachers and students were thrilled to have a wider variety of books available. More importantly, teachers felt they had been given permission to let kids read "easy" materials. They began to understand the reasons for reading easy materials, and that it was not a matter of not having "high standards." It was, in fact, allowing children to have what they need—the opportunity to practice, apply strategies, build fluency, and operate as competent readers. We knew that our intermediate students also needed the opportunity to practice strategies at an independent level. When Pat talked with our intermediate teachers last spring, she told them that they simply had to make time for Self-Selected Reading. "You can't afford not to," she said. That single comment spoke volumes for our teachers.

Kindergarten

Our kindergartens have been moving in a parallel path with the implementation of the Four-Blocks over the past few years. We have had an amazing program in place for years—literacy-rich and developmentally-appropriate. We didn't have to add much to make it consistent with the Building Blocks™ framework. We began to use environmental print on our Word Walls. We did some predictable charts and expanded our use of poetry and big books. We looked for more ways to build phonemic awareness; in fact, one of our kindergarten teachers has taken this on as her mission—she is now our resident "expert"! Our kindergarten teachers constantly seek out new information, so when they heard others were going to visit Four-Blocks classrooms, they wanted to go, too! They visited the kindergarten classes at Mason Ridge (Parkway School System) and were very impressed with what the students there were doing in writing. They came back and adjusted their writing program, making it more multilevel to meet the needs of the wide range of levels of their students. When *The Teacher's Guide to Building Blocks™* book came out this year, they were thrilled to have a new resource. We have the six components of Building Blocks™ in place already, but the book provides a rationale and framework, as well as lots of new ideas.

I can personally attest to the success of our kindergarten teachers because each fall I help screen students for Reading Recovery. We choose the lowest 20% of the class, and this year, even these lowest students were able to write more words, recognize more letters, and hear more sounds than students I have tested in past years. Building Blocks™ does indeed provide a good foundation for future success.

Parent Involvement

We have always done a lot of parent involvement activities, but have really "stepped it up" since we began implementing Four-Blocks and got our grant. We sponsored evening reading activities and gave books to parents and children to take home. We sent home reading activity packs with books, magnetic letters, wipe-off boards, and word cards. Our students were thrilled to have fun packs to take home, and our parents were most appreciative to have materials to use with their children.

Where We Are

As the year ended, we made plans for reapplying for the second year of our grant. Enthusiasm was growing, and more plans were taking shape for next year. Most teachers volunteered to work on summer curriculum projects and planning sessions for implementing next fall. Teachers were embracing the program and becoming the experts. Three of our teachers helped present at summer workshops for other district schools who are starting Four-Blocks this fall. We used videotapes from our classrooms, taken last May, as examples of what the program implementation looks like. These teachers did a wonderful job, speaking from their own experiences and sharing their own stories of the Four-Blocks. This was the point at which I realized we really had made a change. A large staff in a school of 670 students was united behind a goal, energized and enthused, and focused on making it become a reality.

I see now that change has come slowly, and it has also come quickly—in a few defining moments. We have a terrific staff of teachers, a supportive principal and assistant principal, a commitment from the district, and, of course, wonderful children and parents who are counting on us to provide the tools of literacy to make these children successful, productive members of society. Everything that we had been talking about and searching for over the past ten years is becoming a reality.

In a staff our size, there are always changes; many names and faces have changed; teachers have retired, teachers have relocated, teachers have stayed home with families, and new teachers have come to fill those empty spots. But, the program is in place, and we are developing ways to train our new teachers so that the quality of the Four-Blocks™ Model remains constant. It is never about just one of us, it is always about all of us and what we can accomplish together. So this is our story of the Four-Blocks at Walnut Grove Elementary. It is a story of change, and more importantly, of people.

Looking Forward to Next Year

As the school year begins in the fall of 2000, we have been approved for the second year of our grant. Our plans include full implementation of the Four-Blocks in our third-grade classrooms. These four teachers have become the best ambassadors of the program. We also have five teachers new to our first- and second-grade classrooms. They all come with some experience, and most importantly, a wonderful commitment to the Four-Blocks. Bringing two teachers into a grade-level team is easier when there is a defined framework around which to plan the day. It helps teachers to plan together and to provide a consistent framework for all our students. We also try to set up visits, coaching, and mentoring within our building to help support the new people.

We are using many of the new resources, including the *Four-Blocks™ Planbook "Plus"*, *Guided Reading the Four-Blocks™ Way*, and *The Teacher's Guide to Building Blocks™*. The teachers love having them. Since our grant funds have provided expanded classroom libraries, we now have a wide variety of leveled books in all of our classrooms. We want to help teachers use them most effectively with students—how to assess reading levels, how to conference with students, and how to match students with books. At our teachers' requests, we are planning staff development in the Writing Block. We hope this will benefit our students in developing skills and strategies, as well as help them prepare for the state tests. We have many things on our agenda for the coming year. It will, undoubtedly, be exciting, busy, and rewarding.

How Ron McNair Elementary Became a
Four-Blocks™ School: A Principal's Point of View •••••••••••

by Patty Schaffer (With Pat Cunningham)

I had known about Ron McNair Elementary School for several years before I finally got to visit in February, 2000. I had heard about Camp Read A Lot and talked to many people who had observed their excellent Four-Blocks™ instruction. I had read Patty's practical advice, which she freely shared with teachers at the Teachers.Net mailring. As I entered the old but well-kept building, I had high expectations for the instruction I would see and the teachers and children I would meet. I spent the day, trying to keep up with the pace Patty set, visiting classrooms, watching lessons, and observing the children reading and writing. I have never spent a more inspiring day in a school. In classroom after classroom, I saw busy, happy children who loved to read and write and talk with you about books and share their writing. The children at Ron McNair, by any criteria, would be considered at-risk for reading and school failure. They live in public housing, are poor, and are mostly being raised by single moms or grandmothers. These are children who are beating the odds because they have a principal and teachers who believe that all children can and deserve to become literate. Here is Patty's story of how Ron McNair became a showplace for literacy and Four-Blocks. I know it will inspire you as my day there inspired me.

In 1990, I became the principal at Ron McNair Elementary school in Charleston, South Carolina. I was sent there to fill in for a few months while the real principal was away. I have been principal at Ron McNair for 10 years. Ron McNair is a large, schoolwide Title I school. One hundered percent of our children qualify for free and reduced lunch; 98% are African-American. When I arrived, we had 13-year-olds in our fifth grade. Our achievement test scores were almost all single-digit numbers

Folks there were not sure what to make of me. I know the parents were skeptical because they told me so. I was the first white principal the school had had in years and years. One parent told me straight up that a white woman would not be able to be the principal at McNair, "This school needs a black person." I told her I would only be there for a short while, but that I would be fair and honest with each child, and if I needed help, I would call on the community. She said, "OK!" but went down the steps mumbling, "A white woman...I don't think so!"

I spent a lot of my time wandering around the building and doing things that would make the staff and children feel better about being without their principal. We presented a Christmas program, celebrated Ron McNair Day with a skit written by one of the teachers, and began an Advisor-Advisee program. One of the teachers had written a grant for this program, and it was a good outreach effort on the staff's part to help some of our most needy children. Each staff member had an adopted student. The goal was to have contact with the student once a week and to recognize the child on holidays with something small. At the end, there was funding for an Advisor-Advisee banquet. The staff members had gifts for their advisees. I had made wooden apple thank-you gifts for each advisor, and we all dressed up to the nines and attended the banquet. Every advisee that attended brought their "guest" (Mom) with them. It was wonderful. We also invited some district office people (many of them had never been to McNair!). A children's Sunbeam choir came from a lowcountry church and sang their little hearts out. It set the tone for the evening.

The event was magic. Everybody felt like they had made a difference in a child's life. The keynote speaker was Tony Campbell, a black Episcopal priest doing work for the diocese. He grew up in a large housing authority complex, went to the Naval Academy, and later became a priest; he was a good friend of one of our teachers. The parents loved him, and the children thought he was neat.

Laying the Foundation for Change

One thing I quickly learned was that in a school like McNair, one principal could not do all that needed to be done. The school alone could not do it, either. We needed help. To get this help, I wanted to establish a liaison relationship with a college and to network with other agencies that had the same goals as the school.

I had identified some outstanding teachers. I began to "court" some of the folks I knew at the College of Charleston and to ask for student teachers. I called on the college to send us presenters for professional development, to join us in some planning sessions, and to come visit our school. We had student teachers assigned the next year. These student teachers are a big help to us, and we prepare them for the "real world." Many of them take jobs at McNair after they graduate.

We began to network with community agencies that had the same goals as the school and that were targeting the same people. The Department of Health Education, for example, had a clinic in North Park Village. They were doing things that focused on student health. We were, too. Our target was a shared group of people. If we could work together and support each other, we could make an impact that would be significant.

We put a parenting position in our schoolwide Title I project. The parent educator worked hard to identify the agencies that were working with our children. We established the McNair Family Council and invited everyone to join us. Soon, our council had as members such diverse groups as the Department of Social Services, the Department of Health clinic in the housing community, a local church, the city of North Charleston businesses, the Navy, an advertising agency, the HUD office, and Taco Bell. The Council also included teachers and parents. Parents must be a part of the process for change to be significant.

Our mission statement for the council was simple, "to make the McNair community the best learning environment for children." We all were working for this to happen. And things did begin to happen. A full-time nurse from DHEC was assigned to the school clinic. A Department of Mental Health worker was site-based at our school. The Department of Social Services placed two youth specialists at the school to work with the CIS (Communities in Schools) program. We also received a $25,000 grant from the City of North Charleston to improve the playground facilities.

We are constantly looking for help and community support. Just this past year we started work with a church, Celebration Station. They sponsored Kid's Cafe, an after-school tutoring program. They were joined by the Lowcountry Food Bank. Children receive a well-balanced meal during this after-school time.

At the school level, we established the McNair Student Assistance Team (SAT). Members on the SAT include the principal, administrative assistant, school psychologist, guidance counselor, attendance clerk, DMH mental health therapist, CIS youth specialist, resource teacher, nurse, parent educator, and computer proctor. We meet for one hour every Wednesday morning. Our purpose is to coordinate services, do staffing, and to put game plans together to offer support to parents. It is kind of like working with a team of doctors to come up with a recommendation for a patient. It is a time for the professionals to meet with teachers and to plan interventions.

How Ron McNair Elementary Became a
Four-Blocks™ School: A Principal's Point of View •

Finding a Focus and Four-Blocks™

Once we had some help and the community and college working with us, we began to look more closely at academics. We tried all kinds of things—parallel block scheduling, reading and math pullouts, readiness teachers for first grade, parent education programs, etc. We were doing a lot of what looked like good stuff, but we were not moving our test scores at the rate we thought that they should move.

Jean Murray, the area superintendent, gave me the best advice, "Patty, you need a focus at McNair, and it needs to be simple. Everyone ought to be able to tell you what the focus is, and everyone ought to know what you are doing to make the focus become real and seen in the halls, in the classrooms, and in the test scores."

We visited other schools in our state that were similar to McNair. We wanted to know what these schools were doing that worked. We wanted to know what they were doing that was not working. We sent teams of teachers and sometimes parents to these schools. At all the successful schools we visited, we kept seeing a strong emphasis on reading. Everywhere we went, schools were putting their dollars and efforts on improving reading. We had always believed that reading was the key to student learning, and that children who cannot read have academic problems throughout their years in school and often become dropouts. We decided to make reading our focus and to focus our budget, resources, and operation on reading.

As we were making site visits and talking with consultants and folks in our Title I office, we kept hearing about a book titled *Classrooms That Work*. The title itself seemed to capture what we wanted for our school. We wanted every classroom to be a classroom that worked. We were planning to do a book study and *Classrooms That Work* won the vote. Our Title I consultant facilitated the study. (I wanted her to do this so that I could be a participant. I think teachers need to see their principals participating in learning along with them.) We worked through the book, chapter by chapter. Each week the teachers would go back and try something from that chapter in their own classrooms. I would do an administrative activity related to each chapter.

We began to look closely at our classrooms and what was available in them. We even counted and categorized the kinds of books in each classroom library.

No surprise here—poetry and nonfiction were our weakest areas. When it came time to spend money, we ordered poetry and nonfiction. This was just one of the ways in which we matched the budget and the needs of the school in relation to the school's focus—reading.

After reading the comprehension chapter of *Classrooms That Work*, we worked together to learn how to effectively use graphic organizers. The teachers each designed a graphic organizer to use, and included a minilesson outline for it. I collected them and produced a booklet of suggested graphic organizers for each teacher.

The book study took more than 10 weeks. We committed 1½ hours a week for the study until we got through. We then wanted to find out more. This is when we visited Brockington Elementary School and several other schools that were using the Four-Blocks™ Model. We saw powerful instruction and came back ready to try it at McNair.

Getting Started with Four-Blocks™

About this time, the state announced a state-wide training program for Four-Blocks. We begged to be included in the training and were first told that we were not getting in. We continued to beg, and finally were accepted. Four McNair teachers were selected as the demonstration team for Four-Blocks, and I joined them at every session of the state training. We committed a summer to getting ready.

That next year, the four teachers began implementing Four-Blocks in their class-rooms. Annette Gadsden, a teacher leader, and I worked closely with these four teachers. We observed the teachers and arranged for them to observe each other. We met together every week to share ideas and solve problems.

One of the first things the teachers said about Four-Blocks was that their class-room discipline was so much better than it had been in past years. Could it be that all four of them had gotten "better kids?" We dismissed this possibility and decided that the improved discipline had more to do with the engagement of the kids in the activities, the regular routines, the variety of activities in the different blocks, and the success all the children were experiencing.

Towards the end of the year, we began to do grade-level planning to include the other teachers in the school. We created our own pacing charts for planning guides. We made sure that our special area teachers had copies of these pacing charts, so that they knew what was happening in the classrooms and could make connections with their instruction. Our first Four-Blocks year flew by, but it was a year to remember!

Camp Read-A-Lot

The next summer we began to train our staff by teaching our own course, modeled after the state training we had attended. We invited teachers from other schools to participate, and 70 teachers signed up to learn how to do Four-Blocks. We piggy-backed the training with Camp Read-A-Lot, our summer school reading program. Our experienced Four-Blocks teachers taught the children who came to Camp Read-A-Lot on Mondays, Tuesdays, and Wednesdays. Teachers from another school who wanted to implement Four-Blocks assisted our teachers. Teachers taking the course came and observed the teachers and children in their Four-Blocks instruction.

On Thursdays, the teachers met for the course meetings. We read and discussed *Classrooms That Work*, talked about what we had experienced in the classrooms on Monday, Tuesday, and Wednesday, and made all kinds of stuff—author's chairs, charts, Making Words letters, etc. At the end of the summer, our teachers were ready to go with schoolwide implementation.

In the fall, we opened McNair to Four-Blocks site visits, and most of the 70 teachers who had taken the course came back to visit. They also participated in problem-solving sessions we call "Pat Chats" throughout the year as they began implementation. These visits and discussions gave the teachers opportunities and time to learn the "How To Dos," to work out the kinks, and to share ideas with peers. It was also wonderful for our McNair teachers, who got to spotlight "the way we teach reading." We were experiencing a lot of success and had the missionary zeal to share with others.

We continued Camp Read-A-Lot each summer and trained hundreds of teachers in Four-Blocks. In the summer of 1998, we ran three graduate courses—a Four-Blocks course, a Four-Blocks practicum, and a Four-Blocks leadership course. All of these were sponsored by a local college. It was a powerful staff development opportunity, and a lot of folks were trained in ways that offered real hands-on experiences.

Supporting Teachers Through Coaching

As we began schoolwide implementation, I set up a regular schedule for coaching teachers. As we continued coaching, we found a format that worked well for everyone. On the day before the conference, I hold a pre-observation conference with the teacher. In this conference, we discuss what the teacher will be doing and what I can expect to see. I then go in and observe for 20 minutes, a "snapshot" of the lesson. That afternoon, we hold a 20-minute post-observation conference. The time limits are important because, just like the kids in the blocks, teachers know that "nothing will last too long!"

My goal is for teachers to leave the coaching sessions feeling good about opening the door to their classrooms and talking about the teaching act. I want them to be proud of themselves and their classes, and I make a big deal over the coaching experience. I rave about how much I enjoy doing it. Also, I take off my "evaluation hat" and leave it in the office. After the coaching is complete, I give them all my notes or scribbles made during the observation. If I see something that needs to be addressed as evaluator, I revisit the classroom. I am sure to see it again. Then, I address it. Teachers are not so willing to open their doors to coaching with the principal if she is going to zap them and put their jobs at risk.

Once I and my teacher leaders felt that we had the coaching process well established, we began inviting other teachers to "co-coach" with us. We both did the pre-observation conference and observed the teacher. We then coached the teacher who was the co-coach about ways to handle the post-observation conference. It is my goal that all my teachers will feel comfortable being coaches, and that coaching will strengthen our instructional program and empower teachers to make changes on their own to make their lessons more meaningful.

Supporting Teachers with Materials

One of the things we learned early is that if we could reach some consensus about how we were going to share materials, we could get a lot more for our dollar. We were never going to have enough books if everyone had to have their very own copies of everything. So, we organized "share closets." Two grade levels share a closet and store some materials there. When I first announced that we were going to organize share closets and asked teachers to bring everything that the school had purchased to their share closet, folks said, " Not I." Then, one teacher who was leaving started bringing her things to the closet. Little by little, others started contributing. Now, the share closets are stuffed with wonderful materials for grade level teams to use.

When funding comes available, monies are not allocated to each individual teacher in the building. Instead, funding is allocated to each team. The team makes a plan for how funds will be spent. Wise spending of our dollars has provided us with lots of instructional materials for our teachers. We also do bulk orders of things needed to implement Four-Blocks, including writing notebooks, red pens, baskets, sentence strips, magic markers, sticky notes, and index cards.

Book vendors can be a great resource for free books. We have worked with Troll and Scholastic Book Fairs. They will match books instead of money for book fair profits. This has been a big source of books for us. Also, we have written to several of the vendors we use to order supplies. They have been responsive by providing us with free books or discounts. It is important during implementation that you keep your vendors informed about your mission and to help them understand what you are trying to do at the school to improve reading. Many of our vendors are former teachers and are more than willing to join us in the full implementation of Four-Blocks.

One vendor in our area sells books and puppets. We host her visit and invite other schools to come and shop. She always leaves nice puppets or books for the school. This is such a treat for teachers. She comes in and shares the new things. Often, she even reads aloud and models how to let the puppet read the story.

School district personnel in our district like to be included from the ground up in making something wonderful happen at a school. When we started Four-Blocks, we went to the district folks and shared our plan. We invited them to join us. This was smart on our part, because the payback was support. Just last week, I got a big crate of books from one of the district level administrators. They were left over from another project, and she knew we looking for books for our upper-level book baskets.

Self-Selected Reading Is My Favorite Block

Pat always warns teachers that since the Four-Blocks are really four different approaches to reading and call on different teaching styles, most teachers will have a favorite block and a least favorite block. That has been true for my teachers, and even though I like all the blocks, I have to admit that Self-Selected Reading is my favorite.

The teacher read-aloud has given us the opportunity to let our students see the teacher reading and enjoying a book. The silent reading time allows the students to be readers, too. The conferences during the block give the teacher time to work with students to meet their individual needs. This was always a goal for us, but, try as we might, we often could not fit one-on-one time into the schedule.

Our children do not have many books at home, and few of our parents read to them regularly and help them establish the reading habit. Self-Selected Reading provides for these children what many of us experienced at home. It is impossible to overestimate the importance of being read to, having time to read what you want to read, having lots of books to choose from, and having people listen to what you think about reading. The children learn to read during the other three blocks—they *become* readers during Self-Selected Reading.

I am always looking for ways to support my teachers, and sometimes it is the little things that have the greatest impact. One of those little things that had a big impact was buying chairs for each classroom (used chairs or even new, inexpensive plastic ones), along with spray paints, ribbons, and other decorative materials. Teachers came to one of our workdays to find the chairs and decorating stuff, and we all had a good time making a Reader's Chair for the sharing segment of Self-Selected Reading. The chairs in the classrooms are beautiful and help us provide just the right look that sends the message, "Reading is important and fun, and we want to hear what you have to say about it!"

One day, my teacher leader and I were visiting in classrooms shortly after we had implemented the Four-Blocks schoolwide. We walked into a second-grade classroom, and I was thrilled to see that the children were doing Self-Selected Reading. When their reading and conferencing time ended, a few children shared their books with the class. One little boy came to the Reader's Chair to share his book. It was one of those very easy-to-read, first chapter books. He was not a good reader, but it was obvious he had something to share, and he was so proud of himself. He held the book up and said, "This is a chapter book." He pointed to the title and said, "This is the title." Then, he opened the book and found the table of contents, "This is the table of contents—1,2,3,4,5. There are five chapters in this book." Then he turned to the page where chapter one began. He pointed to the words, Chapter One, and said, "This is Chapter One." This continued, "This is Chapter Two," and so on. He continued to show the children every chapter that was in the book. Then, he said again, "This is a chapter book."

True Stories from Four-Blocks™ Classrooms

How Ron McNair Elementary Became a
Four-Blocks™ School: A Principal's Point of View ●

Next, it was time for the children to make comments and ask questions. One little girl asked, "What do you like most about reading this book?" The little boy quickly responded, "I like this book because it is a chapter book."

I left the room and chuckled with my teacher leader in the hall. We both had experienced a precious moment. This little boy, through Self-Selected Reading, had been introduced to the world of chapter books. He knew everything about every part of his book, and this is what was most important to him.

Self-Selected Reading gives children the opportunity to discover books on their reading level and that are of interest to them. And, they read!

How We Know Four-Blocks™ Works at McNair

Come to visit McNair and you will know Four-Blocks works. Our children are all readers and writers, and they are all willing to show off their reading and writing to anyone who will listen. The first year I was at McNair, the children lined up early in the halls outside my office and the line continued all day. They were there to "see the principal" for disciplinary problems! Now, the children still line up in the halls outside my office, but they come to read books to me and show me their writing.

In addition to the visible and obvious signs, we also have test data. As I mentioned earlier, when I came to McNair, almost all our test scores were single-digit numbers. Our 1998 MAT-7 scores indicated that 44% of our first-graders and 38% of our second-graders read above the national average. Visitors often ask if Four-Blocks is helping our best students. In 1998, 17% of our second-graders scored in the top quartile on this test. (In 1995, sadly, only 3% of our second-graders were in the top quartile.)

Looking Forward to Next Year

Just when I thought I could sit back and relax, things changed at McNair School. Eleven of my experienced Four-Blocks teachers left. I should feel good about where they went. Some retired. Some moved to other states and other districts and the magnet schools in our county. One was hired as the literacy coach for the state reading initiative. I should feel proud—and I do. But, we will miss their strengths, and we are beginning again with a very small cadre of experienced Four-Blocks teachers. Research shows that schools like ours are the places that first-year teachers are most likely to be hired, and that is certainly true here. I did discuss our Four-Blocks reading program with all of them during our interviews, and they are all eager to learn how to do it.

Because we have so many new teachers, we hired a Literacy Coach. This coach agreed to work with 10 teachers—20 signed up. I think this speaks well for the kind of teachers that came on board.

In the past, coaching has been somewhat institutionalized at McNair. I hope to foster the growth of peer coaching at the school. I am convinced that when teachers can begin to open their doors and learn from one another and engage in meaningful discussion—even debate—about the teaching act, then the instructional program strengthens. This takes time. It takes a listening ear. We started coaching the first week of school. We began by visiting in a teacher's classroom who was returning from the previous year and is well respected at the school. She has helped set a positive attitude about the coaching experience with the younger staff members.

It is hard work starting again to implement Four-Blocks in our classrooms, but we have eager and willing teachers, and we are making progress. One advantage we have this time is that lots of our children have been in Four-Blocks classrooms, and they know the routines. We are encouraging teachers to learn from the kids, and the kids love being the "smart" ones! Even though we are all exhausted at the end of the day, we know where we are heading, and we know why we are going there. We know Four-Blocks will help us meet our goal of teaching all our children to read and write as well as they possibly can.

Professional Works Cited •

Awakening the Heart: Exploring Poetry in Elementary and Middle School by Georgia Heard (Heinemann, 1996).

Basic Reading Inventory: Pre-Primer Through Grade Twelve by Jerry Johns (Kendall Hunt, 1997).

"Building Blocks: A Framework for Reading and Writing in Kindergartens That Work" (video) by Patricia Cunningham and Dorothy Hall (Windward Productions, 1996).

Classrooms That Work: They Can All Read and Write by Patricia M. Cunningham and Richard L. Allington (Addison Wesley Longman, 1998).

Craft Lessons by Ralph Fletcher and JoAnn Portalupi (Stenhouse Publishers, 1998).

"Developmental Spelling Test" from *Teaching Kids to Spell* by Richard Gentry and J.W. Gillet (Heinemann, 1993).

The Differentiated Classroom: Responding to the Needs of All Learners by Carol Ann Tomlinson (Association for Supervision and Curriculum Development, 1999).

Four-Blocks™ Plan Book "Plus" compiled by Joyce Kohfeldt (Carson-Dellosa, 2000).

Guided Reading the Four-Blocks™ Way by Patricia Cunningham, Dorothy Hall, and James Cunningham (Carson-Dellosa, 2000).

Guided Reading: Good First Teaching for Children by Irene C. Fountas and Gay Su Pinnell (Heinemann, 1996).

Hearing Sounds in Words Test by Marie Clay (from the Observation Survey).

Implementing the 4-Blocks™ Literacy Model by Cheryl Sigmon (Carson-Dellosa, 1997).

Invitations to Literacy (Houghton Mifflin Reading Series).

Literacy Place® Phonics Book by John Shefelbine (part of a K-5 Reading and Language Arts program offered by Scholastic, Inc.).

Professional Works Cited

Literature Circles: Voice and Choice in the Student-Centered Classroom by Harvey Daniels (Stenhouse, 1994).

Making Big Words by Patricia Cunningham and Dorothy Hall (Good Apple, 1994).

Making More Big Words by Patricia Cunningham and Dorothy Hall (Good Apple, 1997).

Making More Words by Pat Cunningham and Dottie Hall (Good Apple, 1997).

Making Words by Pat Cunningham and Dottie Hall (Frank Schaffer Publications, 1996).

Month-by-Month Phonics for First Grade by Patricia Cunningham and Dorothy Hall (Carson-Dellosa, 1997).

Month-by-Month Phonics for Second Grade by Dorothy Hall and Patricia Cunningham (Carson-Dellosa, 1998).

Month-by-Month Phonics for Third Grade by Patricia Cunningham and Dorothy Hall (Carson-Dellosa, 1998).

Month-by-Month Phonics For Upper Grades by Patricia Cunningham and Dorothy Hall (Carson-Dellosa, 1998).

Month-by-Month Reading and Writing for Kindergarten by Dorothy Hall and Patricia Cunningham (Carson-Dellosa, 1997).

The Morning Meeting (Strategies for Teachers Series) by Roxann Kriete (Northeast Foundation for Children, 1999).

Mosaic of Thought: Teaching Comprehension in a Reader's Workshop by Ellin Oliver Keene (Heinemann, 1997).

A Multiage Classroom: Choice and Possibility by Maureen McCann Miletta (Heinemann, 1996).

No Quick Fix: Rethinking Literacy Programs in America's Elementary Schools edited by Richard Allington and Sean Walmsley (Teachers College Press, 1995).

Nonfiction Matters: Reading, Writing, and Research in Grades 3-8 by Stephanie Harvey (Stenhouse, 1998).

An Observation Survey of Early Literacy Achievement by Marie Clay (Heinemann, 1993).

Oo-pples and Boo-noo-noos: Songs and Activities for Phonemic Awareness by Hallie Yopp (Harcourt Brace, 1996).

Phonemic Awareness: Songs & Rhymes Series by Kimberly Jordano and Trisha Callella-Jones (Creative Teaching Press,1998).

Phonics Fundamentals by Bob DeWeese (Evan-Moor, 1994).

Phonics They Use by Patricia Cunningham (Addison Wesley Longman, 1999).

"Preventing Reading Difficulties in Young Children" by the Committee on the Prevention of Reading Difficulties in Young Children edited by Reg Griffin and Susan Burns (National Academy Press, 1998).

Starting Out Right: A Guide to Promoting Children's Reading Sucess edited by Susan Burns, Catherine Snow, Reg Griffin, Betty Alberts, and Bruce Alberts (National Academy Press, 1999).

Strategies That Work: Teaching Comprehension to Enhance Understanding by Stephanie Harvey and Anne Gouvis (Stenhouse, 2000).

Sunshine Assessment Guide (The Wright Group,1996).

The Teacher's Guide to Building Blocks™ by Dorothy Hall and Elaine Williams (Carson-Dellosa, 2000).

The Teacher's Guide to the Four-Blocks™ by Patricia Cunningham, Dorothy Hall, and Cheryl Sigmon (Carson-Dellosa, 1999).

Three Voices: An Invitation to Poetry Across the Curriculum by Bernice Cullinan, Marilyn Scala, and Virginia Schroder (Stenhouse, 1995).

What a Writer Needs by Ralph Fletcher and Donald Murray (Heinemann, 1993).

Professional Works Cited

Words Their Way: Word Study for Phonics, Vocabulary and Spelling Instruction by Donald Bear, Marcia Invernizzi, Shane Templeton, and Francine Johnston (Prentice Hall, 1995).

Words, Words, Words: Teaching Vocabulary in Grades 4-12 by Janet Allen (Stenhouse, 1999).

Children's Works Cited

25 Emergent Reader Mini-Books by Maria Fleming (Scholastic, 1997).

Alexander and the Terrible Horrible No Good Very Bad Day by Judith Viorst (Simon & Schuster Children's, 1976).

Alexander Who Used To Be Rich Last Sunday by Judith Viorst (Simon & Schuster Trade, 1980).

Angel Child:Dragon Child by Michele Surat (Scholastic, 1990).

Annie and the Wild Animals by Jan Brett (Houghton Mifflin Co., 1989).

As the Crow Flies: A First Book of Maps by Gail Hartman (Simon & Schuster Children's, 1993).

Bats by Gail Gibbons (Holiday House, Inc., 2000).

Beaver Stream by Marilyn F. Holmer (Soundprints, 1994).

The Best Way To Play by Bill Cosby (Scholastic, Inc., 1997).

The Big Red Apple by Robert McCracken (McCracken Education Services, 1995).

Black Lagoon Series by Mike Thaler (Scholastic, Inc.)

The Boxcar Children Series by Gertrude Chandler Warner (Albert Whitman)

The Chalk Box Kid by Clyde Robert Bulla (Random House, Inc., 1987).

Chicka Chicka Boom Boom with Me: And Other Phonemic Awareness/Phonics Songs and Activities by John Archambault (Creative Teaching Press, 1999).

Clifford and the Grouchy Neighbors by Norman Bridwell (Scholastic, 1984).

The Crayon Box That Talked by Shane Derolf (Random House, Inc., 1997).

Dragonflies by R. Hugh Rice (Richard C. Owen Publishers, Inc., 1996).

Ducks Don't Get Wet by Augusta R. Goldin (HarperCollins Children's Book Group, 1999).

Even Steven and Odd Todd by Kathryn Cristaldi (Scholastic, Inc., 1996).

The Farmer and the Skunk by Robert McCracken (McCracken Education Services, Inc., 1983).

Children's Works Cited

Friends by Helme Heine (Scholastic, 1999).

Frog and Toad Are Friends by Arnold Lobel (HarperCollins Children's Books, 1979).

From Peanuts to Peanut Butter by Melvin Berger (Newbridge Educational Publishing, 1992).

Gunnywolf retold by A. Elizabeth Delaney (HarperCollins Publishers, 1992).

The Hat by Jan Brett (Putnam, 1997).

Honest Abe by Edith Kunhardt (Greenwillow Books, 1992).

Howdi Do by Vladamir Radunsky (Candlewick Press, 2000).

There Was an Old Lady Who Swallowed a Fly by Simms Taback (Viking Children's Books, 1997).

It's Best To Leave a Snake Alone by Allan Fowler (Children's Press, 1992).

It's Mine by Leo Lionni (Alfred A. Knopf, 1996).

Junie B. Jones and the Stupid Smelly Bus by Barbara Park (Random House, 1992).

Junie B. Jones Series by Barbara Park (Random House)

Lazy Lion by Mwenye Hadithi (Little, Brown & Co., 1990).

Little Celebration series by Scott Foresman.

Little Critter's This Is My School by Mercer Mayer (Western Publishing Co., 1990).

The Little Engine That Could by Watty Piper (Grosset and Dunlap, 1978).

Little Nino's Pizzeria by Karen Barbour (Econo-Clad Books, 1999).

The Little Red Hen by Brenda Parkes and Annette Smith (Rigby Literacy Series, 2000).

Long Way to a New Land by Joan Sandin (HarperTrophy, 1986).

Magic Schoolbus Series by Joanna Cole (Scholastic, Inc.)

Maps by Joellyn T. Cicciarelli (Creative Teaching Press, Inc., 1996).

Me On the Map by Joan Sweeney (Random House, 1996).

The Meanest Thing To Say by Bill Cosby (Scholastic, Inc., 1997).

The Mitten by Jan Brett (Putnam, 1996).

More Than Anything Else by Marie Bradby (Orchard Books, 1995)

"The More We Get Together" from the *Impressions* Basal Series (Holt, Rinehart, & Winston, 1984).

Mouse Paint by Ellen Stoll Walsh (Harcourt Brace & Company, 1995).

My Father's Dragon by Ruth Stiles Gannett (Alfred A. Knopf, 1987).

My Little Island by Frané Lessac (HarperCollins Children's Books, 1987).

Owl Moon by Jane Yolen (The Putnam Publishing Group, 1987).

The Popcorn Book by Tomie de Paola (Holiday House, Inc., 1988).

Pumpkin, Pumpkin by Jane Titherington (William Morrow & Company, 1990).

The Rainbow Fish by Marcus Pfister (North-South Books, 1992).

'Round and 'Round the Money Goes by Melvin and Gilda Berger (Chelsea House Publishers, 1998).

Sing, Sing, Sing a Song by June Meiser (The Wright Group, 1990).

Souvenirs by Jennifer Beck (Shortland, 1990).

Spider's Web by Christine Back and Barrie Watts (Silver Burdett Press, 1989).

Tale of a Tadpole by Karen Wallace (Eyewitness Readers, 1998).

There's A Wocket in My Pocket by Dr. Seuss (Random House, 1974).

Through Grandpa's Eyes by Patricia MacLachlan (HarperCollins Children's Books, 1996).

Children's Works Cited

The Very Hungry Caterpillar by Eric Carle (Scholastic, 1987).

Whose Mouse Are You? by Robert Kraus (Simon & Schuster Children's, 1996).

The Wild Christmas Reindeer by Jan Brett (Philomel, 1990).

Young Amelia Earhart: A Dream to Fly by Sarah Alcott (Troll Communications, 1992).

Young Clara Barton: Battlefield Nurse by Sarah Alcott (Troll Communications, 1996).

Young George Washington: America's First President by Andrew Woods (Troll Communications, 1992).

Young Helen Keller: Woman of Courage by Anne Benjamin (Troll Communications, 1992).

Young Jackie Robinson: Baseball Hero by Edward Farrell (Troll Communications, 1992)

Young Orville and Wilbur Wright: First to Fly by Andrew Woods (Troll Communications, 1992).

Zoo-Phonics by Georgene E. Bradshaw and Charlene Wrighton (Zoo-Phonics, Inc., 1986).

Spanish Resources

Dulce Es La Sal, Antologia de Poesia by Alam Flor Ada y Francisca Isabel Campoy (Harcourt Brace and Company)

Rimas Y Risas Series:

Cuento de Nunca Acabar by Alma Flor Ada (Hampton Brown, 1989).

Pinta, Pinta, Gregorita by Lada Josefa Kratky (Hampton Brown, 1989).

¿ Veo, Veo, Que Veo? by Lada Josefa Kratky (Hampton Brown, 1989).

"Lyric Infantil," Children's Folklore Tape: Volume 1 - 4 with Jose Luis Orozco (Arcoiri's Records, 1986).

"Language Minority Student Achievement and Program Effectiveness: Research Summary of Ongoing Study—Results as of September, 1995" by Wayne P. Thomas and Virginia P. Collier (George Mason University, 1995).

Crossroads Publications:

Explores (Weldon Owen Inc./Shortland Publications, 1999).

Storytellers (Shortland Publications, 1998).

Tortillitas Para Mama by Margot C. Greigo, Betsy Buck, Sharon S. Gilbert, and Laurel H. Kimball (Henry Holt and Company, 1981).

Mi Libro Rimas y Canciones (Houghton Mifflin Company Publications, 1977).

Cuentamundos Reading Inventory (MacMillan/McGraw-Hill).

True Stories from Four-Blocks™ Classrooms